Preface books

A series of scholarly and critical studies of major writers intended for those needing modern and authoritative guidance through the characteristic difficulties of their work to reach an intelligent understanding and enjoyment of it.

General Editor: MAURICE HUSSEY

Available now:

A Preface to Wordsworth   JOHN PURKIS
A Preface to Donne   JAMES WINNY
A Preface to Milton   LOIS POTTER
A Preface to Coleridge   ALLAN GRANT
A Preface to Jane Austen   CHRISTOPHER GILLIE
A Preface to Yeats   EDWARD MALINS
A Preface to Hardy   MERRYN WILLIAMS
A Preface to Pope   I.R.F. GORDON
A Preface to Dryden   DAVID WYKES

Other titles in preparation:

A Preface to Spenser   HELENA SHIRE
A Preface to Dickens   ALLAN GRANT

A Preface to Dryden

David Wykes

Longman

LONGMAN GROUP LIMITED
London

Associated companies, branches and representatives throughout the world

Published in the United States of America
by Longman Inc. New York

This edition first published 1977

ISBN 0 582 35101 4 Cased
ISBN 0 582 35102 2 Paper

Printed in Hong Kong by
Dai Nippon Printing Co. (H.K.) Ltd.

Library of Congress Cataloging in Publication Data

Wykes, David.
    A preface to Dryden.

    (Preface books)
    Bibliography: p.
    Includes index.
    1. Dryden, John, 1631–1700. I. Title.
PR3423.W9   821'.4 [B]   76–12598
ISBN 0–582–35101–4
ISBN 0–582–35102–2 pbk.

For Viva Shelley Corrington

DAVID WYKES read English at University College, Oxford, and then
went as a Fulbright student to Miami University, Oxford, Ohio. He
was awarded a Ph.D. in English by the University of Virginia in 1967.
Since then he has taught at the universities of Nottingham and
Trondheim (Norway), and has been a Junior Research Fellow of
Trinity College, Oxford. At present he is an Assistant Professor of
English at Dartmouth College, Hanover, New Hampshire.

Contents

Foreword

Though it has not always been recognized, a poetic justice must have been in operation in 1700 when John Dryden died unaware that a boy of twelve, Pope, already able to 'lisp in numbers' would be his successor in the realm of poetic satire. Even so, the two have been frequently bracketed together, as when, for instance, and doubly unfairly, Matthew Arnold described them both as 'classics of our prose'. As David Wykes ably demonstrates, Dryden was a Laureate of his own century, ready to appraise all contemporary issues in the arts, linguistic development, politics, religion and philosophy, not a prophet. He left to Pope the task of dealing with eighteenth-century problems. Dryden's imagination, as the biographical sections show, was trained in a demanding school, Westminster, and an equally celebrated college, Trinity, at Cambridge. Such an education was the making of seventeenth-century intellectuals, not proleptic Popes.

To have lived through, at one moment, the execution of Charles I, and through the Commonwealth to the Restoration of Charles II by the time he was thirty meant that Dryden had already felt the impact of two major changes of feeling and thinking. He then went on to support the last period of English absolute monarchy in works that Professor Wykes submits to vivid interpretation and analysis. Having been converted to Catholicism when James II took the throne Dryden had the grace not to turn coat again during the reign of William III and forfeited his Laureateship to his enemy, Thomas Shadwell, the hero of *Mac Flecknoe*. All these shifts can be traced in the different strata of his poetic output. Its principal colouring, however, comes from his respect for the past and the moderation and stability of earlier days; he and his essentially conservative audience shared a view that can be defined as right-wing satire, the opposite of the more modern style of left-wing satire familiar to most of us. But Dryden also wrote in other forms, deriving from metaphysical lyrical style and Cavalier masques and poems, not to mention the heroic plays and influential critical essays, all of which are part of the argument below.

Moving from background to foreground Professor Wykes is anxious above all else to show exactly how we should interpret and read Dryden's couplets with their turning of frequent allusion into poetic metaphor. The whole book is marked by the author's eye for the individual elements in the work of his subject and his gift for vividness of expression and aptness of illustration.. He will make what is admittedly a difficult task into one that is recognizably more rewarding and this is precisely the task of a *Preface Book*.

MAURICE HUSSEY
General Editor

List of illustrations

Acknowledgements

One of my greatest debts of gratitude is to Anne and Irvin Ehrenpreis for the education, the friendship, and the example they have given me. I record the fact fearfully, knowing how they feel about such things, but I will not be denied and hope to be forgiven. This book was begun at Trinity College, Oxford, 'to which foundation I gratefully acknowledge a great part of my education.' I am especially thankful to Dennis and Eleanor Burden for many kindnesses.

Dr Bernard Richards of Brasenose College gave me valuable assistance and precious time on the appropriate topic of noses.

Maurice Hussey was always willing to expand his terms of reference as General Editor of this series to cover whatever difficulties I brought to him. Anything of value here is in large part his.

I thank the Committee on Research of Dartmouth College for making available funds for typing costs.

My wife has faithfully stood godmother to this little book, though it must often have seemed an ugly child to her. The contributions she has made to my work include the index and many things of greater value. The dedication is to her in being to her namesake.

We regret we have been unable to trace the copyright holder of various extracts from *The Letters of John Dryden* edited by Charles E. Ward and would appreciate any information that would enable us to do so.

The author and publisher are grateful to the following for permission to reproduce photographs:
Bodleian Library, Oxford, pages 50 *top left* and 54; British Library, pages 32, 51, 104, 105 and 106; British Museum, pages 34, 60 and 79; Christ Church, Oxford, page 13; Her Majesty the Queen, pages 144 and 148; L.E. Jones, page 7; Mansell Collection, page 187; National Maritime Museum, page 78; National Portrait Gallery, pages 46, 102, 182 and 213; Rijksmuseum, Amsterdam, page 50 *right*; University Library Cambridge, pages ii, 20 and 50 *bottom left;* Victoria and Albert Museum, pages 40, 41 and 146.
The painting of *The Four Days' Battle* by Abraham Storck reproduced on the cover is by courtesy of the National Maritime Museum.

Introduction

A love of Dryden rarely comes at first sight, yet there are few poets better able, on a long acquaintance, to hold a reader's affection. I have assumed that a good purpose for this book, therefore, would be to set out such facts, reasonable guesses, informed opinions, and personal reactions as might help a new reader to establish a long friendship with Dryden. In discussing his work with students, I have repeatedly discovered that Romanticism still supplies the main body of what might be called our unarticulated beliefs about literature, and especially about poetry. The verse of the Augustans is still the writing which demands most adjustment of attitude of the student; it is usually the 'strangest' poetry a student of English meets. My awareness of this fact has to a large extent governed my own attitudes in this book.

Reliable biographical information about Dryden is scarce, and he has attracted few biographers. This in turn means that even the available facts are not so widely known as they should be. Part One of this book attempts to give a brief account of Dryden the man and the writer because I feel that the anonymity which still invests him is by no means unavoidable or desirable.

His literary reputation suffers from undue simplification. He is the man who wrote *Absalom and Achitophel* and who 'precedes' Pope. I have tried, without neglecting either the great satiric masterpieces or Dryden's important Augustan influence, to show that his talents were more diverse than his stock reputation allows, and that it is important to acknowledge that he did not know that he was to be followed by Pope. He belongs as much to his own seventeenth century as to Pope's eighteenth.

Dryden's beliefs in philosophy, religion, and politics have been greatly clarified for us recently by a number of scholars, and it is fortunate that in Part Two I am able to rely on and to help disseminate their findings. In all cases, I have tried to discuss Dryden's ideas as he wrote about them and as they actively affected his work.

In Part Three, *Dryden's Craftsmanship and his Audience*, I have attempted to demonstrate the nature of his work as a literary reformer and as an influence on an important later generation.

Part Four, the *Critical Survey*, has developed from the preceding sections. Of regrettable necessity, it has had to be largely made up of excerpts rather than complete poems, and I have attempted a selection which illustrates both the celebrated and the shadowed sides of Dryden's reputation and which develops points made earlier in the book. I have sometimes felt it best to depart from a chronological sequence in the arrangement of the poems and prose extracts.

Part Five, the *Reference Section*, supplies biographical details of persons important in Dryden's career.

The spelling (and on occasions the punctuation) of quotations has been modernized in accordance with the policy of the series.

Chronological Table

(All dates are Old Style, except that the year is taken to begin on 1 January.)

	DRYDEN'S LIFE	PUBLIC EVENTS
1630	October: Dryden's parents married.	
1631	9 August: Dryden born at Aldwincle, Northamptonshire, eldest of four sons and ten daughters.	
1640		The Long Parliament (evicted October 1659).
1646	A King's Scholar at Westminster School.	
1649	First published poem, 'Upon the death of the Lord Hastings'.	Execution of Charles I.
1650	Elected Scholar of Trinity College, Cambridge.	
1651		Hobbes, *Leviathan*.
1654	March: Dryden takes his degree. Father dies.	
1656		Davenant, *The Siege of Rhodes*.
1658		September: Cromwell dies.
1659	*Heroic Stanzas*, Panegyric on Cromwell published. Dryden apparently living in London.	

1660		Restoration of Charles II.
1662	Elected a Fellow of the Royal Society.	Samuel Butler, *Hudibras*.
1663	First play, *The Wild Gallant*, acted. December: Dryden marries Lady Elizabeth Howard, daughter of the Earl of Berkshire.	
1664	*The Rival Ladies* published, first of Dryden's plays to have a prose preface. Elected to the Language Committee of the Royal Society.	
1665–66	The Drydens retreat to Wiltshire.	Plague in London; theatres closed.
1665–67		Second Anglo-Dutch War.
1666	September: Charles Dryden born.	Great Fire of London. Bunyan, *Grace Abounding*.
1667	January: *Annus Mirabilis* published. October: Dryden dropped from the Royal Society for non-payment of dues.	*Paradise Lost* published. Jonathan Swift born.
1668	Second son, John, Jr (Jack) born. Dryden appointed Poet Laureate. Acquires one and a quarter shares in the Theatre Royal and becomes a contracted dramatist to the King's Company. *Essay of Dramatic Poesy* published. Dryden first attacked at length in a pamphlet.	

1669	Living in Longacre, London. Third son, Erasmus-Henry born.	
1670	July: Dryden appointed Historiographer Royal, with no increase in salary.	May: Secret Treaty of Dover between Charles II and Louis XIV.
1671	December: *The Rehearsal* (satirizing Dryden as 'Mr Bays') acted at the Theatre Royal.	March: Duchess of York dies.
1672	January: Theatre Royal burnt. King's Company perform in a tennis court.	Declaration of Indulgence by Charles II. Provocation of Dutch leads to third Anglo-Dutch War; England allied with France.
1673	Pamphlet attacks on Dryden continue.	King forced to cancel Declaration of Indulgence. Parliament passes Test Act. Duke of York resigns as Lord High Admiral. York marries Mary of Modena. Shaftesbury dismissed and goes into Opposition.
1674	Dryden turns *Paradise Lost* into an opera, *The State of Innocence* (not performed, published 1677). New Theatre Royal opens.	Peace Treaty between England and Holland. *Paradise Lost* (in twelve books) published. Death of Milton.
1676	Dryden's mother dies.	
1677	*All for Love* acted.	

1678	Quarrels with the King's Company and leaves the Theatre Royal. (?) *Mac Flecknoe* written (published 1682).	Bunyan, *Pilgrim's Progress*. August: Beginnings of the Popish Plot.
1679	Dryden's association (since 1659) with the publisher Herringman ends. Begins association with Tonson. December: Dryden beaten up in Rose Alley, Covent Garden.	
1680	Translation of Ovid. Charles Dryden a King's Scholar at Westminster School.	November: Defeat of the Exclusion Bill in the House of Lords.
1681	9 November (?): *Absalom and Achitophel* published.	March: Oxford Parliament. July: Shaftesbury sent to the Tower on a charge of high treason. 24 November: Middlesex Grand Jury sets Shaftesbury free.
1682	Jack Dryden a King's Scholar at Westminster. March: Dryden's satire *The Medal* published. 28 November: *Religio Laici* published.	February, March (?): Medal struck by Whigs to commemorate Shaftesbury's release. November: Shaftesbury flees to Holland.
1683	Erasmus-Henry (Harry) Dryden admitted to Charterhouse.	Death of Shaftesbury. Rye House Plot against the King and the Duke of York.
1684	*Miscellany Poems* (large contribution by Dryden).	

1685   *Sylvae* (second miscellany, including seventeen new poems by Dryden.)

February: Death of Charles II. James, Duke of York, becomes King.

At the King's death, arrears on Dryden's royal salaries total £1075.

April: Dryden reappointed Poet Laureate and Historiographer Royal.

June: Monmouth's rebellion.

At about this time, Dryden converted to Roman Catholicism.

July: Monmouth executed.

October: Louis XIV revokes the Edict of Nantes, which guaranteed religious toleration of Protestants.

November: Dryden's *Ode to the Memory of Mrs Anne Killigrew* published.

1686

November: King James prorogues his Parliament.

1687

April: Declaration of Indulgence.

May: *The Hind and the Panther* published. *The Hind and the Panther Transversed*, a satirical parody of Dryden's poem, by Prior and Montague.

Newton's *Principia*.

November: *A Song for St. Cecilia's Day, 1687.*

1688	The Drydens move from Longacre to Gerrard Street, Soho.	Alexander Pope born. June: Birth of a son and heir to James II. Trial and acquittal of the Seven Bishops. Secret invitation by both Whigs and Tories to William of Orange, asking him to 'mediate' between King James and his people. William prepares an invasion of England. 5 November: William lands in Devon and marches on London. James flees to France.
1689	February: Dryden loses his public posts. Shadwell appointed Poet Laureate. December: *Don Sebastian* acted.	Convention Parliament proclaims William and Mary joint sovereigns. Catholics suffer civil disabilities. May: England joins the alliance against France. (Hostilities end 1697.)
1690	Harry Dryden goes to Rome.	Locke, *An Essay concerning Human Understanding.*
1691	*King Arthur*, by Dryden and Purcell.	
1692	*Satires of Juvenal and Persius*, translated by Dryden and others, with essay on satire by Dryden (dated 1693).	

1693	Charles and Jack Dryden go to Rome. *Examen Poeticum*, third miscellany, with ten pieces by Dryden.	
1694	*Love Triumphant*, Dryden's last play, published. Fourth *Miscellany*, two poems by Dryden.	Foundation of the Bank of England.
1695	Du Fresnoy's *Art of Painting*, translated with a preface by Dryden.	November: Death of Henry Purcell.
1697	Translation of the *Works* of Virgil. *Alexander's Feast* performed and published.	
1698		Collier's *Short View of the Immorality and Profaneness of the English Stage* attacks Dryden and other dramatists.
1700	Dryden's *Fables*. 1 May: Death of Dryden. 13 May: Dryden buried in Westminster Abbey.	

THE STUART MONARCHY

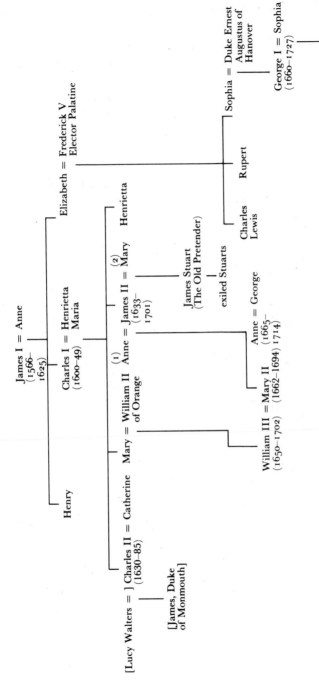

James I = Anne
(1566–1625)

Henry

Charles I = Henrietta Maria
(1600–49)

Elizabeth = Frederick V Elector Palatine

[Lucy Walters =] Charles II = Catherine
(1630–85)

Mary = William II of Orange
(1)

Anne = James II = Mary
(1633–1701)
(2)

Henrietta

[James, Duke of Monmouth]

William III = Mary II
(1650–1702)   (1662–1694)

Anne = George
(1665–1714)

James Stuart
(The Old Pretender)

exiled Stuarts

Charles Lewis

Rupert

Sophia = Duke Ernest Augustus of Hanover

George I = Sophia
(1660–1727)

House of Hanover

Part One

Dryden's Life and Circumstances

I Early Career

By accident and by design John Dryden is one of the hardest men to know among the English poets. The documents on which a full and detailed life of Dryden should be based, and which should explain to us his opinions and justify his deeds were never written or have not survived. His biographers, therefore, produce volumes in which there has to be a disappointingly large amount of hesitation and conjecture. Lives of Dryden seem full of conditional clauses. John Aubrey, the author of the invaluable *Brief Lives*, unwittingly wrote the epigraph for much study of Dryden. At the top of a blank page among his papers—a page dear to students of Dryden—is the heading, 'John Dryden, Esq. Poet Laureate. He will write it for me himself'.

Given the centuries between them, it is startling that we know so little more about Dryden than we know about Chaucer, but the fact may serve as a reminder that the art of biography in England has its real beginnings only in Dryden's lifetime. The desire to preserve personal documents which is stimulated by a tradition of biography and the subsequent tendency to preserve a poet's papers as national treasures belong substantially to a later generation. Alexander Pope, by the publication of his letters, was one man who gave great impetus to the notion. Dryden and Pope, as is inevitable, are often driven in tandem by literary historians, but the difference between them in available biographical material is one of many which should be emphasized to display the real nature of their literary relationship. Dryden's poetry is of the seventeenth century, though its influence on other poets was mainly felt later. To see him aright, we must try here to preserve the balance between his seventeenth-century environment and his 'Augustan' influence.

The corpus of Dryden's work is very substantial indeed. The edition now in progress at the University of California will have twenty volumes when completed, for Dryden wrote, alone and in collaboration, more than twenty plays, more than a hundred prologues and epilogues, several political pamphlets, biographies and translations (including the *Works* of Virgil), as well as the poems for which we chiefly remember him. In these writings he frequently mentions himself, though never at length. Since many of the works deal with topics of religion and politics they tease us by hinting how Dryden arrived at the positions he asserts and defends, yet they never let us into the evolution of his opinions on topics where the evolution means so much. We know that he defended the Church of England in one poem and three years later defended the Roman Church in another, having become a Catholic in the meantime. The causes of the conversion are never explained, and though we now refuse to leap to the hostile conclusions drawn by his enemies, we have no more to go on than they in attempting to say why he changed. In fact, the one great service which Dryden's modern biographers have been able to do him has been to scrape from the events of his life a layer of gossip and rumour. Dryden was certainly beaten up by three men in Rose Alley, Covent Garden, on the night of Thursday, December 18th, 1679; we now know that the scandalous and glamorous Earl of Rochester was *not* responsible for the attack. Yet we know no more than earlier generations did of the identity of the thugs or the reason for the attack. We seem doomed, quite properly, to lose the 'fine fabling' that has surrounded many of the events of Dryden's life, but without gaining much positive truth in its place.

The poet's own letters, the usual lifeline of the literary biographer, are of little help in Dryden's case. Those which survive, and only about eighty do, are frequently business letters to such persons as Tonson, his publisher. Dryden, rather like Dr Johnson after him, seems to have considered the private letter to be no place for consciously fine writing. He was professional enough to know when to conserve his energy. Most of the letters we have are from the later years of his life, written when the political and religious storms which threw up his best poetry were past. They provide an interesting picture of the old poet, working hard on his Virgil and very much 'in exile' as far as the public life of the day was concerned. Many people would prefer, however, to know more of the contentious decade which produced the great satires and poems of argument.

In such circumstances, the wouldbe critic is inclined to make a virtue of necessity. Finding himself alone with the poems, he stresses that it is the poems that are all-important. In Dryden's case, such enforced purism sounds a little hollow. At the height of his powers, Dryden held the posts of Poet Laureate and Historiographer Royal to Charles II and James II. He was a poet with the functions of official apologist and propagandist, and a man writing with those functions is virtually inviting his readers to enquire into his motives. Such enquiries lead only a little way, and if curiosity remains unsatisfied, it is apt to seek other outlets rather than return in quiet submission to 'the poems themselves'. Thus in the twentieth century studies of Dryden have investigated largely the 'intellectual milieu' of his writings, their 'historical background', and the foundation of reading which must underlie his work.

It sounds enormously dull, yet the attempt to come at Dryden by looking at the social and intellectual world in which he lived is a truly virtuous necessity, and it produces a desirable result. The inner heart of Dryden is always kept from us, but we come to know the public man. All his work is public utterance, most of it on public themes. To the modern reader, this fact is the most difficult to assimilate, for

4

it denies so many assumptions we bring to poetry and which are part of our post-romantic inheritance. One objective of this *Preface* is to introduce Dryden as the master of a kind of poetry which is hardly ever attempted in our own day, the lack of which impoverishes our literature.

A modern poet attempting to write a poem representative of public sentiment on a public issue is wilfully putting his reputation in peril. (The elegies for John F. Kennedy are a horrid example.) The very concept of a 'Poet Laureate' is discredited nowadays since it evokes the heresy of 'hack work,' poetry written to order and not to inspiration. A Poet Laureate to us is a 'lost leader', one who has sold out to the Establishment, and Browning's lament, 'Just for a handful of silver he left us', blends with the sort of contempt voiced in Robert Graves's 'The Laureate':

> Once long ago here was a poet; who died.
> See how remorse twitching his mouth proclaims
> It was no natural death, but suicide.

A modern Poet Laureate may keep our respect by *not* writing birthday odes or royal elegies. He is, of course, in effect prohibited from writing poems about Britain's entry into the Common Market or similar topics. In putting itself above party politics, the British monarchy has taken from the Laureate the function of official apologist for the acts of government. In so doing, strangely enough, it has cut off the source of the job's vitality. Poetry is now 'above' politics, too, yet if Dryden as Poet Laureate had been restricted in his choice of subjects to royal births and deaths, the only poems by him under those auspices would be *Threnodia Augustalis* and *Britannia Rediviva*, not the foremost of his works. As it is, the greatest of his poems, *Absalom and Achitophel*, is the work of the Laureate who was able to see Charles II as head of the government, father of his people, and God's vicegerent in England—as well as the Merry Monarch. Dryden is the greatest English Poet Laureate because he was committed to royalism at a time when the king was far more—for better or worse—than the respected figurehead of a liberal democracy. The first steps to bring about that revolution in royal status were taken in Dryden's lifetime. His greatest poem is the conservative manifesto against the change.

If the public nature of Dryden's work were restricted to his great satires it is unlikely that modern taste would resist him, for they are passionate poems of brilliant wit, at times funny, at others truly dignified, striding easily from epic and tragedy to bawdy comedy. It is when we look at the less famous areas of his work that we are most confined in response by our unconscious assumptions. Dryden wrote two poems which set out his religious views, *Religio Laici* and *The Hind and the Panther*. The assumption which tends to operate when we first come to them is that these works will be in essence spiritual autobiographies. We expect something like Browne's *Religio Medici*, but what we encounter is closer to *The Laws of Ecclesiastical Polity*. Dryden patently loved his three sons; he wrote no poems to say so. He may have quarrelled with his wife; he wrote nothing like the fine 'Lines on hearing that Lady Byron was ill'. He wrote many love lyrics for his plays, but wit and the dramatic situation keep them at a distance from the reader, the sort of distance that Byron's 'We'll go no more a roving' seeks to eliminate. The personal to Dryden and to many who followed him was the 'merely personal'. To be interesting, a poem had to appeal to the common, unchanging humanity shared by the moderns, the men of antiquity, and the generations to come. To generalize was wisdom. Even in partisan satire, Dryden believed himself to be defending divinely ordered institutions against the innovations of those who had lost sight of divine wisdom and the unchanging ideal order of the world. The lack of biographical detail forces us —and we should be grateful—to consider Dryden as predominantly a public man and the public writer he wished to be.

The lack of a great public literature in our own day is perfectly explicable, but the fact that we can see why it is unlikely to be written should not necessarily make us glad that we do not have it. Before we congratulate ourselves on limiting our taste, it might be worth asking if the status of poetry in Dryden's heyday, when a good poem could serve the immediate ends of party politics, was greater or less than in our own time, when even many intelligent people assume that a poet is, in Randall Jarrell's words, 'a maker of stone axes'.

Northamptonshire

Dryden was a Northamptonshire man, and in important respects he remained one all his life, despite his metropolitan education and forty years of residence in London. In his old age he looked forward to regular visits to his Northamptonshire relations, where he could escape the discomforts of summer in London and get down to some steady writing. He enjoyed fishing and the unadventurous but refreshing routine of country life, and presumably he enjoyed being the great man of his family home on a visit.

Yet Northamptonshire means a lot more in Dryden's life than a place for a vacation. He had done an unusual thing for one of his origins in going to London to follow a literary career, but his family's place in the Northamptonshire squirearchy gave him the all-important status of gentleman, as well as providing the basis of his income throughout his life. At a time when 'social mobility' within the class structure was common but highly suspect, the 'Esquire' after Dryden's

All Saints' Church, Aldwincle, exterior.

name had a real meaning and dignity. He was in effect a professional poet, yet he was a gentleman, of standing enough to be able to marry an earl's daughter and to associate on equal terms with men of rank. He may have been close to Grub Street, but his talent and his birth made sure he was never of it. His career is the bridge between the gentleman-amateur poet and the gentleman-professional, the gentleman-of-letters.

The Drydens had been settled in Northamptonshire since the mid-sixteenth century. They and the families with whom they intermarried were typical landed gentry, knights and baronets, J.P.s, sheriffs, and M.P.s. They sent their sons to the university and to the Inns of Court, which in those days were virtually universities in their own right and where the legal training was very useful in the education of a young landowner. The thing about the Drydens, however, which has most interested students (and enemies) of the poet is the fact of the family's Puritanism and its support for Parliament in the Civil War. The accusations that Dryden was a turncoat start with the assumption that by birth and breeding he was the last man who should have been a royalist and an orthodox Anglican.

The Puritanism of Dryden's family would have meant to his enemies that they were 'fanatics', to be recognized after the Restoration as Dissenters, Protestants who refused to be communicants of the Church of England. This is in fact unlikely. Dryden was baptized in the village church of Aldwincle All Saints (near Thrapston) where his maternal grandfather, Henry Pickering, was Rector. The religion of his youth, about which we know nothing, may have been 'puritan' in its determination to refuse the 'Romish' ceremonies of the Church's hierarchy under James I and Charles I. It is likely to have been strongly Calvinist in its theology. Erasmus Dryden, the poet's grandfather, was put in gaol in 1604 for circulating a petition in support of Puritan clergy. Such 'dissent', however, was still within the Church of England, and to assume that these attitudes would have projected themselves in a straight line through the upheavals of the Civil War, and that John Dryden would have been totally shaped by them, is to ignore the length of time involved and to simplify the effect of events on opinion. It implies a determinism by environment, and yet we can only guess what that environment was like.

The parliamentarianism of the Drydens has been another unfounded cause for reproach. In 1628 Dryden's grandfather was in gaol again, this time in a civil rather than an ecclesiastical cause. He and Dryden's uncle, Sir John Pickering, refused to meet the loans demanded by Charles I without the authority of Parliament. The issue was the King's prerogative, as it was to be for so long after.

All Saints' Church, Aldwincle, plaque in interior.

JOHN DRYDEN, POET LAUREATE, WAS BORN ON THE
9TH DAY OF AUGUST 1631 IN THE RECTORY HOUSE
OF ALDWINCLE ALL SAINTS AND WAS BAPTIZED
IN THIS CHURCH. HE WAS THE ELDEST SON OF
ERASMUS DRYDEN OF TICHMARSH AND GRANDSON OF
SIR JOHN DRYDEN BARONET OF CANONS ASHBY. HIS
MOTHER WAS MARY, DAUGHTER OF HENRY PICKERING, D.D.
FOR FORTY YEARS RECTOR OF THIS PARISH.
JOHN DRYDEN DIED IN 1700 AND WAS BURIED IN
WESTMINSTER ABBEY. THIS TABLET WAS PLACED
HERE TO HIS MEMORY IN ACCORDANCE WITH
THE DESIRE OF HIS COLLATERAL DESCENDANT
PERCY CHARLES DRYDEN MUNDY OF CALDRESS
MANOR, ICKLETON IN THE COUNTY OF CAMBRIDGE,
WHO DIED ON THE 2ND DAY OF SEPTEMBER 1959.

In supporting Parliament against the King, the Drydens and Picker-
ings did not automatically become caricature Roundheads or eager
regicides. There is nothing to suggest that they were theoretical
republicans. They were English county gentry defending their
interests. Events led to a republic and eventually to a Restoration. If
Dryden's family came to see the Restoration as being in their interest,
their minds 'changed with the nation', as Dr Johnson said. After the
Restoration, when Dryden was involved in public life, the images of
the Cavalier and the Roundhead were simplified for propaganda
purposes. What had been many subtle shades of opinion became melt-
ed into extremist caricatures. Samuel Pepys illustrates nicely the
power of these caricatures. On 1 November 1660, he was in company:

> Among the rest, Mr Christmas, my old school-fellow, with whom
> I had much talk. He did remember that I was a great Roundhead
> when I was a boy, and I was much afraid that he would have
> remembered the words that I said the day the King was beheaded
> (that, were I to preach upon him, my text should be—'The memory
> of the wicked shall rot'); but I found afterwards that he did go
> away from school before that time.

Nothing survives to show that Dryden was 'a great roundhead' when
he was a boy (even his poem on Cromwell supplies far less evidence
than might be supposed). He may have worked for the Cromwellian
civil service, but the fact is still unproven. What matters to us is that
throughout the whole of his life after the Restoration, he was a Tory
and a royalist. And so was Samuel Pepys.

In his last years, when writing his fine poem 'To my Honoured
Kinsman, John Driden, of Chesterton', Dryden looked back to the
1620s when his grandfather and uncle were gaoled. He sees them as
patriots, and discusses their stand quite openly and without shame.
Dryden associates himself with his cousin; they are both country
gentlemen and patriots.

> Between the Prince and Parliament we stand,
> The barriers of the state on either hand.

In time of war, the Prince is to be dominant and to have their support,
but

> Patriots, in peace, assert the people's right;
> With noble stubbornness resisting might:
> No lawless mandates from the Court receive,
> Nor lend by force; but in a body give.
> Such was your gen'rous grandsire; free to grant
> In Parliaments, that weighed their Prince's want,
> But so tenacious of the common cause,
> As not to lend the King against his laws.

The law is here above the King, and though one can see royalist sympathy in the implication that decent Parliaments will come up with the money, Dryden praises patriotism that resists the monarch in certain circumstances. In 1699, when he wrote the poem, events had made it easy for him to express himself in these terms since he regarded William III as a usurper, but one need not suppose that he was ever anything but proud of his Puritan, parliamentarian ancestors. On the other hand, the Restoration Settlement of 1660–61 laid out the terms on which King and Parliament could live together, neither having supremacy over the other. Dryden certainly supported that settlement, and it is an injustice to him to assume that he ever wished it away.

Westminster

Our seminaries of learning do not exactly correspond with the precept of a Spartan king 'that the child should be instructed in the arts which will be useful to the man' since a finished scholar may emerge from the head of Westminster or Eton in total ignorance of the business and conversation of English gentlemen in the latter end of the eighteenth century. But these schools may assume the merit of teaching all that they pretend to teach, the Latin and Greek languages: they deposit in the hands of a disciple the keys of two valuable chests; nor can he complain if they are afterwards neglected by his own fault.

EDWARD GIBBON, *Memoirs*, 1796.

Dryden's boyhood in Northamptonshire is almost completely hidden from us. It seems likely that he attended a local grammar school, for there was one in Aldwincle village and Dryden seems to have been well prepared for his admission to Westminster. From hints that he dropped later, he seems to have been a keen reader. He tells us that he read Spenser and Sylvester's Du Bartas as a child, although at that time he preferred the translation of Du Bartas's long poem on the seven days of the Creation to the 'inimitable Spenser'. Dryden tells us, too, that before he was ten he read an English translation of Polybius, the Greek historian of the rise of Rome. He later remarked that history 'has always been the most delightful entertainment of my life'.

We do not know when he started at Westminster School in London. We know that in 1649, when Charles I was executed, Dryden was in the last form and soon to leave for the university. He probably left home for school in 1646, and so may have been still in Northamptonshire when the decisive parliamentary victory of Naseby occurred in June 1645, some miles across the county from his home. In 1644, when he was thirteen, a group of parliamentary infantry on a tax-gathering expedition was billeted on his uncle, Sir John Dryden, at Canons Ashby. There, in the night, it was attacked by a superior force of Royalists and took refuge in the nearby church. After the door of the building had been hoist with a petard, the King's men took their opponents prisoner and removed them to Banbury. But if the battle and the skirmish were features of Dryden's young life he left no record of their effect on him, and we may reasonably suppose that life in Titchmarsh was fairly peaceful in those years. Northamptonshire was universally for Parliament, or nearly so, and the Civil War in England was not the thoroughgoing blight of the wars of religion on the Continent in the seventeenth century.

Dryden's years at Westminster were passed under the headmastership of Dr Richard Busby, one of the greatest of English schoolmasters. Busby's reputation as a flogger should not lead us to believe that, like Thwackum's, 'his meditations were full of birch'. Like many great schoolmasters, he seems to have had the gift of endearing himself to the boys he apparently terrorized. The best of his pupils at least, were superbly taught, and although Dryden's university years were of great value to him, I think it possible to say that when he left Westminster much of the 'purely literary' aspect of his education was complete. A comparison with Ben Jonson suggests itself. Jonson, many years earlier, was at Westminster under the guidance of a similarly dynamic headmaster (and a better scholar), William Camden. Jonson never went to the university, yet the fact is hardly evident in his work. The schooling he got was very similar to Dryden's, and with the desire to write poetry and the intellectual curiosity, there is little to suggest that Dryden left school any less well equipped for a literary career than Jonson did. Richard Busby, like Camden before him, became a man of importance to English literature.

Dryden's education at Westminster was strongly humanist in form and content, but before discussion of the meaning of that term an account of the boys' routine will be useful. The only full account we have of the daily timetable of a young Westminster student comes from the second decade of the seventeenth century, twenty years before Dryden's time. (It is said to be in the handwriting of Archbishop Laud.) The routine, however, is likely to have been much the same for Dryden. For the sixth and seventh forms, the main items of study were the classical languages, Latin and Greek, and their literatures. Classes began at six in the morning, with two hours of Greek or Latin grammar, which included repetition of the rules, the extempore making of verses, and the giving of explanatory commentary on classical authors. After breakfast, for another couple of hours, the previous night's preparation was read and corrected. After lunch the master, in his turn, would give a critical commentary on some classical author. The final class of the day included repetition of short texts or figures of rhetoric, and ended with the assignment of prepara-

Dr Richard Busby, Headmaster of Westminster School.

tion for the next day. The school day ended about six in the evening. Overnight the pupils had to produce prose essays or verses in Greek or Latin, on topics selected by their teachers, or translations of classical texts. These were taken very seriously, and when Dryden published his translation of the Third Satire of Persius in 1693, he included a headnote in which he remembers translating it at Westminster 'for a Thursday-night's exercise; and believe that it, and many other exercises of this nature in English verse, are still in the hands of my learned master, the Reverend Dr Busby'. Apart from the classics, room was found in the curriculum for history, geography, and study of the Scriptures. Any boy with the aptitude would be given tuition in mathematics, and one of Busby's innovations was the teaching of English grammar to the lower forms.

Such zealous compulsion would meet with little favour nowadays among educators. No doubt a lot of boys were harried and flogged into a permanent loathing of Greek and Latin, but the good pupils would have been very good indeed. Dryden was one such, and the nature of his life's work testifies to his absorption in the literature of Greece and Rome. Yet his surviving comments on education are bewildering in that they are by no means wholly favourable. In his 'Life of Plutarch' (1683) he seems to regard with disapproval the fact that 'the greatest part of our youth is spent in learning the words of dead languages'. The phrase 'dead languages' is the war cry of the anti-classicist, which Dryden certainly was not. Perhaps he put the emphasis on 'words', meaning the mechanical acquisition of vocabulary or grammar, but, still, it is not the comment one expects from him. He seems to have been consistent, however, in his opposition to pedagogical flogging, which may be based on personal experience. The only unflattering reference of his to Busby which survives is from a letter of 1699: 'Our Master Busby used to whip a boy so long till he made him a confirmed blockhead.'

Dryden was clearly one of Busby's 'white boys' or favourite pupils, and he was very glad to send two of his sons to Busby in the 1680s. It will be worth while to ask, therefore, what it was that Dryden found valuable in his education and what its ultimate purpose was thought to be.

The term 'humanist' in this context connects the education Dryden received to the revival of the learning of ancient Greece and Rome which we call the Renaissance. The great English humanists, who brought England into the current of Renaissance thought, Colet, More, Linacre, Cheke, Grocyn, and others, were motivated by more than the simple desire for learning. They were chiefly educators and they gave English humanism an educational bias which had enormous impact on the national life for centuries. Colet established a humanist curriculum for St Paul's School which became a widely copied model.

Humanist education fulfilled the demand of Tudor society for a ruling and administrative class which could cope with those conditions of political and social life which had brought the Tudors to the throne. Medieval patterns of education, the highest aims of which might be said to have been the training of the chivalrous knight or the saint, were not capable of supplying administrators fluent in the Ciceronian Latin of diplomacy, sharing a common cultural heritage with the rulers and diplomats of continental Europe. The Tudor monarchs centralized their government, choosing their servants, men such as Wolsey, More, and Cromwell from among the humanistically educated gentry or even merchant classes, passing over the hereditary aristocracy whose training fitted them only for battlefield or hunting-field and whose feudal power had been greatly diminished by the Wars of the Roses. When the aristocracy realized what was happening, and that the power of the humanistically trained upstarts was real and lasting, they reacted with the adaptability and willingness to compromise for survival which have characterized the English upper classes ever since. They learnt their lesson both figuratively and literally, and their sons were soon crowding out of the schools the sons of tradesmen for whose benefit the schools had been founded. For the first time in English history learning became a desirable attribute in a gentleman, and the grammar schools, where the sons of local merchants and lower gentry went to learn their Latin, were on the way to becoming 'public' schools, the training grounds of the ruling class.

The ideals which informed this new education bring us closer to understanding the meaning of the actual term 'humanism'. All the humanists and their pupils were Christian, but under the canopy of Protestant orthodoxy the education they gave and received was basically secular. Many of the boys trained at Westminster went from there to a university and thence into the Church of England. Busby once boasted that he had taught many who sat on the 'bench of bishops', and that phrase gives us a clue to his part in their education. Theology was a matter for the university; at Westminster the wouldbe parson learnt the ideals of the gentleman in public life, so that when ordained he was able to take his place as one of the governing class. The ideal eighteenth-century clergyman of the Church of England was much more than a preacher or a priest; he was often a landlord and a magistrate, and, if he became a bishop, a member of the House of Lords. The reality was often an abuse of the ideal, as Fielding shows so often in *Joseph Andrews*, but the political and literary sides of Swift's career or Gilbert White's *Natural History of Selborne* show that the 'squarson' is not the whole story.

The humanists stressed the rationality of man, the attribute of reason—God-given of course—which was held to separate mankind from all other earthly creatures. It was reason which made a man human or 'humane': the two terms were identical until quite recently. To be a 'humanist' was to glorify in what was, after all, mankind's divine attribute, the thing which, with the immortality of his soul, he shared only with divine beings. In the classical learning of Greece and Rome, the men of the Renaissance found an image of the ideal man, one who treasured his human rationality, and who, with the addition of the truth of Christian revelation, would provide the pattern for an ideal modern man.

The central cluster of Renaissance humanist ideals was gathered, therefore, about man's social attributes stemming from his reason: ideals of ethics, politics, and education. The view was that rational conduct was measured by a man's relationships with other men, whereas the state of his soul could be gauged only by his relation to God. (Since there is no way for an individual to demonstrate quantitatively the state of his soul in God's eyes, it is no wonder that many humanistically educated men of the seventeenth and eighteenth centuries tended to distrust individual religious fervour and to esteem only the rational approaches to salvation.) The main emphasis of humanist education was on the production of a class of men trained to take their place as the ruling elite of a state which wanted to draw analogies between itself and the Greek city states (the Athens of Pericles, for example) or the Roman Empire in the time of Augustus. Between the invariables of a sovereign head and a plebeian mass were to stand the well-born and well-educated 'governors', which in English terms frequently meant the class of J.P.s, High Sheriffs, and Members of Parliament from which Dryden came.

To the humanist educators, the key to a good society was the proper education of the ruling class, and in the educational writings of the ancients, such as Quintilian's *De Institutione Oratoria*, they found a model they could adapt to their own purposes. Quintilian is concerned with the qualities of good oratory, and the good orator in the classical world was the good man, made good by the right education, able to apply the wisdom derived from a universal range of study to the problems of politics. Oratory, and in this context poetry is to be considered a branch of oratory, was the eloquence of expression used to translate specialist learning into political action. English life in Dryden's day may have provided few opportunities for the orator, the master of the spoken word, to be decisive in political affairs, yet the man trained in the qualities of the orator could intervene to great effect in the public world by means of poetry, including the theatre, and prose pamphlets. Dryden's education at Westminster fitted him superbly for the career he was eventually to make for himself. The Countess of Breadalbane and Holland expressed precisely the objectives of that schooling when she wrote, about 1687: 'They are bravely taught both to be scholars and orators at Doctor Busby's school at Westminster, where my son is.'

The production of poets was not a principal aim of Westminster School, despite a number of distinguished poets among past pupils, notably Ben Jonson and Abraham Cowley. To modern eyes, the curriculum described above may seem highly specialized, a rigorous and almost exclusive training in the classical languages, yet its ultimate objective was to produce, not an academic specialist nor even a specialist man-of-letters, but a widely educated man of action, able to take his place in the public life of the community and able to build on the foundations laid at Westminster virtually any kind of subsequent career. That Busby had his great realizations of this ideal is demonstrated by the later careers of two others of his pupils: John Locke, a coeval of Dryden's, and Christopher Wren. Locke was a physician who became the greatest philosopher of his age. Wren was an astronomer who made himself the greatest architect of his time. Busby taught them neither medicine nor philosophy, neither astronomy nor architecture, yet he helped greatly to prepare their minds for their later achievements. He taught them humane letters— *litterae humaniores*, the name given to the modern descendant of the humanist curriculum at Oxford. The Latin and Greek in which they were so fiercely drilled made available to them the wisdom of classical antiquity, and having learnt to be good 'governors', able to take their places in the public life of the kingdom, they were free also to turn their minds on the problems of more specialized disciplines, relying on their rational abilities to solve their difficulties.

In fact, one of the greatest testimonies to the freedom of mind which the humanist curriculum strove to give is Locke's own rejection of it. When he wrote his *Thoughts concerning Education*, it is clear that Locke regarded much of the education he had himself received as useless, particularly for the concerns of the ordinary gentleman as opposed to the scholar. Locke asked himself most of all how education could be of practical application in life, and his utilitarian criteria led him to draw up a model of education very different from the humanist one. Latin, for example, was absolutely necessary for a gentleman, because it was the international language of Europe, the language, indeed, of business. Greek, on the other hand, though necessary to the scholar, had no place in the schooling of a gentleman. It was not firsthand acquaintance with the wisdom of the ancients *via* their literature that Locke sought in a language, but its current usefulness.

It should not be thought, however, that in saying so Locke was desecrating an ideal of education that was being realized everywhere in England as he wrote. What is to be inferred from the cold light which he throws on education in his day is that in most cases the humanist ideal was ill-understood by many schoolmasters and in practice had degenerated into just the kind of self-involved study, totally lacking in ideal justification, which we find condemned as 'Gothic barbarism' by the early humanist reformers, such as Erasmus.

(Pope complained of modern education in much these terms in *The Dunciad*. In Book IV the spectre of Busby appears to defend the 'tyranny' of a narrow schooling—'Words we teach alone'—and plenty of birch. Pope was educated at home.) A 'gentleman's calling', according to Locke, was 'to have the knowledge of a man of business, a carriage suitable to his rank, and to be eminent and useful in his country, according to his station'. The desired objectives were generally the same as those of humanist education, but the terms are subtly different. Locke wanted to produce 'useful' citizens, and his was undoubtedly the way of the future. If, despite the good sense and compassion of many of his 'thoughts', he was the precursor of Bentham and of Dickens's Gradgrind, part of the blame, if blame it is, must lie on the humanist plan of education which, in spite of its ideals, and in spite of the usefulness of learning for a 'bookish man', like Locke himself, failed too many of those it tried to educate.

From all we know Dryden was one of the successes of that form of schooling, and its ideals inform his poetry. Locke and Defoe and many others wanted education to be 'modernized' and suggested that gentlemen should avoid Greek and learn to keep accounts, but the opinion of the majority of the gentry seems to have been otherwise. Even if the ideal of the humanist 'governor' was lost to sight, the knowledge of classical languages became a useful barrier against social upstarts. It was Lord Chesterfield, the self-proclaimed authority on matters of gentility, who defined 'illiterate' as 'ignorant of Greek and Latin'.

Until quite recently, the schooling of the English upper class remained markedly similar to that which Dryden received, for in the eighteenth and nineteenth centuries the acquisition of an empire made the training of a ruling elite even more of a priority than it had been in the seventeenth century. The classical model of the 'governor' served the English, almost unchanged, for over three hundred years.

It will be clear at once that an educational system which saw as its first duty the inculcation of public spirit could help produce in Dryden a poet of the public mode. The particular period in which Dryden and his Augustan successors lived, an age of commercial expansion and of great difficulty for the lesser gentry, the governor class, helps explain in turn why it was the humanistically educated writers—those, that is, who did not repudiate their schooling—who became the Tory satirists. Their ideal lay in the past, in Periclean Athens, Augustan Rome, or even in Elizabethan England, and they saw the busy world about them as a negation of nearly all they thought good in a society. Swift, Pope, Gay, Arbuthnot, and Bolingbroke are Augustans and satirists because their humanistic ideals made them misfits in a world dominated by Locke in ideas and by Walpole in politics. Their literary eminence may distort for us the nature of

18

eighteenth-century England if we think they represented the views of most of their countrymen.

Cambridge

A man should be learned in several sciences, and should have a reasonable *philosophical*, and in some measure a *mathematical* head to be a complete and excellent poet. And besides this should have experience in all sorts of humours and manners of men, should be thoroughly skilled in conversation, and should have a great knowledge of mankind in general.

'Postscript' to *Notes and Observations on the Empress of Morocco*, DRYDEN, SHADWELL, CROWNE, 1674.

Dryden tells us that he read Plutarch in the library of Trinity College, Cambridge, 'to which foundation I gratefully acknowledge a great part of my education'. Unfortunately, but typically, we know little more than this for certain about his university years. Modern research has discovered that in July 1652 he was punished by the governing body of the college for some unknown offence, that when punished he disobeyed the Vice-master and was contumacious in taking his punishment, and that he was in consequence 'gated' (confined to the college), prevented from taking meals in hall, and finally had to read a public confession. All efforts to discover the cause of this rebellion have failed, but its occurrence gives comfort to anyone who might feel that Dryden was too tame a person to be a great poet. The offence was not, however, of a kind to ruin his career at Cambridge, and he received his BA in due course without special distinction and without apparent difficulty. Trinity College was willing to keep a place open for him had he wished to continue as a postgraduate student, but by that time his father had died and he left the university for good in March 1654.

To write about the influence of Cambridge on Dryden's intellectual life, on the basis of such facts as there are, is bound to be a venture in speculation. Yet that influence may well have been considerable, and it would be misleading to pass over those years in silence. The discussion which follows is largely guesswork, but it is guesswork based on Dryden's subsequent writings. What was available in the intellectual life of Cambridge in the early 1650s which Dryden seems to have found useful for poetry?

It cannot certainly be proved that he was influenced by any of the ideas or movements which scholars tend to say 'must' have affected him. Any don or any student knows that it is possible to pass through a university totally untouched by the new ideas or the influential research to be found there. All that can be shown is probability, based on the certainty that Dryden had an enquiring mind and did live an intellectual life.

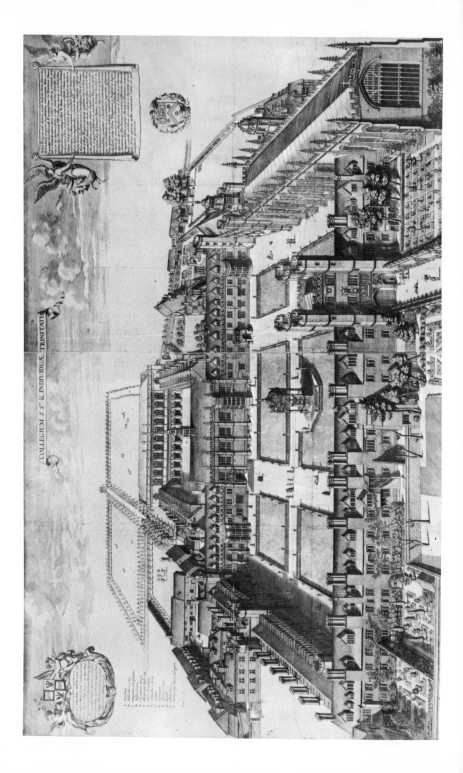

COLLEGIUM S. S. & INDIVIDUÆ TRINITATIS

This granted, there are three aspects of Cambridge thought and teaching which seem to participate in the making of Dryden's poetry (though his desire to write poetry antedated his stay at Cambridge, since he had already, in 1649, published his elegy 'Upon the Death of the Lord Hastings'). Those aspects are the standard curriculum of the undergraduate student, the influence of the so-called 'new science' at Cambridge, and the presence of the Cambridge Platonists as an active and notable force in theology and philosophy.

But before this trio of possible influences can be discussed yet another proviso is necessary. The history of the English universities in the sixteenth and seventeenth centuries has recently become the subject of much research and debate, and ideas about the purposes and methods of a university education in those times—who went there, what was studied, and why—are changing rapidly. The process is as yet unfinished, and the stability of conclusions reached here may prove to be illusory in the light of future research. I have tried to take into account the conclusions which seem to have achieved fairly wide acceptance by historians, without overemphasizing any particular influence on Dryden to make him fit a predetermined theory.

THE CURRICULUM. The standard patterns of university study in the seventeenth century were those of scholasticism, the all-pervading philosophy of Europe in the Middle Ages. Scholasticism was the philosophy of the Catholic Church, having as its object basically the same which Milton took in *Paradise Lost*, to justify God's ways to men and to teach man how and where his reason should properly be applied. Its greatest figure was St Thomas Aquinas, who flourished in the thirteenth century, and its presiding genius was Aristotle, whose writings became a sort of unofficial holy writ on all kinds of topics. The Reformation effectively removed the Roman Catholic Church from England, but the scholastic methods of teaching and enquiry, built up over centuries, remained largely unchanged in the universities. By Dryden's day scholasticism was a system of thought and enquiry rather than a philosophy of belief.

In the seventeenth century Englishmen who were critical of the education provided by the universities—Bacon, Milton, and Hobbes are the most prominent—attacked the still-prevailing methods of scholasticism. In the logic and disputations of the orthodox curriculum they saw intellectual sterility and pointless argument—'logic-chopping'. (The popular idea that scholastic methods could lead to grandiose debates as to the number of angels who could dance on the point of a pin seems to stem from this contempt.) Modern historians have only recently set themselves to discover what facts lie behind the controversies and the myths. What they have found concerning the

Trinity College, Cambridge, 1690.

years of Dryden's young manhood is that scholasticism retained a strong hold on the forms, methods, and ends of the curriculum, but that changes of all kinds were continually occurring as the universities adapted themselves to a changing world. Changes were slow in coming, but such used to be the way of universities.

We are fortunate to possess documents which show something of the routines followed by Cambridge students in the 1650s when Dryden was there. James Duport, a Fellow of Trinity, drew up some 'Rules to be observed by young pupils and scholars in the University' which are very revealing. His are in the main rules of religious observance, morality, and daily conduct. Obviously, Duport would have seen himself as describing an ideal rather than a reality, but his exhortations in the section devoted to studies, 'De exercitiis Scholasticis', show that, for him at least, it was a scholastic ideal which still prevailed.

> Use often to dispute and argue in logic and philosophy with your chamber-fellow and acquaintance when you are together.
> Let your declamations be filled and condensed with arguments, thick and threefold, and objections answered as fast as you can.
> A sober, calm, sedate deportment of speech is the best, even in disputing.
> Yet when you dispute, think it not enough barely to pronounce and propound your arguments, but press them, and then urge them home and call upon your adversary for an answer, and leave him not till you have one.
> Dispute always syllogistically, at least enthememalically and as much as you can categorically.
> If at any time in your disputation you use the authority of Aristotle, be sure you bring his own words and in his own language.
> In your answering reject not lightly the authority of Aristotle, if his own words will permit of a favourable and a sure interpretation.

(Though much has changed, it is evident from Duport's preferences that, in other respects, dons and undergraduates are still the same.

> Be not too spruce, curious or fantastic, nor yet too careless, supine, and slovenly in your apparel.
> Refrain football, it being as it is commonly used a rude, boisterous exercise, and fitter for clowns than for scholars.)

The terms Duport employs here are those of the scholastic methods of teaching and it seems clear that, however many reforms had come about and however much the older methods were neglected, Dryden as an undergraduate must have followed an essentially scholastic pattern of education at Trinity.

The subjects of the undergraduate arts curriculum were logic, rhetoric and ethics, and the methods of teaching (apart, of course, from the students' all-important reading) were the lecture, the disputation, and the declamation. All forms of instruction emphasized the spoken word, and we should recall at this point the importance of the figure of the orator in humanistic education. Though the forms were medieval in the universities, the humanist ideal could be served by them.

The lecture was, of course, delivered orally, and, properly presented, it was meant to be retained easily in the memory of the audience. (The taking of notes was sometimes discouraged.) Clarity of style and orderliness of presentation were thus held up to the students as an ideal. Lectures were by no means always formal affairs, but could be semi-private meetings in a tutor's room. In Dryden's day, the colleges had become markedly independent in their teaching, and this freedom allowed considerable differences in method between college and college and permitted the introduction of subjects not prescribed by the university or the neglect of subjects which the statutes required.

The disputation, a formal or semi-formal debate between students, could be required by the university to qualify a student for his degree (though, in the main, degrees were taken only by those entering the Church), or could be held in a tutor's chamber or in the college hall. The disputants argued for or against a question proposed for debate, and they used the syllogistic method favoured by the schoolmen. Learning the syllogistic method, and learning to detect false syllogisms, was a major part of a student's work in logic; the disputation put him to the test.

The syllogistic method, whereby a logical argument proceeds from a major universal premise to a minor individual premise to a conclusion is a form of argument well adapted to systematic debate. The proponent's or opponent's strategy was to get assent for syllogisms which would eventually lead his antagonist to accept as truth a conclusion opposed to his own thesis. And not only was the dispute logical and learned, it was frequently witty too. When King James I visited Cambridge in 1614, a formal disputation was staged before him in which the question was 'Whether dogs can make syllogisms', a topic which could be handled either as a deliberate *jeu d'esprit* or as an investigation in animal psychology. The disputants fought hard, and when the moderator seemed to sum up for the negative, the King asked how it was that, without reason, one of his hounds was able to start a hare and then, realizing it needed help, summon the pack by baying. The answerer answered the King, saying 'that his Majesty's dogs were always to be excepted, who hunted not by Common Law, but by Prerogative'.

Dryden as a poet is famous for his ratiocination, his ability to argue in verse. It is unlikely that the disputations he took part in as a student did not help that ability. Yet we must be cautious. One important function of such debates, especially when they took place in public, was to instil poise. A tutor at Queen's College, Oxford, wrote in a letter of 1678 that one of his pupils lacked courage, 'but I hope that disputing in Hall will put some briskness into him'. Dryden was all his life notoriously diffident and shy in public, and it seems unlikely that he was ever a happy disputant, much as he may have profited by the effort.

This 'training toward expert contentiousness' plays a role, too, in the general character of seventeenth-century literature. One thing easy to get in those days was an argument, and the element of debate present in so much writing is shown by the numerous 'answers' to poems, for instance, or by the fact that pamphlet warfare was a major literary activity. A number of Dryden's own works are answers to criticisms of his plays, and when, as Historiographer Royal, he was called upon to write political pamphlets, he was able to do so expertly and effortlessly.

To be able to argue, to understand the psychology and techniques of reasoning and to be able to conquer an opponent were some of the objectives in studying logic and in disputing. But to make one's reasons prevail it was necessary to add the study of rhetoric, the art of persuasion. Skill in eloquent presentation was stimulated by the writing of declamations, polished speeches in which the student drew on his reading for examples of effective language and in which the highest ideals were elegance of Latin style and clarity of thought. (Although written out, the declamation was intended to be spoken, and it is in fact the ancestor of the weekly essay at Oxford and Cambridge which the undergraduate still reads aloud to his tutor or supervisor.)

In studying rhetoric—and it was a very important study—the student was encouraged to cull from the works he read eloquent phrases, witty ideas, and telling allusions. To this end he kept a commonplace book, and a modern expert on the curriculum of seventeenth-century Cambridge, Father W.T. Costello, has stated that 'the allusiveness of seventeenth-century style is owed directly to [the students'] commonplace borrowing'. Dryden's critics certainly thought so. In *The Rehearsal*, Bays, who represents Dryden, is made to say,

> Why, sir, when I have anything to invent, I never trouble my head
> about it as other men do, but presently turn o'er this book, and
> there I have, at one view, all that Persius, Montaigne, Seneca's
> *Tragedies*, Horace, Juvenal, Claudian, Pliny, Plutarch's *Lives*, and
> the rest, have ever thought upon this subject. And so, in a trice, by
> leaving out a few words, or putting in others of my own, the business
> is done.

(The skill, of course, was in the tactful and witty use of the common-place book, but hostility would not detect such skill.)

The third art studied by the undergraduates was ethics, the study of moral conduct. With the triumph of Protestantism in England ethics became a most important subject, since the external authority of the Catholic Church was removed and the doctrine of Protestantism, that every man was ultimately responsible for his own conscience, prevailed. Aristotle's works on ethics were the important authorities studied under this heading, and the Aristotelian *via media*, whereby moral conduct is the middle way between extremes of vice, became an almost instinctive part of the seventeenth-century mind. Polonius's advice to Laertes is possibly the only example most of us know of a specifically Aristotelian discourse on ethics, but Polonius is giving the best counsel he knows, and falls back uncritically on the Aristotle he read as a student. Justice, according to Aristotle, is the highest of the ethical virtues. A truly just man was an ethical saint. In the light of this Aristotelian idea, we see why Dryden, in celebrating the restoration of Charles II, called his poem *Astraea Redux*, for Astraea personifies justice and Charles is leading her back to England. We can also see why the King in that poem is given so many attributes of Christ.

SCIENCE. The sciences 'officially' studied at Cambridge as part of the undergraduate curriculum—physics, metaphysics, mathematics, and cosmography—present far more of a problem in evaluation than the undergraduate arts. Apparently, mathematics and cosmography were hardly studied at all by the average undergraduate, and metaphysics and physics were again largely the province of Aristotle, whose scientific works had supreme authority. The scholastic study of the Aristotelian categories of matter would have introduced Dryden to many interesting ideas that he could use in poetry, for an idea does not have to be 'true' to make a good image, but it involved little in the way of scientific study as we know it. The 'new science', taking much of its inspiration from Bacon, rejecting Aristotle as a sacrosanct authority, eventually embodied in the Royal Society in 1662, played no official part in the studies of the Cambridge undergraduate. Yet Dryden became a member of the Royal Society, and when he speaks of himself as a sceptic he means a sceptic in the scientific sense, as we now know.

In actual fact, the 'neglect' of the new science by the universities in the seventeenth century has been shown by modern research to be an unfounded myth. The freedom to teach which the college system gave was employed by tutors to introduce their pupils to new ideas in mathematics, cosmology, medicine, botany, and many other subjects. Duport's rules are not the whole story, for he was a conservative, concerned to see that the established scholastic curriculum got its proper representation in the work of the undergraduates. Trinity attracted and produced many men with what we now recognize as true scientific interests in Dryden's day—Ray, Barrow, Needham, Willughby, Mapletoft, and Allen—and what we have now been taught about the university and science makes the emergence of Newton from seventeenth-century Cambridge seem far less of a mystery of 'pure genius' than it once was. The traditional Cambridge curriculum had an important part to play in the advance of the new science, for it was able to train the minds of undergraduates to receive new ideas in a proper spirit. As the foremost historian of the English universities in the fifteenth and sixteenth centuries, M.H. Curtis, has written,

> to select the significant data from a mass of observations and to plan and execute a critical experiment required wide knowledge, sound grounding in the theories about phenomena, breadth of vision, and disciplined imagination. The formal training of the universities prepared men to recognize a significant new fact and to understand how it affected old ideas. Furthermore, it gave them training in systematic thought so that they could speculate profitably about new theories and could work out the logical consequences of such discoveries.

The great majority of those who were eminent in the scientific advances of the seventeenth century were university men, and it now begins to appear that their university training was a positive help in their scientific work, rather than a hindrance, as has been hitherto the assumption.

Dryden was not himself a scientist, but the universities then as now played a great part in the formation of an 'intellectual class', which, while not making new discoveries or new formulations itself, provides the soil of receptive interest in which new ideas can flourish. There is much scientific imagery in Dryden's poetry, and we shall later look more closely at the nature of his scepticism (see pp. 64–68). At this point, it will suffice to remark that Trinity probably awakened him to the significance of the 'new philosophy' and that his subsequent membership of the Royal Society was the result of that awakening.

One of the most important of Dryden's works for those interested in his views on science is his poem 'To my honoured friend, Dr Charleton' (1663). Charleton had written a book to show that Stonehenge was built, not by the Romans, as Inigo Jones had suggested, but by the Danes. Dryden congratulates his friend on setting aside tradition and on evolving a new theory based on his own observations. He congratulates Charleton, in fact, on being properly sceptical. The poem opens with lines on Aristotle which sum up perfectly the rejection of his authority by the 'new scientists'.

The longest tyranny that ever swayed,
Was that wherein our ancestors betrayed
Their free-born reason to the Stagirite,
And made his torch their universal light.

The ideal of scientific inquiry now was to be, in the words of the Royal Society's motto, *Nullius in Verba*, 'on the word of no one', not even Aristotle's. Yet this rejection of Aristotle's authority in one sphere of human thought does not necessarily mean that his name carried no weight with Dryden in other areas. His literary criticism owes much to Aristotle, for example. Dryden's mind, like anyone else's, had partitions in it, and a rejection of Aristotle in natural philosophy need not overflow into any other compartment. Similarly, his approval of the Royal Society does not mean that he absorbed all its doctrines. He continued, for example, to believe in some forms of astrology, such as nativities, untouched by the contempt of Sprat, the Royal Society's historian, for what he called 'a disgrace to the reason and honour of mankind'. And yet there were other forms of astrology that Dryden despised and satirized.

The Cambridge Platonists

Let us express this sweet, harmonious affection in these jarring times, that so if it be possible, we may tune the world at last into a better music.

RALPH CUDWORTH.

During the Commonwealth and the period following the Restoration, an important element in Cambridge intellectual life was the existence of a group of theologians and philosophers called the Cambridge Platonists. The writings of these men may have been important in the development of Dryden's religious views and especially in the composition of his two religious poems, *Religio Laici* and *The Hind and the Panther*. It is very likely, of course, that Dryden read any books he may have used long after he had left Cambridge, but it seems appropriate to indicate briefly here what the Platonists' beliefs were, since their association with Cambridge was so notable, and since it is at least possible that Dryden learnt something of them while he was an undergraduate. Moreover, the existence of a group of men such as these and their wish to disseminate their ideas tell us a great deal about English religious life in Dryden's day.

The important names among the Cambridge Platonists are those of Benjamin Whichcote, Henry More, Ralph Cudworth, and John Smith. The Platonists had many links with the markedly Puritan Emmanuel College, of which Dryden's father had been a member, and the origins of their religious evolution were Puritan. They were not, however, Puritan 'enthusiasts', for they were specifically opposed to Calvinism and to the divisive notion that true faith meant cutting oneself off from all those whose beliefs were not identical to one's own. They opposed, in fact, one of the main trends of seventeenth-century religious life in England, sectarianism, which had played an important part in bringing about the Civil War. At the same time they opposed the High Church sectarianism of the ill-fated Archbishop Laud, with its strong emphasis on predetermined forms of religious ceremony and worship, and they further opposed the 'atheism', as they called it, of the philosophy of Hobbes, which took the form of determinism and materialism.

It is convenient to define the ideas of the Cambridge Platonists by enumerating the beliefs they opposed, but it should first be made clear why they are called Platonists. The Greek philosopher Plato had described the physical universe as consisting merely of the 'shadows' or imperfect images of a truly real universe of spiritual forms. The truly 'real' was the ideal, which, unlike its physical manifestations, was eternal, unchanging, and possessed a greater beauty than even the most beautiful of physical things. The soul of man was his 'real', immortal self. The Platonic view of existence was, therefore, essentially spiritual, and it had long been brought into the tradition of Christian theological discussion. In seeking for an authority to support their views in religious philosophy, the Cambridge thinkers turned naturally to Plato, whose standing in the eyes of educated men was high, second only to that of Scripture, and equal to that of Aristotle in secular philosophy.

Religious controversy in the seventeenth century had been a process of continuing fission, as Protestants split into mutually exclusive groups, each claiming the true way for itself. The Cambridge Platonists argued that the best course of religious enquiry was to find those beliefs held in common by all Christians and to emphasize them in order to bind believers together. The Platonic ideals of proper religious conduct were available to all men, since every man was endowed with reason, and the end of theology and preaching should be to open men's eyes to the essential beliefs and to turn them away from doctrinal disputes, arguments about the meanings of 'inessential' passages of Scripture, and from all views which tended to make man grovel in a knowledge of his baseness. The Cambridge Platonists wished that man should see himself as 'deified', to use their own term, meaning that man should recognize the seeds of the divine within him, which it was God's intention to raise to full participation in His nature. 'The Gospel is nothing else but God descending into the world in our form, and conversing with us in our likeness, that he might allure and draw us up to God, and make us partakers of his Divine Form' (Cudworth). The doctrines, derived from St Augustine and reinforced by Calvin, of man's inescapably degenerate nature and the view that man could do nothing to aid his own salvation were vigorously refuted by the Cambridge group. They claimed that God had supplied man with an inborn, or innate, ability to find his way to God, and their famous slogan for this was a verse from Proverbs, 'the spirit of man is the candle of the Lord'. Whichcote added that it was 'lighted by God and lighting us to God'.

This gift of God to man was reason, and reason was the main instrument at man's disposal for finding his way to God. The emphasis they gave to reason causes the Cambridge Platonists to be called 'rational theologians', but in their vocabulary 'reason' meant far more than the rational ability, the mere processes of logical thought. To them, reason was as much a spiritual faculty as a mental one. It combined the innate ideas within man's mind with the ordinary rational powers and the truths of revealed religion to lead him to God. No spectacular mental abilities were required of the believer. If he trusted to the promptings of his innate dispositions towards salvation, he would attain it. (The stress on the 'more than rational' nature of this 'higher reason' led, in fact, to a certain anti-intellectual strain in Cambridge Platonism.) Basil Willey summarizes thus: 'The appeal to Reason, then, meant an appeal to that which was common to all mankind, that which transcended the particularities of time, race, and denomination.' It was not opposed to the spiritual, for reason and faith were mutually interdependent. One of Whichcote's most famous pronouncements was, 'I oppose not rational to spiritual; for spiritual is most rational.'

'Salvation', too, was a concept which the Platonists somewhat redefined. Besides being a state beyond this life, salvation was evident in life by conduct. Whichcote asked for a religion 'that doth attain real effects', and an important sign of salvation in life was virtuous conduct. Instead of squabbling over doctrines, Christians should be concerned to live good lives. Thus Cambridge Platonism acquired an emphasis on conduct which separated it even further from the doctrines of 'faith before works' held by the Calvinists.

The Platonists rapidly acquired the name of 'latitudinarians' or 'men of latitude', and although 'latitudinarianism' eventually extended far beyond the confines of the group, the name tells us how they were seen by their contemporaries. They were men who wanted to make Christianity as inclusive as possible, rather than exclusive. To this end they eulogized reason, though finding it innately present in all men by God's gift, 'the candle of the Lord'. 'Universal charity is a thing final in religion,' said Whichcote, and thus the spirit of toleration was given a theological basis. (Lady Masham, Locke's patron, was Cudworth's daughter; the author of the *Letters on Toleration* is linked through her to Cambridge Platonism, though Locke's rejection of 'innate ideas' indicates the wide gulf between him and much Platonic thought.) The emphasis given to conduct opened the arms of Christianity still wider, since the effective primacy of right conduct permitted the salvation of the 'virtuous heathen' to whom revelation was unavailable.

The Cambridge Platonist movement helped English thought along the road of liberal enquiry which we call 'the Enlightenment' by helping to do away with the reactions of fear and suspicion which had, before its rise, tended to accompany all kinds of speculation. It also had what its founders would undoubtedly have seen as bad results. The importance it gave to innate ideas and good conduct helped the establishment of deism, the belief that the knowledge of a Supreme Being does not need to be revealed to man by scriptural means and that virtuous behaviour is instinctive in man. A remarkable feature of eighteenth-century Anglicanism is 'the disappearance of Christ' from much religious discussion, and the Church followed the Platonists in not emphasizing the evangelical aspects of Christianity, the fall of man, the necessity of grace, and the all-important doctrine of the redemption. If the Cambridge men helped to weaken sectarianism in the seventeenth century, they also helped create a need for Methodism in the eighteenth.

Dryden, however, was a man of the seventeenth century, and although by the end of his life he actively repudiated many of the beliefs held by the Cambridge Platonists, there are certain aspects of their thinking which always remained congenial to him. In his earlier writings there are signs of a flirtation with deism, which the Cambridge school may have unwittingly encouraged. Attitudes of toleration are common in his writings, though always within limits, and naturally they are most emphasized when, in his later, Catholic years, he was himself a member of a suspected minority. The ideas of Platonism in general are frequently encountered in his writings, and Platonic habits of figurative thought appear often in his poems. Professor Miner has said that 'Dryden's use of controlling metaphors to suggest steadfast values seems to involve Platonism: whether in satire or panegyric, he compares the individual event or person in time to ideal values or beings above time'. It seems likely that these habits of thought were started during Dryden's Cambridge years.

There remains to add one very large agreement between Dryden and the Platonists, where both he and they can be seen to be moved by and to be giving impetus to a major tendency of late seventeenth-century intellectual life: the appeal to reason. An unmistakable and unchanging element in Dryden's thought is his abhorrence of anarchy, an abstraction which had been all too concrete in the middle years of his century. He sought, like the Platonists, a permanency of ideas and ideals above sectarian brawls and party politics. The desire for stability, naturally but ironically, led him to espouse beliefs and causes which involved him deeply in the metaphorical warfare of politics and religion, but the desire remained. Basil Willey expresses well the sentiment which, most of all, Dryden shared with certain of the leading men of his university.

In appealing to Reason, in trying to represent religion as rational, the Cambridge Platonists were obeying a profound instinct, and at the same time adding momentum to the master-current of thought in their time. The instinct was the instinct to cling to some 'ever-fixed mark', something high and lifted up above the flux and chaos of religious disputes.

As a satirist, Dryden took the offensive against those he saw as enemies of true religion and good government. He could have found a justification in an aphorism of Whichcote's: 'Enthusiasm is the confounder, both of reason and religion; therefore nothing is more necessary to the interest of religion than the prevention of enthusiasm.'

To 'prevent enthusiasm' by poetry, however, would have seemed a contradiction in terms to the Cambridge Platonists, for despite their use of metaphor and their strongly poetic tendencies, they distrusted eloquence and the literary arts. Imagination and passion were to them the opposites of reason and truth, and figurative language was one of the earthly 'shadows' which 'stained' the pure and eternal light of truth. 'Christian religion,' said Whichcote, 'is not mystical, symbolical, enigmatical, emblematical; but unclothed, unbodied, intellectual, rational, spiritual'.

After Cambridge

In the period between Dryden's departure from Cambridge in 1654 and the publication of his poem on Cromwell in 1659 he disappears totally from sight, to the great frustration of his biographers. His father died in June 1654, and Dryden became the head of a large and young family and inherited the farmland which was to provide him with a steady though inadequate income for the rest of his life. One might guess that, in the circumstances, he would stay some time at home in Titchmarsh before going to London to make a career for himself. He seems to have been in London for certain in 1659, and for the rest of his life had his home there. That he should have gone to London at all is somewhat surprising, since he was the eldest son and quite entitled to take his father's place in the Northamptonshire community. When one considers, however, that the family estate had to support a large number of children and their widowed mother, it becomes reasonable to suppose that John would decide to seek employment away from home.

Dryden's enemies said that in this period he was employed in Cromwell's administration. His modern biographer, Charles E. Ward, has decided that there is not enough evidence to support this contention, and it is true that we cannot prove the claim. It seems to

AN
ELEGY
ON THE
USURPER O.C.
BY THE
AUTHOR
OF
Abfalom and Achitophel,

publifhed to fhew the Loyalty and Integrity of the POET.

AND now 'tis time for their Officious haft,
Who would before have born him to the Sky
Like eager *Romans* e're all rites were paft,
Did let too foon the sacred Eagle fly.

Though our beft Notes are Treafon to his Fame,
Joyn'd with the lowd Applaufe of publick Voice,
Since Heaven the praife we offer to his Name,
Hath rendred too Authentick by its Choice.

Though in his Praife no Arts can lib'ral be,
Since they whofe Mufes have the higheft flown,
Add not to his Immortal Memory,
But do an Act of Friendfhip to their own.

Yet 'tis our Duty and our Intereft too,
Such Monuments as we can build to raife,
Leaft all the World prevent what we fhould do,
And claim a title in him by their praife.

How fhall I then begin or where conclude,
To draw a Frame fo truly circular?
For in a Round what Order can be fhew'd,
Where all the parts fo equal perfect are?

His Grandeur he deriv'd from Heaven alone;
For he was great e're Fortune made him fo,
And Wars like Mifts that rife againft the Sun;
Made him but Greater feem, not Greater grow.

No borrow'd Bays his Temples did adorn,
But to our Crown he did frefh Jewels bring;
Nor was his Vertue poifon'd foon as born,
With the too early thoughts of being King.

Fortune (that eafie Miftrefs of the young,
But to her Antient Servants coy and hard;)
Him at that Age her Favorites ranck't among,
When fhe her beft Lov'd *Pompy* did difcard.

He private, mark't the Faults of others fway,
And fet as Sea-marks for himfelf to fhun,
Not like rafh Monarchs who their youth betray
By Acts, their Age too late would wifh undone.

And yet Dominion was not his defign,
We owe that Bleffing not to him but Heaven,
Which to fair Acts rewards unfought did joyn;
Rewards which lefs to him than us were given.

Our former Cheifs like Sticklers in the War,
Firft fought t'enflame the Parties, then to poize,
The Quarrel lov'd, but did the Caufe abhor,
And did not ftrike to hurt, but make a noife.

War, our Confumption, was their gainful Trade,
We inward bled whilft they prolong'd our pain,
He fought to end our Fightings, and Effaid
† *To ftanch the Blood by breathing of a Vein.*

Swift and refiftlefs through the Land he paft,
Like that bold *Greek* who did the *Eaft* fubdue,
And made to Battle fuch Heroick hafte,
As if on Wings of Victory he flew.

He fought feeure of Fortune as of Fame,
'Till by new Maps the Ifland might be fhown,
Of Conquefts which he ftrew'd where e're he came;
Thick as the Galaxy with Stars is fown.

His Palmes though under weights, they did not ftand,
Still thriv'd, no Winter could his Lawrels fade,
Heaven in his portraict fhew'd a Workmans hand,
And drew it perfect yet without a fhade.

Peace was the Price of all his Toyls and Care,
Which War had banifht and did now reftore,
Bolognia's Wall thus mounted in the Air,
To feat themfelves more furely than before.

Her

me, and to many other students of Dryden, however, that there is enough of a basis for reasonable probability that he was in some way connected with the Protector's government.

His cousin, Sir John Pickering, was Cromwell's Lord Chamberlain, and it seems natural that a young man needing a job should turn for assistance to a relative so well placed. Payments to a certain 'Dryden' for public service were made in 1656 and 1657. A 'John Driden' signed an official receipt in 1657. (The handwriting resembles Dryden's attested signatures in certain details, but this signature is too isolated in time to be definitely identified as his.) When arrangements were being made for Cromwell's funeral in 1658, a list was drawn up of government employees to be allotted 'mourning cloth' to be made up into suits to wear at the ceremony, and it included the name of 'Mr Draydon'. Two of those who applied for grants were Milton and Marvell, but 'Mr Draydon's' request for nine yards was refused. In reports of the actual procession, among the group of 'Secretaries of the French and Latin tongues', appear the names of Milton, Marvell, and 'Mr Dradon'.

It seems likely, therefore, that Dryden had some employment, perhaps of a literary nature, in Cromwell's administration. The fact that his request for mourning cloth was turned down suggests to the California editors 'that his services to the government were regarded as occasional or unimportant, or that he was not looked upon as a man who had identified himself with the party or the cause'.

John Aubrey tells us that in 1676 Dryden had what seems to me to be the astounding temerity to ask Milton's permission to turn *Paradise Lost* into an opera and its blank verse into couplets. If the story is true, it may well be that he was capitalizing on his earlier acquaintance with Milton in making the approach, for the old, blind, and surely somewhat forbidding poet is said to have given Dryden leave to 'tag' his verses.

The certain fact which ends this period of anonymity in Dryden's life is that, in 1659, he published a panegyric on the dead Lord Protector, 'Heroic Stanzas to the Glorious Memory of Cromwell'. It appeared in a volume with two other poems on the same subject, by Edmund Waller and Thomas Sprat respectively, and it marks the real start of Dryden's career as a poet. Later he was much abused for this poem, especially for some lines, distinguishing Cromwell as the one 'chief' of the Parliamentary party who truly wanted peace, and which Dryden's enemies misconstrued as approval of the King's execution (see illustration, p. 32).

> He fought to end our Fightings, and Essaid
> To stanch the blood by breathing of a vein.

Dryden had, in his elegy for Lord Hastings, ten years earlier, disapproved of the execution, and does not seem to have changed his mind.

33

Ivy Lane

Bedford

Durham house

Iork house

White Hall

Aske

We should not let ourselves think, however, that the poem's place as one of Dryden's earliest works means that it was written by a very young man. Dryden was nearly twenty-eight when it appeared, an age by which many poets have done their best work. In the period since leaving Westminster he must have written and torn up a great deal. On the eve of the King's return he was ready to start out on his career in the public world, to become the poet of Restoration England.

Whitehall from the Thames in 17th century.

2   Making a Living

Patronage

Dryden's land in Northamptonshire meant that he never had to write to survive, but he was never rich enough to write without taking care to see that the work brought the best possible reward. Such rewards, of course, are not always financial, and the poems Dryden wrote between the Restoration in 1660 and his appointment as Poet Laureate in 1668 show his awareness that he had to establish himself with the body of readers best able to appreciate him and to show their appreciation by several kinds of support. The right audience would provide not only money but friendship, protection, influence with those still more powerful and introductions to such persons—all the aspects which are grouped under the invidious term 'patronage'. Dryden was in effect a professional poet at a time when that profession, in the sense of a respectable arrangement between author, publisher, and purchasers, did not exist. In his later career he helped to bring it into being, but he was always a master of the art of dedicating his works to the powerful and influential, and his unremitting commitment to achieving his literary ends made him the best—and perhaps, therefore, the worst—writer of flattery of his age or any other.

Dr Johnson kept some of his best thunder for Dryden's 'meanness and servility of hyperbolical adulation', and the passage makes delightful reading.

> When once he has undertaken the task of praise, he no longer retains shame in himself, nor supposes it in his patron. As many odoriferous bodies are observed to diffuse perfumes from year to year, without sensible diminution of bulk or weight, he appears never to have impoverished his mint of flattery by his expenses, however lavish. He had all the forms of excellence, intellectual and moral, combined in his mind, with endless variation; and when he had scattered on the hero of the day the golden shower of wit and virtue, he had ready for him, whom he wished to court on the morrow, new wit and virtue with another stamp. Of this kind of meanness he never seems to decline the practice, or lament the necessity: he considers the great as entitled to encomiastic homage, and brings praise rather as a tribute than a gift, more delighted with the fertility of his invention than mortified by the prostitution of his judgment. It is indeed not certain, that on these occasions his judgment much rebelled against his interest.

Dryden's greatest crime as a flatterer—his willingness to prostitute his judgment or even genuinely to hold it suspended—is here properly censured, yet, as in so many passages where a great critic analyses in a spirit of hostility, much is indicated which might serve a more charitable interpretation. If one's moral loathing of flattery overrides all other considerations, as perhaps it should, then there is no more to be said, but Dryden and his patrons are long dead and time's winnowing lets us see them fairly plainly. We might be able to get the flattery into perspective, too.

Johnson reminds us that Dryden's wit and imagination were always engaged when he wrote a dedication. (The reminder is in part implicit. Johnson's elaborate simile of the undiminishing 'odoriferous bodies' is a compliment to Dryden's wit in the form of parody, conscious or unconscious. One can easily imagine Dryden applying it to a patron, with no ironical intent. He came close in *Eleanora*.

> As in perfumes composed with art and cost,
> 'Tis hard to say what scent is uppermost;
> Nor this part musk or civet can we call,
> Or amber, but a rich result of all;
> So, she was all a sweet; whose ev'ry part,
> In due proportion mixed, proclaimed the Maker's art.
>
> (lines 154–9)

These lines, to complete the sequence of influence, are greatly indebted to Donne in *The Second Anniversary*.) Johnson despised Dryden for being good at dedicating, and he was good at it because he made it new. Yet though Dryden is deplorably willing to suggest that the feeble poems of a titled patron are great works of art, his own literary skill as he does so, particularly in panegyrics in verse, sets a standard which tells the truth. In his New Year's gift poem to Lord Chancellor Clarendon (1662), Dryden alludes to Clarendon's youthful efforts in poetry.

> The Muses (who your early courtship boast,
> Though now your flames are with their beauty lost)
> Yet watch their time, that if you have forgot
> They were your mistresses, the world may not:
> Decayed by time and wars, they only prove,
> Their former beauty by your former love;
> And now present as ancient ladies do
> That courted long at length are forced to woo.
>
> (lines 5–12)

The personification makes human and dramatic one of the most frequent of topics on which poets commended their patrons in the world of affairs. Though by no means extraordinary, the lines involve Clarendon with poetry while complimenting him in verse, and two of Dryden's favourite manoeuvres in flattery were to dramatize himself and his patron and to raise the status of poet by attaching it to the particular star he is describing. The playfulness is not ironic, but it seems to be a justification in itself and for itself, as Johnson saw when he described Dryden as 'delighted with the fertility of his invention'. There was no one great individual patron, no Maecenas, in Dryden's life, but each time he writes a flattering dedication he creates for himself the role of a Horace or a Virgil approaching one of those classical benefactors. The recipient was then expected to play his part and return a gift for the honour. This 'classical' licence for what was, in Dryden's time, a much debased practice, can be seen in the Preface to Virgil's *Pastorals* (translated 1697). It is addressed to Lord Clifford, whose father had patronized Dryden.

> You have besides the fresh remembrance of your noble father, from whom you can never degenerate. *Nec imbellem, feroces prognerant aquilae columbam.*
>
> [The quotation, to flatter his lordship's abilities, is from Horace, who had the most famous patron of all—see Reference Section, Maecenas, pp. 217–8—and means 'Nor do fierce eagles beget the timid dove.']
>
> It being almost morally impossible for you to be other than you are by kind [that is, by nature], I need neither praise nor incite your virtue. You are acquainted with the Roman history, and know without my information that patronage and clientship always descended from the fathers to the sons; and that the same plebeian houses, had recourse to the same patrician line, which had formerly protected them, and followed their principles and fortunes to the last. So that I am your Lordship's by descent, and part of your inheritance.

Dryden's pretence to be the property of Clifford in fact makes Clifford his. (Johnson writes of Dryden's 'golden shower of wit and virtue', but it will be recalled that Zeus took possession of Danaë by descending on her as a shower of gold.) A refusal to pay would have been felt as a disclaimer to these honours, and no one seems to have protested at receiving such public adulation.

We know of disappointments, however. In 1693 Dryden dedicated *The Third Miscellany, or Examen Poeticum* to Lord Radclyffe, who seems to have failed to reward him. In a letter to Tonson, Dryden shows us the practical realities of the business of dedications. 'I am sure you thought my Lord Radclyffe would have done something. I guessed more truly that he could not, but I was too far engaged to desist, though I was tempted to it by the melancholic prospect I had of it.' To some this will seem sordid, but I take comfort in such realism, and since Dryden was a skilful flatterer, I take pleasure in observing his skill, playing his role, displaying his wit, exercising both his capacity for absurd fancy and his dramatic power. Eventually the flattery accumulates into a sort of reversed *Dunciad,* in which fictional characterizations of various notables are preserved to surprise future ages with the contrast between such adulation and sober fact. Charles Sackville, Earl of Dorset, had a small talent for poetry and is remembered in anthologies for one song, 'To all you ladies now at land'. To find Dryden saying that Dorset's lyric poems 'are the delight and wonder of this age, and will be the envy of the next', and that 'Donne alone, of all our countrymen, had your talent', is to enter a realm of absurd comedy where it would be pompous to protest. One reservation alone is important. In his verse Dryden almost always builds his praise on a foundation of serious ideas, and ultimately he wishes to be taken seriously. One must keep separate criteria for judging praise of a patron in a prose dedication and that which is given to the royal party in *Absalom and Achitophel* or to cousin Driden. The two kinds of praise approach and mingle in only a few poems, one of which is discussed in the Critical Survey ('To the Duchess of Ormonde', pp. 185–9).

The Patronage of the Theatre

On 9 April 1668 Sir William Davenant, Poet Laureate and manager of the Duke's Theatre, died. On 13 April the warrant was drawn up which conferred the Laureateship on John Dryden (an action, incidentally, which made Dryden the first official, 'signed and sealed' Poet Laureate). The salary of £200 a year (when the Treasury could be persuaded to part with it) was a valuable addition to his income, but the Laureateship may also be seen, as Dryden no doubt saw it, as the public sign of his 'arrival' as a writer. He was making his way.

By April 1668 Dryden had written and published three plays all his own: *The Rival Ladies, The Indian Emperor,* and *Secret Love.* (His first play, *The Wild Gallant,* was apparently an adaptation of an earlier work, author unknown even perhaps to Dryden, who said that the plot was not originally his, but 'so altered by me that whoever the author was, he could not have challenged a scene of it'. Adaptations were a frequent resource of the Restoration dramatist, and Dryden made several more.) Two of these plays had been very successful with their audience—Charles II had called *Secret Love* 'his' play and had greatly admired *The Indian Emperor,* with which Dryden made himself the master of the shortlived but highly characteristic Restoration genre of the 'heroic play'. Since 1660 he had collaborated with Sir Robert Howard on *The Indian Queen,* with the old Duke of Newcastle on *Sir Martin Mar-All* (though Dryden did so much of the work that the play is usually assigned to him alone), and with his predecessor as Laureate, Davenant, on an adaptation of Shakespeare's *The Tempest. Sir Martin Mar-All* had been a great success at the box

Exterior of Dorset Gardens Theatre.

40

Interior of Dorset Gardens Theatre, showing visual resources: proscenium, scenery and backcloth.

office, and everyone knew that it was really Dryden's skill that made them laugh till their heads ached, as did Samuel Pepys's when he saw it. The profit that came to Dryden for his work, however, must have been in part the advantage of Newcastle's support, and this is even more true in the case of *The Tempest*, which was deservedly no great success. Apart from performances at Court, Dryden's own plays had hitherto been performed at the King's Theatre, to which he had been introduced by Howard, but the collaborations with Newcastle and Davenant in 1667 allowed him to work with and for the Duke's Company, which meant that he had good relations with both the customers of a dramatist with a play to sell. His professional prudence in this matter is notable, though it may have paid off both indirectly and after a considerable time. Ten years later Dryden did switch to the Duke's Company.

In the meantime, the King's Company at the Theatre Royal took steps to see that his plays should henceforth be their property alone, and the success of *Sir Martin Mar-All* at the Duke's Theatre may have helped them make up their mind. Soon after Dryden's appointment to the Laureateship they succeeded in placing him under contract by making him a shareholder in return for three plays a year from his pen. Dryden received one and a quarter shares, which was the proportion held by each of the three main actors in the company. When he and the company fell out in 1678, it was claimed that Dryden's share had brought him as much as £300 or £400 a year. The sums were probably less, but they were surely far from negligible, and in 1668 Dryden must have been very happy to have assured himself of such an income.

For ten years Dryden wrote plays exclusively for the King's Theatre, but as time went on feelings on both sides about the arrangement must have changed. The company had Dryden's talents to draw on, but his output, as is the way with literary eyes and literary bellies, fell far short of three plays a year. In his ten years under contract, Dryden wrote ten plays, nine of which were performed. Some were very successful—*Tyrannic Love*, *The Conquest of Granada* (a two-part work), *Marriage a-la-Mode*, and *Aureng-Zebe*—while only one, *The Assignation*, was a downright failure. *All for Love*, the play of Dryden's which has had the greatest reputation with posterity, was the last play of his to be given by the King's Company. Dryden's biographer, Charles E. Ward, suggests that its failure to make any impact may have been due to a mediocre production in December 1677 and that this helped Dryden decide to move over to the Duke's Theatre.

His dissatisfaction at the Theatre Royal is easy to understand, for the company there was cursed by ill-luck and bad management. In

1672 the theatre had burned down, destroying with itself between fifty and sixty houses around Drury Lane, and the situation was made more painful for the company by the fact that the Duke's Company had just moved into a large, well-appointed and brand new building in Dorset Garden. The King's Company had to take over the tennis court from which the Duke's had just moved and their productions for a while thereafter were hampered by lack of scenery and costumes. When a new building was completed in 1674 (for which the shareholders were assessed), it was still inferior to the Duke's Theatre, and from then until 1682, when the King's Company was absorbed by the Duke's to make the United Company, affairs went from bad to worse and the King's people must always have felt overshadowed by their rivals. There seems to have been much squabbling among the shareholders and actors in those years and by the time Dryden came to make his move the company was in debt, its actors were getting on in years, and it suffered as a result of uninspired artistic direction. Since so much of his income depended on the theatre, he can hardly be blamed for moving. And since the life of a playwright was harassing and insecure—Dryden seems to have had no contract with the Duke's Company and so was back in the position he had had before 1668, at the mercy of the management with only his reputation to protect him—it is no wonder that he was eventually happy to renounce the theatre and concentrate on work he enjoyed more and thought he could do better.

Between his adaptation of *Troilus and Cressida* in 1679 and his 'return' to the stage with *Don Sebastian* in 1689, Dryden wrote only three plays: *The Spanish Friar*, *The Duke of Guise* (in collaboration with Nat Lee), and *Albion and Albanius* (which was in fact an opera, music by the Frenchman Grabu, Master of the King's Music). All three of these works contain an important political element, for in these years Dryden's involvement with public affairs engrossed him and he produced most of the poems for which he is now remembered, from *Absalom and Achitophel* in 1681 to *A Song for Saint Cecilia's Day* in 1687. When he lost his official appointments in 1688 he also saw defeated and proscribed by the Revolution the causes for which he had worked in his public poems. Satire of contemporary public events could appear thereafter only if heavily veiled, and Dryden went back to writing plays. It is notable, however, that he did so only until another expedient could be found. Dryden the translator of Juvenal and Persius, of Virgil and the *Fables* comes into his own after 1688, and once the translations were well under way the theatre was renounced again. After *Don Sebastian* there were four more plays, and in the Prologue to *Love Triumphant* (1694) Dryden announces his retirement and writes his theatrical last will and testament. Yet that was not, as it happened, his last work for the stage. At the very end of his life, a benefit performance of Fletcher's *The Pilgrim* was given for him, and he wrote for it a new Prologue and Epilogue and a *Secular Masque*, which proved to be his last word on his art and his times (see Critical Survey, pp. 192–5). In view of what was, despite himself, a lifetime in the theatre, it was fitting that his final work should have been for the stage.

In 1668, though, when the task of picking a new Poet Laureate was in hand, Dryden's theatrical abilities must have counted a great deal in his reputation. As Laureate, he made public poetry outstanding in the literature of his age, yet the abilities he so displayed were never seen as indispensable for a Laureate. The fact that he was preceded by Davenant and succeeded by Shadwell, the butt of *Mac Flecknoe*, and that both these men were chiefly men of the theatre, shows that a playwright as Laureate was quite the usual thing. Ben Jonson had occasionally cursed a situation which made him the literary accompanist of Inigo Jones in the production of masques for the Stuart court, but the kings he and Dryden served felt that the ability of the Laureate to help in a royal entertainment was useful, perhaps essential.

Dryden, therefore, would probably have got the job had he been only a playwright in 1668. His plays had pleased the court and the rather select audience of the public theatres. Apart from his poem to Cromwell—and a lot of men now well placed in public life had written admiringly of Oliver—all his work showed the 'right attitude'. *An Essay of Dramatic Poesy* displayed him as an analytical theorist of his art with the graces and deferences of a courtier. No one else in 1668 could claim to be a more eminent writer, for eminence is a matter of public agreement and persons so obviously unaccommodating as Milton and Marvell had only the wrong kind of repute in politics and poetic fashion. Dryden it should be, and Dryden had also written *Annus Mirabilis*.

In looking back at the entirety of Dryden's career with the Laureateship in mind, it seems self-evident that *Annus Mirabilis* was the work which secured the appointment for him. Of his works before 1668 it alone has in large proportion the important characteristics of his later, famous poems: grandeur, historical and spatial sweep, heroism, and satire, all in the service of the public life. Yet this obviousness in our estimate is the distortion of hindsight. Dryden was to prove in his poems that *Annus Mirabilis* pointed the way; the fact may not have been so apparent in 1668, particularly since the poem's 'prophetic' features are to some extent obscured by mannerisms that the fully mature Dryden shed. The poem could certainly have done him no harm with the Court; equally certainly, it was not the most important element in the decision to make him Laureate. For that the theatre was responsible.

44

Dryden and Tonson

> Those who with nine months' toil had spoiled a play,
> In hopes of eating at a full third day,
> Justly despairing longer to sustain
> A craving stomach from an empty brain
> Have left stage-practice, changed their old vocations
> Atoning for bad plays with worse translations.
> (MATTHEW PRIOR, 'A Satire on the Modern Translators', 1685)

In 1679 Dryden's version of Shakespeare's *Troilus and Cressida* was first printed. Hitherto Dryden's works had been put out by Henry Herringman, but *Troilus and Cressida* was the venture of a pair of 'stationers' or booksellers, Abel Swalle and Jacob Tonson. Swalle disappears immediately thereafter from Dryden's career, but Tonson was associated with Dryden for the rest of his life, and that association is of great importance to English literature and to the history of business.

Tonson was just out of his apprenticeship in 1679; he was twenty-four years old and Dryden was forty-eight. It is a mark of Tonson's acumen and drive that he became the publisher of the chief poet of the day almost as soon as he went into business for himself. Despite the difference in age and the social distinction between the Poet Laureate and the son of a respectable and prosperous cordwainer of the City of London, it is a mark of Tonson's character that he and Dryden always did business together, agreed and disagreed, as equals.

We should, perhaps, be cautious of the word 'publisher', which did not come into general use in its modern sense until the nineteenth century. Yet it is quite fair to speak of Tonson as a 'publisher', or even as 'the first English publisher', since in fact he performed most of the functions of modern publishers. A publisher nowadays occupies all the middle ground between authors, printers and bookbinders, booksellers, and the reading public. He commissions books, accepts or rejects manuscripts for publication, employs the printers and binders, supplies the booksellers, and arranges the advertising of his publications. Tonson, as a 'stationer', sold the books he published at his own shop, and the financial arrangements of his business did not permit him to make to his authors the 'advances' which publishers now make to support authors during the writing of books. In these respects alone Tonson differed from a modern publisher; in all other respects his relationship with Dryden was much like that between a modern publisher and a distinguished writer. Similarly, Dryden's attitudes towards Tonson are reminiscent of those which an established modern poet might display towards his publisher. Tonson's reliance on Dryden's judgment and the way in which they developed projects together suggest that, in the twentieth century, Dryden might

easily have been a poet-publisher himself, in the manner of a T. S. Eliot or a C. Day Lewis.

Herringman had never really made much of Dryden. He had never collected his works or done much to 'sell' him by way of advertisement. If he called on Dryden's judgment in his publishing ventures he kept quiet about it. Tonson changed all that. At his initiative, there came into being something like a firm of 'Tonson and Dryden', and Dryden's name was frequently in the public eye in connection with a book of Tonson's. Nearly everything Dryden wrote from 1679 until his death was 'Printed for Jacob Tonson', who carefully acquired the copyrights of those of Dryden's works published before Tonson went into business. He was thus able to issue the collected *Works* of Dryden in the poet's lifetime and after his death. (Dryden's estate received payment for the second edition of *Fables* in 1713.)

Dryden's talent repaid Tonson well. The decade of the 1680s, the first half of the period of the partnership, saw Dryden at his peak as a poet. Tonson, despite his Whiggish principles, found himself publishing the Tory Laureate's best-selling satire *Absalom and Achitophel* in 1681. (Although the poem was anonymous in the early editions, everyone knew it to be Dryden's; Tonson prudently abbreviated his own name to 'J.T.' for this poem.) The success of *Absalom and Achitophel* meant that Dryden's dependence on the theatre was lessened and he was encouraged to produce the series of public poems on which his fame still rests. All were published by Tonson.

At this time, too, Tonson and Dryden thought up a publishing project which was to have very important results for them both, and it may well be that this —the series of volumes known as the *Miscellanies* —really did more to 'liberate' Dryden than his satires did.

In 1680 Tonson had put out *Ovid's Epistles, Translated by Several Hands*. Dryden translated two of the epistles and collaborated on a third with the Earl of Mulgrave. He also wrote the preface for the volume and clearly had a large part in its inception and preparation. This first translation work for Tonson was popular and in 1683 a similar, collaborative translation of Plutarch's *Lives* was begun by Tonson. For this, Dryden wrote his 'Life of Plutarch'. Then, in 1684, came the first of what were to be annual miscellanies, collections of short poems by various authors. The first, *Miscellany Poems By The Most Eminent Hands*, was followed in 1685 by *Sylvae: or, The Second Part of Poetical Miscellanies*. The importance of these volumes is manifold. They provided a place of publication for short poems which might otherwise have circulated only in manuscript and have been lost in time; they permitted new, young poets to get into print early in their careers and in the company of their elders; they allowed a poet to provide an authoritative text of a poem earlier printed in

Jacob Tonson, Dryden's publisher.

corrupt form (as happened with *Mac Flecknoe*, printed first by a mysterious 'D. Green' and included, with Dryden's corrections, in *Miscellany Poems*) and, most important of all, they tested further the public taste for translations.

The first miscellany included *Absalom and Achitophel*, *Mac Flecknoe*, and *The Medal*, all preserving the fiction of their author's anonymity. Prologues and epilogues by Dryden appeared. All these were proven successes. The presence of two of Virgil's eclogues, an idyll of Theocritus, and an elegy of Ovid in Dryden's verse translations, as well as many other verse translations by the other contributors to the volume, was a way of confirming the public's taste for such versions, already demonstrated by *Ovid's Epistles* four years earlier. In *Sylvae*, the second miscellany (1685) Dryden wrote a preface in which he followed up his remarks on translation made in the preface to the Ovid. One-third of *Sylvae* was Dryden's and was made up of translations from Virgil, Theocritus, Lucretius, and Horace. Dryden's only 'original' contributions—though in this context we must revise our idea of 'originality'—were two songs. The 'disease of translation', as he wryly called it, had a strong hold on him. A few years later he would be grateful that he was bitten by that bug, for with the Revolution of 1688 and the accession of William and Mary, Dryden's original public poems, written, one might say, in his combined role of Poet Laureate and Historiographer Royal, were at an end with the termination of those appointments. Dryden's commitment to Catholicism and James II meant that some of his boats were burned. Two, however, were still seaworthy: the old vessel of the theatre and the new one of translation.

It is probably testimony to Dryden's financial plight after the Revolution that his first play on his return to the theatre should have been published by Joseph Hindmarsh rather than by Tonson. Hindmarsh presumably offered more for the copyright, but with the next play, *Amphitryon*, Dryden went back to Tonson—or, more accurately, to the Tonsons, Jacob and his elder brother Richard, also a stationer. We must presume that the Tonson brothers found a little more money and that Dryden found that there were advantages in being associated with them.

The writing of plays, however, was inferior to translation in the reliability of its profits. Translation promised better, and it is to the combined circumstances of Tonson's genius, commercial and literary, and the political events of 1688 that we owe some of the greatest verse translations in English. Satire of contemporary events was now no longer possible for Dryden as a major undertaking, but his talent for satire, discovered so late in life, was not to be suppressed. It gets very full expression in his marvellous translation of Juvenal and (less marvellous) Persius in 1692. *Examen Poeticum: Being the Third Part of Miscellany Poems* came out in 1693. Dryden contributed fifteen pieces, most of them translations. The fourth miscellany appeared a year later, but by then Dryden was much less involved, having embarked on the most ambitious of the projects he carried out with Tonson—his translation of the *Works* of Virgil.

Since the story of that translation supplies much of what we know of the personal relationship between Dryden and Tonson, it is as well to bear in mind at the outset that the relationship was of far greater extent and duration than the period covered by the *Virgil*. Many of the surviving letters of Dryden and Tonson relate to that particular transaction, and since a quarrel occurred about it, the conclusion is often drawn, with the natural sympathy of posterity for the poet rather than the publisher, that Tonson was all at fault and that he habitually maintained a mercenary stance—'poetry by the yard'—in his attitude towards Dryden. (On the one known occasion when Tonson thought he had paid for more lines than he received, Dryden wrote more without demur.) Tonson was not really so crass, and his biographer, Kathleen M. Lynch, has rightly stressed that the remarkable thing about the two men is that their obvious differences did not drive them apart, even over the *Virgil*. The nature of that quarrel is still obscure, and need not concern us much. It seems that there was a genuine ambiguity in the contract between the men which led Dryden to believe that he was to receive more money from the second subscriptions than Tonson assumed. The quarrel, as far as one can judge, lasted quite a while, but it did end, though a trifle sourly. In January 1695 or thereabouts Dryden wrote in a letter to Tonson, dealing with arrangements for the Virgil: 'Upon trial I find all of your trade are sharpers and you not more than others; therefore I have not wholly left you.' He concludes that he is 'not your enemy, and may be your friend'. Thereafter the breach mended, and Tonson continued as Dryden's publisher and perhaps as his friend, serving him by collecting his rents, for instance, or by publishing the only play written by John Dryden, junior, in 1696. Tonson published *The Works of Virgil* translated by Dryden in 1697.

The method followed by Tonson and Dryden to finance their version of Virgil deserves attention, since nothing illustrates better the changing relationship between the poet, the patron, and the public. Dryden started on the work in 1693, and in the four years when it absorbed most of his time he lived on the £200 which Tonson gave him, in instalments, for the 'copy' and the subscriptions of two lists of 'subscribers'. Like the miscellany, which Tonson did not invent but which he perfected, subscription publishing was nothing new, but until Tonson it had never been used for English literature and had never been so successful. In 1687 Tonson published by subscription the fourth edition of *Paradise Lost* (it was actually dated 1688) and Milton's poem, which had never till then 'moved' well, was assured of a success. In extending the subscription method to Dryden's

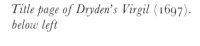
Title page of Ogilby's Virgil (1654).

Title page of Dryden's Virgil (1697).
below left

Ivory medallion of William, Prince of
Orange. below

Virgil, the work of a living English poet, Tonson took a step of great importance in English literary history.

Subscription publishing allowed the production of large books, often those including many plates or special illustrations. Before the middle of the seventeenth century, the method was used particularly for books of science, geography, and law, and for large theological works, especially those by nonconformist clergymen, those, that is, who had no established stipends. John Ogilby's *Virgil* in 1654 was the first translation of the Latin poet to appear by the subscription method and is in many ways an important precursor of the Dryden-Tonson version. (Dryden mocked Ogilby in *Mac Flecknoe* as a poetaster, but when, in making his own translation, he was stuck for a rhyme or generally tired, Ogilby's version was among those from which he stole.) Ogilby's version had been illustrated by a series of engravings which Tonson, in an uncharacteristic piece of cheese-paring, lamented by bibliophiles, took over and used for the Dryden edition. (Tonson had wished the book to be dedicated to William III but Dryden resisted successfully. Yet as a letter to his sons shows, the vestiges of Tonson's ambition were still to be seen. '[Tonson] has missed of his design in the dedication, though he had prepared the book for it; for in every figure of Aeneas, he has caused him to be drawn like King William, with a hooked nose.' The altered noses [see p. 50] are perhaps the most oblique tribute ever paid to royalty.)

Moreover, like Ogilby, Dryden and Tonson opened two subscription lists. The first, of one hundred names, was to commit the subscribers to a down-payment of three guineas and a final payment of two guineas on delivery of the book. The subscribers would receive copies on fine paper and each person on the list would have his name, coat-of-arms, and titles placed below one of the engravings. The subscribers on the second list, who were not limited in number, paid a guinea down and a further guinea on receipt of the book. Their copies were similar to those of the first subscribers, with fine paper and engravings, but their coats-of-arms were not included. (The book, of course, then went on sale to the general public at Tonson's shop.)

The significance of these arrangements may not be apparent at first sight, but will appear if we add some details. The idea of a translation of Virgil by Dryden was public property for some time before the contract was drawn up. Dryden and Tonson doubtless talked about it to others, and the *Miscellanies* had carefully prepared the ground. In the *Gentleman's Journal* in June 1694, just when Dryden and Tonson were drawing up their contract, Peter Motteux is found hoping 'that Mr Dryden will undertake to give us a translation of Virgil; 'tis indeed a most difficult work, but if anyone can assure himself of success, 'tis doubtless the Virgil of our Age, for whose noble pen that best of Latin poets seems reserved'. The public was ready for Dryden's attempt and wanted it to succeed. In fact the subscription

John Dryden
To translate Ecl. Georg.
& Eneids of Virgil.

to do nothing in ye mean
time, except the Transla-
tion of Fresnoy, or any Poem
or Book in Prose, not above
ye price, when printed

for the sole Benefit of
Jac. Tonson.

Mr Tonson to pay to
Mr Dryden £200. viz.
50 in ye when the Ecl.
& Georg. are done: 50£
when ye first 4 Æn. ar
finished. 50£ at ye end
of ye 9th book: & 50£ when
ye whole is compleated.

Tonson to provide 100
Plates, used formerly in ye

Imprimis The said
the said John Dryden shall
with such notes preface or
and agree in manner afo
thing to be printed Except
agreed by and between the
Gentlemen Subscribers and
And Excepting also his p
Item It is herein and he
Jacob Tonson his Exers & Ad
under the agreem ts herein
Item It is herein and he
herein and hereby coven
said John Dryden for the
From the said John Dryden th
Shop in Fleetstreet And also
soe translated as aforesaid
said John Dryden of the Fift
at the place aforesaid And a
or upon the delivery of the
Item The said Jacob Tonson

lists, particularly the first, and Dryden's attitude towards them show that the public knew that it had its part to play in what was seen as an enterprise of importance to the nation. The first subscription list was to provide evidence in its roll of prominent names that the nobility and gentry of England supported Dryden, both financially and morally. In that respect the provision beneath the plates of the coats-of-arms is not a trivial matter. It showed that genuine 'quality', one hundred armigerous persons, stood behind the translator. On 29 October 1695 Dryden said in a letter to Tonson,

> I must have a place for the Duke of Devonshire. Some of your friends will be glad to take back their three guineas.... I find my Lord Chesterfield and my Lord Petre are both left out, but my Lady Macclesfield must have a place.

Nowadays when we have to find the money to save a beautiful Leonardo or an ugly Titian for the nation, a public appeal is launched and lists of subscribers appear in the press *pour encourager les autres*. The first subscription list for Dryden's *Virgil* was in some ways similar, and Dr Johnson remarked on the kind and quality of additional support that Dryden received.

> The expectation of his work was undoubtedly great; the nation considered its honour as interested in the event. One [Gilbert Dolben] gave him the different editions of his author, and another helped him in the subordinate parts. The arguments of the several books were given him by Addison.

Addison wrote the 'Essay on the Georgics'. Knightley Chetwood wrote the 'Life' of Virgil and the 'Preface on Pastoral' for the volume, while Congreve checked the whole of the translation in manuscript against the Latin original and helped Tonson compose the advertisements. Dryden was invited to Denham Court and to Burghley to work on the translation in peaceful and elegant surroundings. All in all, the volume was a communal effort, and that fact might somewhat alleviate the sting of another of Johnson's remarks. Dryden dedicated each main section of the *Works* of Virgil, the *Pastorals*, the *Georgics*, and the *Aeneid*, to a different nobleman. Johnson asserted that this was so 'that no opportunity of profit might be lost' and that it was the 'oeconomy of flattery, at once lavish and discreet'. No doubt this is true, but it may not be all the truth. Dryden the Jacobite had refused to dedicate the book to William III, and in dividing it between three dedicatees he maintained its communal spirit, in that no one person had pre-eminence. Besides making money for Dryden, the *Virgil* was 'for the nation'.

Dryden's contract with Tonson.

53

The subscription list turned the single patron into a community of support, and in that way the *Virgil* advances a decisive step away from patronage towards modern publishing. The subscribers are collectively responsible for supporting the venture but none of them is the patron. The list of their names confers credit on them, yet it is credit somewhat limited in that the amount they have given is known and fixed. (Dryden did, however, receive many individual gifts besides subscriptions to help him with the work, and of course he received presents from the three dedicatees.) The limitation of the list to 100 persons (though in fact there are 101 names on it) means that the book's producers, stationer and poet, are conferring a distinction of their own on the first subscribers in admitting them to membership. And the fact that, underlying all this, the subscription was simply a fancy way of buying the book meant that the subscribers had more in common than appeared with the ordinary public. Not long thereafter the publisher was able to step in himself and finance the production of books, and the patron-subscriber fell back into line with the rest of the public, except for a specialized existence nowadays as a member of a limited edition book club or as a subscriber to a magazine.

Another point of importance was that Dryden and his supporters clearly felt that the nation was ready for the translation inasmuch as the English language in its recent 'refinement', always a genuine concern of Dryden's, was now capable of equality with the Latin of the Augustan age. In this sense the *Virgil* was a claim for the greatness of the English language and the new 'correctness' of English poetry. Those who had subscribed to Ogilby's *Virgil* had done so to read Virgil in English, but subscribers to Dryden's version were paying for Dryden as much as for Virgil. It must be supposed, whatever was true for the general public, that many of the subscribers would have been insulted had it been suggested that they could not read Virgil in Latin. They subscribed, among all the other reasons for which people do such things, to support English literature and the English language.

Dryden received in all about £1400 for his *Virgil*, which was no fortune. Without knowing it, however, he had shown a way for a poet to achieve independence—financial independence, bringing with it independence of the theatre, of hack work, and of the patron. Alexander Pope's translation of Homer, following Dryden's example and profiting from his mistakes, gave Pope a freedom which Dryden never attained. Like so much in Dryden's life, his relationship with Tonson was truly representative of the experience of his age, especially in that it occurred so obviously in a world of great transition.

John Dryden.

3 Dryden the Man

Dryden was not a very genteel man. He was intimate with none but
poetical men. He was as plump as Mr pitt, of a fresh colour, and
a down look—and not very conversible.

ALEXANDER POPE

Dryden speaks often of himself in his various prose writings, but
almost always with a hint of polemical purpose. Thus he remarks
often on his 'modesty', his lack of ease and boldness in society, his
'bashfulness' we might say. He remarks on it so often, in fact, that one
begins to suspect that he protests too much, and in reading through his
prefaces and dedications one encounters a confidence in his own
talents and a strength of opinion that seem to belie much of what he
says of his manner among people. It is quite likely that he was happiest
on paper, that the confidence and ease of his arguments and wit in
writing were beyond anything he was able to reproduce in company—
in this respect he seems very similar to his friend Joseph Addison—and
that he felt a compulsion to warn the public that they must not expect
to meet in person the man who spoke to them from the page. This
warning may have had special significance for Dryden because of the
importance he attached to the art of conversation as a factor in the
development of sound literary opinions and good style. His reputation
as the 'literary arbiter' of the coffee-house is somewhat qualified by
his tendency to efface himself in polite social gatherings.

Little that is certain is known of Dryden's relations with his immediate family and his kin. There is a family tradition that Lady
Elizabeth was not a good wife to the poet, but there is little support
for it. (See the Reference Section, 'Lady Elizabeth Dryden'.) When
Dryden mentions her in his letters to other persons, he does so in a
perfectly normal and matter-of-fact way. She did not usually accompany him on his regular summer visits to Northamptonshire
and his family there, but again this seems to have been an arrangement quite acceptable to all parties. The glimpses we are given of the
marriage show it to have been a steady and established relationship,
unimpassioned but not therefore unhappy.

Dryden's enemies assiduously spread the story that in the early
1670s he had as his mistress an actress of the King's Company, Anne
Reeve or Reeves, who took part in several of his plays. She became a

nun in 1675, a circumstance which added piquancy to the story and ensured its further propagation. Again, we have to attach a 'perhaps' or a 'probably' to it. There is not enough proof to be certain.

Towards their three sons both Dryden and Lady Elizabeth showed open affection and frequent solicitude. The real instances of royal favour we see at work in Dryden's life almost all relate to his sons. He begged King's Scholarships at Westminster for Charles and John Jr, and Erasmus-Henry similarly went to Charterhouse by the King's favour. All three sons followed their father into the Church of Rome and John Jr was admitted a Fellow of Magdalen College, Oxford, at the insistence of James II during that monarch's great battle with the college. (If this was a mark of the King's favour to Dryden the convert, it rebounded, for John was ejected from Magdalen at the Revolution.) When it was decided that his sons should go to Rome to advance their careers in that Catholic city under the protection of their kinsman, Cardinal Howard, Dryden and his wife wrote to them frequently, though only one letter has survived. On one occasion, in a letter to Tonson, we find Dryden arranging to send to Rome two watches for his sons, made by the famous Thomas Tompion at a cost of £22, which, as Charles E. Ward points out, was 'almost as much as he would receive from two books of the *Aeneid*—four months' work'. It may be that this was an investment for his sons in the form of portable property, but in any case it bespeaks a deal of affection. Dryden's concern for his sons' health at a time when his own was fatally failing is very moving. Of Charles he wrote in 1697: 'If it please God that I must dye of over study, I cannot spend my life better, than in saving his.' Lady Dryden's spelling is more eccentric, but her sentiment is as strong. 'I will Leaf noe ston unturnd to help my beloved sonns.'

The survival of so few of Dryden's letters will always be regretted, but those that still exist show us an attractive personality and one capable of overturning our preconceptions. This is especially true of his letters to Elizabeth Steward, daughter of his cousin Elizabeth Creed and wife of Elmes Steward, of Cotterstock, Northants. There are sixteen letters to her, all from the last few years of Dryden's life. It is clear that Mrs Steward took pains to 'cultivate' Dryden. Most of his replies to her send his thanks for a gift or a favour, and since he felt that he should reward her interest in him with compliments, short accounts of his doings, and tidbits of gossip, the letters nourish our interest more than mere 'bread-and-butter' letters might.

Courtly compliment:
Old men are not so insensible of beauty as it may be you young ladies think. For my own part, I must needs acknowledge that your fair eyes had made me your slave before I received your fine presents.

His work:

> ...betwixt my intervals of physic and other remedies which I am using for my gravel [probably a condition of the urinary tract], I am still drudging on—always a poet, and never a good one. I pass my time sometimes with Ovid, and sometimes with our old English poet Chaucer, translating such stories as best please my fancy; and intend besides them to add somewhat of my own: so that it is not impossible, but ere the summer be passed, I may come down to you with a volume in my hand, like a dog out of the water with a duck in his mouth. As for the rarities you promise, if beggars might be choosers, a part of a chine of honest bacon would please my appetite more than all the marrow puddings; for I like them plain, having a very vulgar stomach.

The theatre (two plays on the same subject were produced in the same week):

> Both the *Iphigenias* have been played with bad success, and being both acted, one against the other, in the same week, clashed together like two rotten ships which could not endure the shock, and sunk to rights.

Wayfaring life:

> My journey to London was yet more unpleasant than my abode at Titchmarsh, for the coach was crowded up with an old woman, fatter than any of my hostesses on the road. I must confess she was for the most part silent, unless it were that sometimes her backside talked, and that discourse was not over-savoury to the nose. Her weight made the horses travel very heavily, but to give them a breathing time she would often stop us, and plead some necessity of nature, and tell us we were all flesh and blood. But she did this so frequently that at last we conspired against her, and that she might not be inconvenienced by staying in the coach, turned her out in a very dirty place, where she was to wade up to the ankles before she could reach the next hedge.

This last extract, particularly in being addressed to a lady correspondent, even now shocks one somewhat by its revelation of Restoration manners. Neither life nor literature was as yet so 'polite' as to exclude such an incident. In the novels of Fielding, fifty years later, it is quite likely that the situation would have exposed the fat woman's fellow passengers to the novelist's irony; in the Victorian novel, it could occur only in considerably expurgated form. One makes allowance for Dryden's ill-health, of course, but perhaps the real point of the extract is that it shows him in transit between country and town. There is a rustic earthiness here which does not fit Dryden's 'town' persona, the frequent indecency of his wit, especially in his plays, not excepted.

Dryden possessed a flexibility of response to his surroundings which gave him different 'voices' or personae when addressing lords or commoners, superiors or inferiors, townsmen or countrymen, men or women. To some extent we all possess it; if it is hypocrisy then it comes very naturally. Dryden responded to such changes of surroundings in a sympathetic way which recalls Keats's description of Shakespeare's 'negative capability', the great poet's power of effacing himself and of responding imaginatively so as to become 'another person' while creation lasts. Shakespeare, it will be recalled, is reputed to have been the same kind of unobtrusive listener in society that Dryden was.

Dryden's annual visits to Northamptonshire, doubtless for the ostensible purpose of looking over his land, were clearly of great importance to him for rest and recuperation. They were, it may be supposed, visits into the past, and in those surroundings he seems to have taken on the role of a member of the local gentry, but by no means the foremost of them, and hardly ever the great man home on a visit. He wrote to Tonson in 1693,

> Having been obliged to sit up all last night almost, out of civility to strangers, who were benighted, and to resign my bed to them, I am sleepy all this day. And if I had not taken a very lusty pike that day, they must have gone supperless to bed, four ladies and two gentlemen; for Mr Dudley and I were alone with but one man and no maid in the house.

I suppose Dryden's motive in mentioning the incident came really from his fisherman's pride in the size of that pike, but the lines show us quite clearly that in Northamptonshire Dryden himself was no stranger. It is only when he writes from the country to a more exalted or sophisticated acquaintance than Tonson that we are truly shown country scenes through city eyes.

> I am now settled in the country, and having given two or three days to idleness, parsons, and my cousin's discourse, which is the worst of the three evils, am going to drudge for the winter... my cousin is to be managed as I please, being sufficiently easy as well in all other things as in his understanding. He talks nothing all day long to me in French and Italian to show his breeding. (To the Earl of Dorset, 1677)

When writing to the libertine Earl of Rochester in 1673, Dryden puts on the mask of the witty cynic (for just about the only time in his surviving correspondence) and speaks of the country in the traditional way of the man-about-town: 'If your Lordship had been in town and I in the country, I durst not have entertained you with three pages of a letter, but I know they are very ill things which can be tedious to a man who is fourscore miles from Covent Garden.'

Tis a strange quality in a man to love idleness so well
as to destroy his Estate by it; and yet at the same time to
pursue so violently the most toilsome, and most unpleasant
part of buisinesse. These observations would easily run
into lampoon, if I had not learnd that dangerous
part of wit, not so much out of good nature, but least
the ill nature of wits, I should show it to others, and
betray my self to a worse mischeif than one of... did to
my Enemy. This has been lately the case of Etherege
who translating a Satyre of Boileau's, and changing the
French names for English, read it so often that it
came to their eares who were concern'd; and forced him
to leave off the designe ere it were half finisht. Two of
the verses I remember.

I call a Spade a Spade, Eaton a Bully
Frampton a Pimp, and Brother John a Cully.
But one of his friends imagind those names not biting
enough for the dignity of a Satyre, and chang'd them
thus.

I call a Spade a Spade; Dunbar a Bully,
Brouncker a Pimp, and Aubrey bere a Cully.
Because I deale not in Satyre I have sent your...
a prologue and an epilogue which I made for our...
when they went down to Oxford. I hear... they
have succeeded; And by the event your Lordship will judge
how easy tis to passe any thing upon an University; and
how grosse flattery the learned will endure. If your
Lordship had been in Town, and I in the Country, I durst
not have entertaind you, with three pages of a letter;
but I know they are very ill things which can be tedious
to a man who is fourescore miles from Covent Garden. Tis upon
this confidence that I dare almost promise to entertain you with a thousand bagatelles every week; and
not fail spriting in any part of my letter, but that
wherein I take leave to call my selfe
                Your Lordships most obedient
                Servant   John Dryden

Dryden's few letters, then, do show us something of the man himself, which his poetry does only rarely or very obliquely. It is necessary to insist on the amount and warmth of friendship which the letters show and to point out that Dryden had many friends and kept them. He was, like all the Augustans, a 'poet militant', to use the description he borrowed from Cowley. To be a poet at that period was to be involved in controversy and animosity almost without intermission, yet, like Dryden, the other great writers of the age were firm and lasting friends with their friends, though enemies to their enemies. To read through the bibliography of 'Drydeniana' in Hugh Macdonald's *Dryden Bibliography* is very instructive, for it shows vividly that Dryden's claim to have been the most abused writer of his time—which is to say the best!—is likely to be the truth, and that the abuse did not start only when he entered the political wars. The literary quarrel with Sir Robert Howard on theatrical matters led to an unceasing war of words (on one occasion, of course, it became blows) which lasted throughout Dryden's career. He gave as good as he got, knowing that this kind of controversy was inevitably a part of his life. The terms of the quarrels seem very harsh nowadays—the personal characters of the combatants were fair game, and few holds of any kind were barred. Dryden's politics and his religious conversion gave much ammunition to his enemies, so much so that a major task of all his biographers has been to find nuggets of truth in a great heap of largely fanciful vituperation. The heap grew even after Dryden's death. One writer, for instance, depicts him in Hell.

> Like Sisyphus a restless stone he turns,
> And on a pile of his own labours burns,
> Whose curling flames most ghastly fiends do raise,
> Supplied with fuel from his impious plays.

And yet the letters show us that this poet militant could put aside such warfare when he turned back to private life and that the battles he fought did not distort his character, though they certainly scarred him.

In the letters some of those scars are visible, particularly those acquired through religion. Dryden never exactly 'explains' his conversion to Catholicism (though one of his best hints is given in a letter to Mrs Steward, when he speaks of the variations of species of Protestantism), but his letters show us the effects of the change. He writes of the fears of the Catholics under William and Mary, emphasizing their disabilities and helplessness. He hints at advances made to him in matters of religion by those in power and states his determination to maintain his stance of tacit obedience to the govern-

Dryden's handwriting: a letter to the Earl of Rochester.

ment in exchange for its toleration of him, though he rumbles a little against the politicians for actions he finds unconstitutional and malicious: 'Our hopes of the House of Commons are wholly dashed. Our proprieties are destroyed, and rather than we should not perish, they have made a breach in the Magna Charta, for which God forgive them.' On religious matters, Dryden in his letters is a sincere convert, willing to endure the penalties of a Catholic with the minimum of grumbling. An inveterate enemy might say again that he is over-insistent on 'not being capable of renouncing the cause for which I have so long suffered', but given the circumstances in which he had to live, such as the special taxes he had to pay, no one could grudge him a little obsessive bitterness. As in all the public quarrels of his life, the remarkable thing is that, with so much cause, there is so little bitterness in Dryden. Finally, one endorses his own words in the dedication to his comedy *Amphitryon* (1690):

> You see, Sir, I am not entertaining you, like Ovid, with a lamentable epistle from Pontus [Dryden refers to the *Epistulae ex Ponto* in which Ovid bemoans his banishment to the Black Sea]; I suffer no more than I can easily undergo, and so long as I enjoy my liberty, which is the birthright of an Englishman, the rest shall never go near my heart. The merry philosopher is more to my humour than the melancholic.

Part Two
Dryden's Beliefs

In retrospect it has seemed to some classical scholars, still under the spell of the Romantic view, that Greek tragedy died of Greek philosophy, that the primitive inspiration which the tragic poets drew from myth and ritual could not survive the destructive talk of Socrates. In the *Phaedo* Plato seems to suggest that Socrates felt a scruple on that account and sang a poetic swan-song before he died, as if to recant his inveterate addiction to reasonableness. He had been visited by certain dreams which intimated that he should 'cultivate and make music': so he composed a hymn to Apollo and turned Aesop's *Fables* into verse. Whether this delightful story is true or not, Plato took the occasion to define the kind of poetry that Socrates would write: it is didactic poetry, a class of literature which every respectable treatise on modern aesthetics has taught us to despise.

EDGAR WIND, Art and Anarchy

4 Philosophy

Dryden's Scepticism

Why should there be any *ipse dixit* in our poetry, any more than there is in our philosophy?

Preface to An Evening's Love

Dryden describes himself several times in his prose writings as a sceptic, one 'naturally inclined to scepticism in philosophy', but this apparently simple term needs careful interpretation. A frank statement by Dryden of the nature of his beliefs is so rare an event that it is quite understandable that his avowed 'scepticism' should have been thankfully grasped as one truly reliable hold on his elusive intellectual system. It can now be said that at last Dryden's scepticism is properly understood, but this degree of certainty has come about only after much misunderstanding. It is also true to say that while we now possess a soundly based estimate of the importance of scepticism in Dryden's thought, it proves in actuality to leave 'unsolved' a number of problems in his thinking which earlier and erroneous misinterpretations were able to 'resolve' with confidence.

The true understanding of what Dryden meant when he applied the term 'sceptic' to himself is the work of several modern scholars, and their investigations are summarized and carried further by Phillip Harth in his book *Contexts of Dryden's Thought*. To his work this *Preface* is greatly and generally indebted, especially in the present chapter. Serious students of Dryden will inevitably wish to examine Harth's work at first hand. My objective here is to help to disseminate his conclusions, to spread the word that a real advance has been made in the study of Dryden's ideas.

As Dryden used it, the term 'scepticism' varies in meaning according to its context. If the context is carefully considered, the two basic meanings separate themselves fairly easily. When writing of ancient times, Dryden can use 'sceptic' in the context of classical philosophy to mean the Pyrrhonists, a sect of philosophers who argued that human reason was so fallible and the evidence of the human senses so unreliable that no valid results could be obtained by such doubtful means as to the nature of truth. As a result, Pyrrhonism was antirational and advocated a perennial suspension of judgment on any question which might have more than one answer. Dryden himself, in his 'Life of Plutarch', paraphrasing the sources on which he relied, described the Pyrrhonists or 'Pyrrhonians' as the 'grosser sort of sceptics, who bring all certainty in question, and startle even at the notions of common sense'. In his 'Life of Lucian' he can define a sceptic as one who 'doubted of everything'.

Since Dryden called himself a sceptic, and since Pyrrhonism would solve so many problems for the understanding of his thought, it has been held until recently that it is proper to describe Dryden as a Pyrrhonist. Thus his tendency to balance conflicting points of view in his writings could be the Pyrrhonist's constitutional inability or refusal to decide. His political conservatism could be the Pyrrhonist's distrust of change or Utopia on the grounds that what already exists has been tested, whereas changes are hypothetical and depend for their attraction on the reasoning and imaginative powers of the fallible mind. His conversion to Catholicism would be the Pyrrhonist's ultimate abandonment of reason by seeking refuge in the infallible authority of the Church of Rome.

The most famous advocate of Pyrrhonism in the modern Western cultural tradition is Montaigne. Dryden wrote of his affection and admiration for 'honest Montaigne'. In English literature, another notable distruster of the powers of reason is Sir Thomas Browne. His position is that of the fideist, the man who says that reason can do nothing in the matter of religion and that faith alone is man's means of knowing God. The title of Dryden's first religious poem, *Religio Laici*, echoes that of Browne's great book, *Religio Medici*. Superficially, Dryden seems to be aligning himself with Montaigne and Browne, and it is no wonder that, until the whole question was reopened and critically re-examined, it was customary to see Dryden as a Pyrrhonistic fideist, a man who could be imagined as saying, 'I do not know; therefore I will believe'. The poet commonly taken as the inaugurator of an 'age of reason' could thus appear as a man with no trust in reason.

Dryden was not as careful as we might wish in his use of philosophical nomenclature, but care exercised on his behalf by recent students of his work has shown us a vital distinction. Three times in his writings he claims for himself the position of a sceptic. In each instance the circumstances are the same, and in each case it becomes clear that he does not wish to declare himself a Pyrrhonist. The first of these passages must here do duty for all of them. It comes in the 'Defence of *An Essay of Dramatic Poesy*' (1668) in which Dryden defends himself against an attack by his brother-in-law, Sir Robert Howard.

> He is here pleased to charge me with being magisterial, as he has done in many other places of his preface. Therefore in vindication of myself, I must crave leave to say, that my whole discourse was sceptical, according to that way of reasoning which was used by Socrates, Plato, and all the academics of old, which Tully [Cicero] and the best of the Ancients followed, and which is imitated by the modest inquisitions of the Royal Society. That it is so, not only

the name will show, which is an essay, but the frame and composition of the work. You see it is a dialogue sustained by persons
of several opinions, all of them left doubtful, to be determined by
the readers in general.

The term 'sceptical' is opposed here by Dryden to the term 'magisterial', and opposed, we note, with something of indignation. The last
thing he wishes to claim for himself is dogmatic authority, which was
the kind of dead hand which, in Dryden's view, Aristotle had laid on
'natural philosophy' or science in the preceding centuries. The 'best
of the Ancients' in this context would not include Aristotle, for the
'way of reasoning' Dryden extols by strong implication here, and
which he calls 'scepticism', is the exact opposite of deference to
authority, such as that given by the schoolmen to Aristotle, and
follows the method of the 'modest inquisitions of the Royal Society'—
Nullius in Verba—of which Dryden had been a Fellow from 1662 till
1666. (His loss of membership came about because he did not pay
his dues. He had no discernible disagreement with the Royal Society's
aims or philosophy.)

The members of the Royal Society were hardly a group of
Pyrrhonists, but they, like Dryden, frequently adopted for themselves
the title of 'sceptics'. One can see the contrast between Pyrrhonistic
scepticism and Royal Society scepticism most vividly in an example
suggested by Phillip Harth. Montaigne, a true Pyrrhonist, could see
no reason to try to decide between the Ptolemaic and Copernican
accounts of the structure of the solar system. Such indifference, and
particularly such an implicit denial of the importance for mankind of
determining the truth of this matter, is entirely opposed to the philosophy and the practice of the Royal Society. Their scepticism was not,
as was Montaigne's, a theory of knowledge or, more properly, a
theory of the impossibility, and therefore the futility, of attempting to
arrive at certainty on such topics. For the Royal Society, 'scepticism'
was a mode of inquiry wherein the inquirer started by doubting and
reconsidering all his information in the light of reason and eventually
hoped to arrive at true and certain knowledge. Lord Bacon, whose
writings set out the methods of enquiry which the Royal Society
followed, described this in a famous remark in *The Advancement of
Learning*: 'If a man will begin with certainties, he shall end in doubts;
but if he will be content to begin with doubts, he shall end in certainties.' Whenever, in the controversies of his literary life, Dryden
had to defend himself from the charge of being 'magisterial' or
dogmatic, he relied on this definition of scepticism. He claimed he
was concerned to find the truth, and that he did so by a tentative,
modest, self-doubting, and basically unauthoritarian approach. After
all had been debated and reasoned, then certainty might be evident.

Such a habit of mind, as we have seen, could easily have been
inculcated by aspects of Dryden's Cambridge education. It is clear,

besides, that a rational, wary, self-doubting tentativeness in method, leading to confidence of ultimate judgment, well suited the personality of the man. In conversation he was generally hesitant to obtrude himself, but after he had studied a question and thought out its implications he was prepared to give his opinion in writing and to 'end in certainties'. His satires show the force of his decision and commitment in politics, and his religious poems are tentative only to serve the ends of certainty.

Scepticism so defined restores one's faith in Dryden's own faith in the power of reason. He need no longer be looked on as a man unwilling to decide between possible alternatives, nor will it be necessary to see his Catholicism as the abandonment of reason and a plunge into fideism. On the other hand, the corrected account of the nature of Dryden's scepticism places back on his readers the duty to understand where and how it operates. In religion, for example, much is, in Dryden's view, 'above' reason. The scepticism Dryden truly advocates covers a smaller area of his mind than the Pyrrhonism which used to be attributed to him. It is a far less extensive, esoteric, or antique mental attitude than it once seemed. In fact, Dryden is sceptical in the way it is generally hoped that any modern, educated man will be sceptical. While he may limit the power of reason, particularly in its application to religion, in all other matters he expects to see and judge for himself, with the right and duty of doubt until certainty is properly demonstrated. If we are tempted to sum this up as 'common sense', then I think Dryden would agree. He describes common sense as 'a rule in everything but matters of faith and revelation', and an understanding of the relationship of scientific scepticism to revealed religion is provided by him in his 'Character of Polybius' (1693):

> He who knew not our God, saw through the ridiculous opinions of the heathens concerning theirs; and not being able without revelation to go further, stopped at home in his own breast, and made prudence his goddess, truth his search, and virtue his reward.

Polybius, in fact, took his thinking as far as he could with common sense and without Christ. He was a sceptic in doubting the claims of the heathen religions, but had no revelation of the true religion. (The fate of such 'virtuous heathens' after death is an important motif in *Religio Laici*.)

As in religion, so in politics. The scepticism operating in Dryden's literary criticism and in the routine problems of his intellectual life is not brought to bear on matters of divine right, the duties of subjects to kings, or the existence of an 'original contract' between ruler and ruled. Other minds in Dryden's day followed that course and wrought great changes in political theory, but Dryden's was not among them. His belief in the value of rightful authority and traditional forms for achieving political stability—his moderate conservatism—was as much an article of faith as his religion. We would nowadays say it was 'instinctive', but whatever the terminology, and however well Dryden called on reason to defend his political beliefs, they were not in their essence open to the criticism of his 'scientific scepticism'.

Scepticism and Literary Form

The forms into which Dryden cast a number of his important works reveal the effect of his 'scepticism in philosophy' on his methods as a controversialist. Yet these forms must be studied with caution, for when Dryden appears most obviously to be the even-handed presenter of opposing views, refusing to interject his own opinions on the matter in question, he is always being deliberately deceptive. He has decided on his own views and one of the participants in the debate will be their advocate. Moreover, that advocacy will be supported by Dryden to the greatest extent compatible with giving the opposed arguments an apparently fair hearing. What happens, in fact, is that we are presented with what appears to be a genuine debate of which we as readers are the judges. Yet Dryden so loads the dice that it is most difficult for any reader to award the victory to the side which Dryden opposes. The form of the work, the debate, is 'sceptical' in that both sides are presented, but the author's verdict was decided before he began to write and the reader is subtly led to agree with him.

The notable instances of the 'debate form' in Dryden's work are the *Essay of Dramatic Poesy*, *Religio Laici*, and *The Hind and the Panther*. In each of these the reader is given an all-important illusion of freedom. He sees both sides presented with apparent fairness and feels he is making an objective decision. In fact, as a study of the way Dryden favours the participants in the debate would show, the reader is being led to the conclusion Dryden wishes him to reach. He is free only to follow or to miss the signs erected to guide him. The method is in many ways like that of the Socratic dialogues. The reader is brought to 'participate' in the debate; his acceptance of the pre-ordained but hidden conclusion will therefore tend to be firm.

The authors of *The Rehearsal* make Mr Bays say, 'Gad, I love reasoning in verse', for Dryden was famous for his ratiocination. Yet what applies to 'debate' also applies to 'reasoning'. Dryden could fascinate an audience by presenting the two sides of a question brilliantly, but he is usually committed to one side. 'Reasoning in verse' in the sense of a genuine investigation into truth is merely apparent. Dryden applies his oratorical skills to fine literary effect, for when he argues in his poetry he is not thinking aloud but guiding his listeners towards a desired conclusion. The greatness of his argumentative style is not that of the original thinker, but that of the orator, selecting and arranging those ideas which will best persuade his readers to follow him.

Moderation

Throughout his intellectual life, Dryden showed a preference for moderation and the avoidance of extremes, and he strove hard against those forces which would have dragged him towards the Scylla or the Charybdis of any controversy. Yet the events of his life, baldly stated, seem to show that he strove ineffectually. His support of Cromwell is followed by the political satires of the 1680s which show us the 'Tory poet', the scourge of the Whigs, and in religion his conversion to the Church of Rome seems to show a move to the right of the religious road, away from the median of Anglicanism. Yet the truth is that Dryden loathed regal tyranny as much as he loathed the anarchy which Shaftesbury seemed to promise, and that as a Catholic he was decidedly a moderate, both in secular and ecclesiastical matters, and must have viewed the political conduct of his King and co-religionist with great perturbation. The inferences which should be drawn from the outward events are not at all those which seem at first obvious. To the world in general Dryden appeared as a political and religious opportunist, but we know better.

To modern minds moderation may seem dull. Romanticism has given extremism an undeniable, though equivocal, blessing. The middle of the road is an unsafe, or at least an unglamorous, place to be. In the Restoration, on the other hand, men had seen extremism at work and at close quarters, and if we cannot feel the attraction which moderation had for Dryden, we should at least make the intellectual effort to appreciate that there was a quality of heroism and plain good sense in his refusal to go to the limit in any direction.

In Dryden's philosophical and intellectual life moderation, as we have seen, takes a 'sceptical' form, and in an earlier section it has been shown how his Cambridge education may have played a part in making his mind receptive to the methods of the Royal Society. Another aspect of that moderation, the choice of the *via media*, is linked to the scholastic curriculum at Cambridge, and particularly to scholastic forms of enquiry and Aristotelian ethics. A man's education is usually a patchwork of experiences out of which he strives to make a garment to fit his needs. Dryden seems to me to have done so with considerable success.

The *via media* of Aristotelian ethics fitted beautifully into the forms of disputation and presentation employed by the student in the scholastic curriculum. The emphasis on arrangement, on the placing of ideas in structures and categories, accords well with the Aristotelian habit in ethics of defining ideal conduct by reference to extremes. Dryden shows the effects of these processes throughout his life as a writer. As a critic especially, he defines the highest excellence by showing how pairs of writers can be used in combination to create an ideal. He admires both Shakespeare and Jonson, for example, but both diverge slightly, though in opposite directions, from the absolute ideal. Had Shakespeare more of Jonson's 'art', and Jonson more of

Shakespeare's 'nature', then each would have been perfect. Such perfection is unlikely to be found in human life, and this recognition of the highest man can achieve as always something below the ideal tells us a fact of importance about the attraction of such schematized accounts for Dryden. Christianity, Aristotelian ethics, and personal history combine in him to stress the duty of man to pursue an ideal while recognizing the impossibility of ever achieving it. In this respect Dryden is the true precursor of the English Augustan humanism of the eighteenth century. Unlike the *philosophes* of France, the great English writers of the eighteenth century maintained a belief in the ultimate impossibility of human perfection. They were but rarely betrayed into utopianism, and like Dryden they found schemes and the use of extremes to point an ideal middle way very attractive. *A Tale of a Tub* and *Gulliver's Travels* are two of the most famous instances. The similarity need not be a matter of 'influence', but it is certainly true that Dryden and Swift shared basic assumptions which connect them more strongly than any personal feelings could separate them.

Dryden did not pretend that moderation came easily to him. He strove to be moderate, but in his satires he was licensed, in the interests of a middle way between extremes, to lash the extremists. Again like Swift, and like the other great satirists who followed, he felt himself permitted, in the cause of moderation, to take a holiday from moderation. Few satirists display conspicuous calmness of temper in their private lives, and this psychological escape mechanism of satire is very important when one tries to understand them. Dryden knew, too, that artistic moderation was not easy for him. When he puts Homer and Virgil together to make an ideal epic poet, he confesses that he feels closer to Homer. He knows that the ideal poet should combine the fire of inspiration with the willingness to revise and polish, yet he himself is by nature reluctant to revise and often sends his work into the world less perfect than it should be. Ideals are important to him, but as a man he is well aware of the difficulty of attainment.

The tendency to schematize and to point to an ideal middle between extremes may seem to support the notion of Dryden's 'Pyrrhonism', a reluctance to decide. Since an ideal of the epic or of political conduct was never realized or ultimately realizable, it has something Platonic about it which might delude one into thinking it does not exist. Later chapters will attempt to define Dryden's opinions in religion and in politics, and to show that he knew very well where he stood.

Poetic Licence

The gravamen of the Romantic complaint against reason, science, and Augustan poetry was that they stifled imagination, producing, in

Arnold's formula, an 'age of prose'. Keats, in a famous passage in 'Lamia', complained that science had murdered the poetic beauty of the rainbow, and in 'Sleep and Poetry' he proclaimed his distaste for the couplet verse of the previous century. Such an attitude was being expressed long before Keats wrote, of course, and in Dryden's views on his rights as a poet to use whatever he found 'poetical' we see an early, though unsystematic and fragmentary, refusal of the poet to permit the limitation of his freedom. This is not to claim a Romantic status for Dryden. His belief in reason, moderation, and his own form of commonsense scepticism, added to his literary preferences, his respect for authority, and his politics, all these lead me to believe that he would have been happy to be acknowledged as the father of the poetry Keats so disliked. Yet attempts to suggest to Dryden that he should deliberately restrict the range of materials on which his sensibility could work were always resisted. Poetry obeyed a reason which overrode the prescriptive formulations of his critics. Poetic licence in his view could be rationally defended, and common sense in that case resided with the defender of the poet's liberty.

In combating those who would limit his poetic licence, it is striking that Dryden puts up a defence which conforms at least superficially to the Royal Society's policy. John Evelyn, the diarist and likewise an F.R.S., could write scathingly of 'chimeras and other things which are not in nature', but Dryden spoke up for the chimera without abandoning the style of commonsense scepticism.

> But how are poetical fictions, how are hippocentaurs and chimeras, or how are angels or immaterial substances to be imaged; which some of them are things quite out of nature; others, such whereof we can have no notion? . . . The answer is easy to the first part of it. The fiction of some beings which are not in nature (second notions, as the logicians call them) has been founded on the conjunction of two natures which have a real separate being. So hippocentaurs were imagined by joining the natures of a man and horse together. . . . The same reason may also be alleged for chimeras and the rest. And poets may be allowed the like liberty for describing things which really exist not, if they are founded on popular belief. Of this nature are fairies, pigmies, and the extraordinary effects of magic; for 'tis still an imitation, though of other men's fancies. . . .
> ('The Author's Apology for Heroic Poetry and Poetic Licence, prefixed to *The State of Innocence, an Opera*', 1677)

Dryden thus 'proves' that almost anything a poet writes is an 'imitation of nature', a criterion which embraces both classical precepts and the rational modernism of the Royal Society. The liberty he claims, when one examines the passage closely, is huge and would satisfy almost any writer, from a Romantic poet to a science fiction novelist. 'Out of nature' becomes a meaningless phrase, since every kind of fictional being can be linked to nature, however tenuously, and to accept 'popular belief' as a 'limitation' is to set very wide boundaries indeed. Elsewhere, Dryden goes even further and claims that poetry provides the best of all ways of investigating mysterious phenomena:

> An heroic poet is not tied to a bare representation of what is true, or exceeding probable: but. . . he may let himself loose to visionary objects, and to the representation of such things as depending not on sense, and therefore not to be comprehended by knowledge, may give him a freer scope for imagination. 'Tis enough that in all ages and religions the greatest part of mankind have believed the power of magic, and that there are spirits or spectres which have appeared. This, I say, is foundation enough for poetry; and I dare further affirm that the whole doctrine of separated beings. . .may better be explicated by poets than philosophers or divines. For their speculations on this subject are wholly poetical; they have only their fancy for their guide, and that, being sharper in an excellent poet than it is likely it should be in a phlegmatic, heavy gown-man, will see farther in its own empire, and produce more satisfactory notions on those dark and doubtful problems.
>
> ('Of Heroic Plays: An Essay prefixed to
> *The Conquest of Granada*', 1672)

The poet thus becomes an ally of the theologian, the philosopher, and the scientist in the search for truth, and his power of 'fancy' gives him distinct advantages on certain subjects. Dryden defends the use of the imagination and the importance of poetry by attaching them to the other arts and sciences on terms of equality. He makes no quasi-religious or mystical claims for the imagination, as the Romantics were to do, but in compensation he insists that the poet's business is essentially the same as that of the scholar or the scientist. In its own insistence on the superiority of imaginative insight over all other kinds of knowledge, Romanticism might be said to have 'priced itself out' of the world of mere learning. Dryden refused to think of poetry as anything but learning applied to human nature, sharing its approaches and its materials on equal terms with all the arts and sciences.

The defence of poetic licence Dryden puts up in the passages I have quoted is, of course, carried out with his particular zest for argument. Its playfulness may be an indication that he is not entirely serious and that he is merely revelling in being able to make a defence of an apparently hopeless position. On the other hand, his poetry— and not just the poetry of his 'heroic' plays—shows that he really did exercise the freedom he claims, and that to accept the limitations against which he argues would have severely cramped him. Yet his respect for the philosophical methods of the Royal Society was genuine (a respect he did not hand on to Swift, Addison, or Pope), so the two things had somehow to be reconciled. If Dryden finds, and like Shakespeare and Milton he often does, that the 'old' cosmology of Ptolemy is of more use to him in a poem than the 'new' cosmology of Copernicus, then he uses the Ptolemaic system unhesitatingly. It is unlikely that he believed in it, but he did believe firmly in the poet's right 'of speaking things in verse which are beyond the severity of prose'.

5   Religion

Religion and politics were woven together for Restoration men in a way which is only occasionally found in the modern world. In England then, as in Northern Ireland today, politics tended to follow religion, though rarely *vice versa*. A man might well be a Whig because he was a Dissenter; he was unlikely to be a Dissenter because he was a Whig. In the present discussion, the political aspects of Dryden's religion will be in the main held back until his political beliefs are examined, but the impossibility of a total separation will serve as a reminder of the very real link between religion and politics in those days.

Dryden's religious beliefs are important to a student of his poetry because at certain points they enter his poetry. He wrote two major poems on religion, *Religio Laici* (1682), and *The Hind and the Panther* (1687). The first he wrote as a Protestant, the second as a Catholic, and each poem will serve here as the opportunity for the examination of his attitudes as a Protestant and then as a Catholic.

These poems take religion for their subject, but we must be cautious of calling them 'religious poems', for they, like so much in Dryden's work, disappoint post-Romantic expectations and demand to be understood and appreciated on their own terms. If the paradigm of a religious poem for the reader is 'The Hound of Heaven', 'The Wreck of the Deutschland', or even a poem by Donne or George Herbert, then Dryden's poems will take some getting used to. They tell us little about the state of Dryden's soul, for their purpose is not to be confessional or to sweep us along with the author's fervour. There is little that is mystical or soaring in them, for they, like all Dryden's poems, are social documents, dealing with ideas as they affect men who have to live with them. If we can clarify at once what these poems are not, then to discover what they actually are can be an enlightening business and not a dull one. Dryden is not half-hearted in *Religio Laici* and *The Hind and the Panther*. His wit, his ratiocinative skills, and his general poetic talents are fully employed. With prejudice laid aside, the beauty as well as the intellectual force of the poems is free to make its impact on us.

The Church of England

Dryden belonged at least nominally to the Church of England all his life until his conversion to Catholicism in 1685 or 1686. He was baptized at All Saints Church, Aldwincle, ten days after his birth, and there is no indication that he was other than a Church of England man until he became a Catholic. The Puritanism of the family in his youth was still within the Church of England, and if he flirted with deism at a fairly early stage of his career, as has been suggested, there is no sign of it outside his works. In 1670 he could write of 'the due reverence of that religion which I profess', though his profession of it was so unostentatious, at least in his writing, that the appearance of *Religio Laici* is still a surprising event in his career. In seeing that work as Dryden's 'Anglican poem', we take it to be generally representative of the religious assumptions of the majority of his countrymen, and this representativeness applies as much to the style and presentation as to the ideas and arguments.

The Church of England had been 'restored' with the Stuart monarchy in 1660, but it was a couple of years before the terms of that restoration were settled by Parliament. Before his return, Charles had issued in Holland the Declaration of Breda, in which he had declared a general pardon, with certain exceptions, and had promised in religion 'a liberty to tender consciences'. This offer of toleration was, however, vaguely worded and would need the ratification of Parliament to become a political fact. Charles himself favoured toleration of differing beliefs in religion, for he himself inclined towards Catholicism and had been well served by his Catholic subjects. (It was well understood both by Charles and his successor, James II, that 'toleration', to preserve the appearance at least of fairness, would have to include both Protestant Dissenters and Roman Catholics.) His Parliaments, however, were to prove much more righteously Anglican than the Defender of the Faith.

The restored Church was presented with the choice of inclusiveness or uniformity. If it could find a place for the large body of Puritans who had agreed to the Restoration and who wished to stay inside the Church, then it could represent virtually all of the English people with the exception of Roman Catholics and extreme Protestant sectaries. If it wished to insist that membership of the Church of England should be confined to those willing to subscribe to a rigidly defined set of Anglican doctrines, then its members would be uniform in belief at the cost of excluding from the communion a relatively large group of dissenting Protestants. Inclusiveness demanded a forgiving and compromising approach. It would mean an abandonment of the very principles for which so many Church of England men had suffered and been exiled. It would change the Restoration from a final Anglican triumph and vindication into a compromise treaty. It would tarnish the cult of King Charles the Martyr. It is no wonder that it came to nothing.

On the Puritan side there were many, especially a large body of Presbyterians, who welcomed the Declaration of Breda as the first step towards the permanent establishment of themselves within the Church, where they would be able to keep the livings they had held during the Interregnum. For that to be possible, the Restoration Church would have to agree to some modifications of doctrine (the High Church insistence that communicants kneel to take the sacraments, for example) and of Church government (such as a scheme of 'modified episcopacy', whereby a bishop's authority would be that of the president of a synod). If such conditions could not be agreed, then the Presbyterians were willing to suffer in their turn.

Until the election of Charles II's 'Cavalier Parliament' in 1661, a compromise solution seemed possible. The Convention Parliament which had invited Charles back was a moderate body by the standards of the time. There was a general assumption that the bishops would be 'restored' too, but very little support for the 'lords bishops' of Charles I's time. When the Convention Parliament passed a bill dealing with the painful matter of replacing evicted ministers in their livings, it provided no protection for the Puritans thus removed, but it did try to minimize the opportunity for evictions. A Declaration on Ecclesiastical Affairs of October 1660 gave temporary latitude in doctrine and forms of worship pending a final decision by a national synod. The Presbyterians must have been comforted, even if Charles was not, by the fact that he began his reign with ten Presbyterian chaplains to minister to his rather rudimentary spiritual needs.

This period of hope for the Presbyterians lasted only until the Cavalier Parliament, which was not dissolved until 1679 and is therefore sometimes called the Long Parliament of the Restoration. The bishops took their seats in the Lords once more, the Commons as a body were fanatically royalist, and there was a general determination everywhere to finish off once and for all the surviving traces of the Puritan experiment in government. 'Setting quickly to work, they added a series of measures to the Statute Book of such a character as to create a second Restoration settlement far more uncompromising than the first' (David Ogg). The national synod for the determining of religious differences failed to reach an agreement; the prayerbook was revised by Convocation of the Church of England.

> The Thirty-Nine Articles, with their affirmation of the doctrine of Predestination, remained unaltered; otherwise the revised formulary succeeded in rejecting everything considered distinctively Puritan or Papist, and theological difficulties were safely navigated by steering between them. 'It hath been the wisdom of the Church of England,' declared the preface, 'to keep the mean between the two extremes of too much stiffness in refusing and of too much easiness in admitting any variation from it.' (Ogg)

This proclamation of the middle way was, however, to be codified by Parliament, and a series of laws, known collectively as the 'Clarendon Code', was enacted to make the Church of England secure in its claim to be the state religion. These laws provided that any clergyman who failed to meet the doctrinal and political demands of the Church (such as the acceptance of the revised liturgy, the repudiation of the Solemn League and Covenant, and the denial of a subject's right to take up arms against the king) should be expelled from the Church. The 'cut-off date' was 24 August 1662, and when it came about one-fifth of the beneficed clergy of the Church of England, nearly two thousand men, were automatically dispossessed of their livings and became Dissenters. The event made the Church for a while into a tightly knit body in terms of doctrine and politics, but it created a large Protestant 'opposition' to itself and sacrificed many men of talent and the vital principle of flexibility, factors which were in the end to cost the Church dearly.

So far as the laity were concerned, the Clarendon Code made communicating membership of the Church of England necessary for the holding of virtually any public office, civil or military. It conferred full English citizenship on Anglicans alone. Moreover, the determination of Parliament that nothing like the 'Great Rebellion' should ever occur again caused the legislature to enact a series of laws making life difficult for the Dissenters. A fairly active persecution of noncon-formists went on steadily for some time, and one very important effect of these laws and their prosecution was that the idea of an indissoluble link between dissent from the Church of England in religion and republicanism (or at least anti-royalism) in politics was hammered home incessantly and became one of the stock ideas of late seventeenth-century English life. The Bill of Indemnity which had been passed in 1660 had made it an offence for anyone to utter 'reproaches tending to recall the memory of the late differences' of the Civil War. The Clarendon Code of the Cavalier Parliament turned such reproaches into an institution.

The Church of England maintained its differences with the Church of Rome just as firmly as it held to those with the Dissenters, of course, but the history of the Civil War made the 'Protestant left', for a while at any rate, seem more dangerous than the 'Catholic right'. Then, as Catholicism triumphant in the person of Louis XIV and suspicions of the Catholicism of Charles II and his court began to force them-selves on the attention of Englishmen, Anglicans again began to feel threatened from both sides. Charles's attempt, like those of his brother, to extend political toleration to both Catholics and Protestant Dis-senters by the exercise of the prerogative in a Declaration of Indulgence was fiercely resisted by Parliament, and that body, which had started the reign in a mood of adulatory royalism, was at odds with the King over the extent of his prerogative. In 1678 the great Popish Plot began to be unfolded, and English politics took a strange turn.

Titus Oates, an entirely repulsive figure and a liar of genius, claimed knowledge of a plot by Jesuits to murder the King and rule

Medal of Shaftesbury, subject of Dryden's poem.

the country as a Catholic state with James as a puppet king who would be murdered in turn if he resisted that role. (In the earlier stages, Oates did not accuse James of complicity in or knowledge of the Plot, but the Duke's religion made him so obnoxious to the anti-Catholic party that a move to prevent his accession was inevitable.) Oates's lies were shored up by some pieces of good—or ill—luck. Sir Edmund Berry Godfrey, the magistrate to whom Oates had told his story in the earliest days of the Plot, was murdered, obviously by the Jesuits. (The identity of the murderers and the real motives are obscure to this day. It is even possible that Godfrey's death had nothing to do with the Plot.) James's secretary, a foolish Catholic convert called Edward Coleman, had written letters to the French king's confessors which, read in the light of the Plot, seemed to corroborate it. They cost Coleman his life. As these events occurred, the Popish Plot became a fact for much of the nation, and an unsurpassed hysteria dominated the life of the country. Other 'witnesses' came forward to support Oates, and trial followed trial. Many 'plotters' went to their deaths.

The anti-Catholic feeling was encouraged by the Earl of Shaftesbury and his supporters, soon to be called the Whigs, who wished to make sure, by an Act of Exclusion, that the Duke of York, whose Catholicism had been publicly avowed in 1673, should not succeed to the throne, but should be replaced, according to one version of the Exclusion Bill, by Charles's illegitimate son, the 'Protestant Duke' of Monmouth. The Parliamentary attempts to pass the Bill were floated on the tide of anti-Catholic feeling set in motion by Titus Oates, but though the Commons passed Exclusion Bills twice (and were about

James, Duke of York, Lord Admiral, in classical pose.

to do so a third time when Parliament was dissolved in 1681), the Lords rejected the only one which reached them. By 1681 the Plot was dying down, and a reaction in favour of royalism and James's succession took place. Shaftesbury was sent for trial on a charge of high treason for 'intending' to levy war against the King. At this point Dryden published *Absalom and Achitophel*, supporting the King and the Duke of York against Shaftesbury, Monmouth, and the Exclusionists. Nothing, not even a great poem, could have persuaded the Middlesex grand jury (selected by Whig sheriffs) to send Shaftesbury for trial, and he was freed, but *Absalom and Achitophel* can be taken as the literary beginning of the Tory counterattack, which is sometimes called 'the Stuart revenge'. When the Whigs struck a medal to celebrate Shaftesbury's release from the Tower, Dryden wrote *The Medal*. And, moving from the political to the religious side of the spectrum of public life, in 1682 he published *Religio Laici*.

'Religio Laici'

The title means 'A layman's faith', and it proclaims, therefore, that it is a non-specialist work, by a layman and for laymen. It has a prose preface in which Dryden rehearses many of the points the poem is to take up; the preface often serves as a useful gloss on the poem. The most important function of the preface, however, is to add a dimension to the poem, for the poem sticks to its subject, faith, but the preface links religious matters with political ones.

Dr Johnson describes *Religio Laici* as Dryden's only 'voluntary effusion', meaning that it was a poem which had no 'occasion', that it was something Dryden simply felt a need to write. That may be so, but it seems more likely that the poem began its existence as the most occasional of occasional works, a commendatory poem.

In January 1682 there was published a translation of a French work, *A Critical History of the Old Testament*, by Richard Simon, a man of great importance in the history of Biblical studies. (Simon's place in *Religio Laici* and in the intellectual circumstances which surround the poem is complicated, but it needs to be understood only in so far as Dryden is concerned, so a full account of Simon and his extraordinary book will not be given here.) The book was translated by one Henry Dickinson, and its publication became difficult because of suggestions that it attacked Christianity. Jacob Tonson, who was involved in it from the first, took over the publication in May of 1682. When his re-issue appeared, it was prefaced by commendatory poems by Nathaniel Lee, Nahum Tate, and Richard Duke, who had all written commendatory poems for *Absalom and Achitophel*. Dryden, who seems to have known Dickinson, and who might well have been called upon by Tonson to help the book along and who probably recruited Lee, Tate, and Duke, did not contribute, but when *Religio Laici* appeared it was at once evident that the whole poem had a relationship to Simon's book, for the poem contained lines commending Dickinson's translation. Phillip Harth has plausibly suggested that Dryden set out to write a commendatory poem of his own to go before Dickinson's work and that the lines grew into *Religio Laici* as we have it.

The lines in question (224–251) are an important structural feature of the poem. If they are taken as the point from which Dryden started, then the lines preceding and following can be imagined as the two 'wings' which the poet built on to the original structure. Dryden acknowledges in these lines that his thoughts were 'bred' by reading Dickinson's translation. He praises his friend for having undertaken such a work in preference to the usual amusements of youth, and he humorously characterizes Simon's book,

> in which appears
> The crabbéd toil of many thoughtful years,
> Spent by thy author, in the sifting care
> Of rabbins' old sophisticated ware
> From gold divine; which he who well can sort
> May afterwards make algebra a sport.

Simon, as the first man to investigate the transmission of the text of the Old Testament in an exact and critical spirit, is imagined as one trying to separate the gold of God's word from the dross which has been mixed with it by the copyists and commentators who have intervened since the word of God was first written down. The central concern of his book in Dryden's eyes, therefore, is to re-establish what is really God's word in the Old Testament. Dryden accepts easily and willingly (as many adversaries of Simon would not) that corruptions of the text have occurred, but he builds his poem on what he sees as certain logical conclusions to be drawn from Simon's demonstration. *Religio Laici* asks what things a Christian must believe to be sure of salvation in the next world, and Dryden uses Simon as the point of departure for a discussion of the claims under that head of the Anglican Church (the Protestant sectaries are dismissed curtly), the Roman Catholic Church, and the 'non-church' of natural religion, the deists. (Deism, as far as Dryden is concerned, was the belief, originating in the seventeenth century and of greatest importance in the eighteenth, that any man could, by the exercise of his innate, native reason, infer from the evident design of the universe that there was a Creator. Rules of conduct for mankind and some form of life after death were equally inferable. Deism got rid of 'special revelation', the Bible, and all ideas of original sin, basic human imperfectibility, and the need for a personal Redeemer. It was a 'natural' religion because it presupposed as necessary only the 'natural' ability of everyman to observe the universe rationally. The Christian churches saw it as an insidious heresy.)

Authority, a proven claim to have the right answer as to what the believer must believe, was the desire of all the groups. There is good evidence to believe that the Church which demonstrated to Dryden the best claim of authority would command his allegiance. In *Religio Laici*, the Church of England does so.

Dickinson's motive in translating Simon's book had been to show its great usefulness in combating the ideas of the deists. Simon's reverence and love for God's word were clear in his book and they inspired his cutting contempt for the commentators, copyists, and translators who had botched and bungled their work from the earliest times. In the first major subdivision of *Religio Laici* (lines 1–223), Dryden too is defending the necessity of revelation, the word of God as presented in the Scriptures, against the claim of the deists that they can know God, and hence be saved, without accepting the Bible as the word of God. When Dryden says that his 'crude thoughts' in the first part of the poem were 'bred' by reading Dickinson's translation of Simon, he means that Simon's concern for the preservation and correct transmission of the text of the Old Testament has brought home to him the indispensability of the text of the Bible as the only means available to man of knowing the true God. But this is a large and general truth which has emerged from reading a closely argued and learned book. Dryden concentrates on using that great truth against the deists in the first part of his poem without dragging in Father Simon. The acknowledgment of his indebtedness is made in lines 226–75, but Father Simon enters the poem (as an adversary) only in the second major part. This means that when Dryden opposes deism in the first section, he approves of Simon and implicitly relies on him. The deist, against whom the poet argues in the first 'wing' of the poem, is a 'nonce adversary', an opponent invented for this particular occasion. In the second part (mainly lines 276–397), when Dryden opposes the Catholic Church's claims for its 'tradition', Father Simon, who supports that tradition, is no longer approved and is used as Dryden's opponent. Simon's dual 'role' in *Religio Laici* has, not unnaturally, caused much confusion.

Religio Laici is a great poem. It is the first panel of Dryden's religious diptych; it dramatizes brilliantly the 'moderate Anglican' position in the Restoration period; it is important in its influence. Its greatness, however, is due not to these important though secondary factors, but to its poetic excellence—a superiority which the twentieth century has only begun to appreciate.

Dryden himself is partly responsible for the ease with which modern readers and Victorian ones have neglected the poem. His conclusion describing 'this unpolished, rugged verse' is a part of his pose of 'modesty', but it provides a sort of justification for dismissing unexamined the poetic qualities of the work. The next line, 'As fittest for discourse, and nearest prose', bangs down the coffin lid. But *Religio Laici* is a superbly and appropriately 'polished' work, a living demonstration of 'decorum' in style, the perfect suitability of manner to matter, which was one of Dryden's definitions of 'wit'. One can test the refinement of one's taste for Augustan verse by asking oneself how and why *Religio Laici* is not only influential or important as 'background', but also beautiful.

As for influence, it should be pointed out that *Religio Laici* is the first eminent example of a genre of Augustan poem—it might be named the 'didactic debate'—which will include Pope's 'essays', *An Essay on Criticism* and *An Essay on Man*. It 'teaches' by involving the reader in an informal and generally good-natured discussion of an important subject and convinces in leading to a carefully prepared conclusion. Its classical ancestors are the verse epistles of Horace, and though it may seem to have few descendants outside its own period, it could plausibly be claimed that it contributed importantly to the long 'meditative' type of poem which became fashionable in the later eighteenth century and which leads in turn to Wordsworth's *Prelude*. *Religio Laici*, in its form perhaps more than in its arguments, is a quintessentially Augustan poem of the English eighteenth century, which it antedates by eighteen years. In that, it contrasts somewhat with *The Hind and the Panther*, which points back to older traditions of didactic verse.

The Church of England and the 'Glorious Revolution' of 1688

When Charles II was succeeded in 1685 by his Roman Catholic brother, James II, the Stuart monarchy seemed to have survived the turmoil which the prospect of that succession had helped to create in the early years of the decade. Anti-Catholic fanaticism had died down with the expiry of the Popish Plot. Exclusion had failed, and the lawful descent of the throne to James was generally welcomed. For his part, James promised to rule his officially Anglican kingdom without bias, and was rewarded with the greatest display of Parliamentary loyalty ever bestowed on a Stuart.

The Church of England had long been preparing itself for a Defender of the Faith who was not actually of the faith. It taught that the throne was James's by right divine, and that the duty of Churchmen was 'Passive Obedience and Non-Resistance'. However bad a ruler might be, the only recourse of the Church, both clergy and laymen, was to suffer in silence. St Paul had prescribed such a course for the Christians of Rome under Nero. The great Restoration preacher, Robert South, drew the traditional distinction between the man and his office.

The baseness of the metal is warranted by the superscription, the office hallows the person; neither is there any reason, that the vileness of one should disannul the dignity of the other; forasmuch as he is made wicked by himself or the devil, but he is stamped a magistrate by God. We are therefore to overlook all impieties and defects, which cannot invalidate the function. Though Nero deserves worthily to be abhorred, yet still the emperor is and ought to be sacred.

This counsel of perfection was easy to uphold when it applied to the distant past of the primitive Church, or even to the more recent past of the reign of Charles I. But when James II, who was hardly Nero, took measures which directly threatened the privileged position of the Church of England, St Paul's advice became harder to follow. In retrospect, the amazing thing is the firmness with which so many Anglican clergymen held to the doctrines of Divine Right and Passive Obedience. James's culminating act of folly was to send seven bishops for trial for refusing to order his Declaration of Indulgence read in Church. The invitation to William of Orange was signed on the very day on which the Seven Bishops were acquitted. Yet five of those seven refused to take the oaths of allegiance to William and Mary and so lost their rank and their livings. A large body of Anglican clergy became 'non-jurors' and their departure was a great wound to the Church. One of these men (he later became a non-juring 'bishop') was Jeremy Collier, who in 1698 attacked the lubricity of Dryden's plays. Dryden himself may be seen as a sort of 'secular non-juror' in the reign of William and Mary.

Dryden's Conversion

Dryden became a Catholic during the reign of James II. The passage in *The Hind and the Panther* in which he refers to the event (I, 62 ff.) is carefully vague on matters of detail. The arguments for Catholicism which seem to have carried most weight with him were the inadequacy of Scripture alone as a rule of faith and the consequent claim of the Catholic Church to be the interpreter of Scripture, by virtue of being in the direct line of descent from the primitive Church. The conversion represents an entire change of opinion from that expressed in *Religio Laici*, but the circumstances which brought Dryden to change his mind are not known. To his contemporaries, the obvious answer was that he changed his religion to keep his posts as Poet Laureate and Historiographer Royal. This has been shown to be untrue, though the inference is at least understandable at a time when conversions were being made for no better reasons. (It is natural to feel, without impugning Dryden's sincerity, that if he had wished not to be misunderstood over his conversion, he could have managed certain aspects of it more prudently.) Dryden himself points out that James II was not, in fact, notably generous in rewarding converts to his religion. The Hind (representing the Catholic Church in *The Hind and the Panther*) is made to say,

> Now for my converts, who you say unfed
> Have followed me for miracles of bread,
> Judge not by hearsay, but observe at least
> If since their change, their loaves have been increased.
> The Lion* buys no converts, if he did,   [*James II]
> Beasts would be sold as fast as he could bid.

(III, 221–6)

It is not wholly true, but it is true so far as Dryden himself was concerned. Indeed, given the attention to detail James was apt to lavish on financial affairs, Dryden might be considered lucky not to have had his stipends reduced.

Dryden's feelings towards the events of James II's reign are political matters and will be considered under that head. Similarly, much of *The Hind and the Panther*, especially Part III, concerns itself with the political relationship of Protestants and Catholics. These parts tell us little about Dryden's feeling for his new religion except that he wished to uphold it in the world. In turning to the poem for evidence of the religious doctrines which attracted him, it must be remembered that the work is no more 'confessional' than *Religio Laici*, and that much of it is not concerned with the private and devotional but with the public and ceremonial.

The Roman Catholic Church in England

The Church which Dryden had joined at some time in 1685 or 1686 was in a strange and uncomfortable position. Since the time of the Reformation it had been an underground organization because it was regarded as the enemy of the English monarchy. Some of its members had been involved in plots against the Crown; many more had been accused falsely of such plotting. Although there were Catholic peers and a relatively large body of Catholic landed gentry, the Catholic proportion of the English population at the time of the Popish Plot has been estimated at less than $1\frac{1}{2}$ per cent (J. Miller, *Popery and Politics in England, 1660–88*, Cambridge, University Press 1973). Catholics, like Protestant Dissenters, were forbidden to hold public employments or to send their sons to the universities. For most Catholics in Dryden's time, life was a mainly domestic affair, passed as much as could be out of the limelight, with all possible done to avoid bringing the wrath of the Anglican powers down on them.

The only really extensive and in any way confident Catholic

community in the country was in London. Foreign ambassadors were permitted their Catholic chapels, which English Catholics often attended, despite occasional attempts to stop them. Among the tradesmen of London, there were many skilled Catholic artisans whose chief desire was to practise their professions and religion undisturbed. (In a letter of 1697, Dryden remarks that he is changing his draper in order to give his custom to one 'who is of my own persuasion'.) To avoid suspicion and publicity was, throughout the Catholic community in general, a fundamental desire. In London, one could do so without the isolation from co-religionists which was often the lot of Catholics in the countryside. When laws against Catholics were made more extensive after the Revolution of 1688, an attempt was made to break up the Catholic community in London. (Pope's father, a linen-draper, went into retirement on a small estate near Windsor, where the poet grew up.) But the law commanding the removal of Catholics from London was never rigidly enforced. Dryden's name was noted as a Catholic inhabitant of Soho, but he was not forced to move permanently from the city. Roman Catholics in London were often to the parish officers good neighbours rather than dangerous Papists.

In 1685 the English Catholics found themselves in a kingdom ruled by a Catholic. It is natural to suppose they rejoiced at this circumstance, but in fact events showed that they were wise to view the accession of James with a degree of foreboding. James promised to uphold the Anglican religion, but his greatest ambition was to rule a Catholic England. His temperament was not that of a patient man, and other circumstances combined with it to make him hurry. He had no Catholic heir; his Protestant daughter Mary, wife of the Prince of Orange, was next in line. Although he was not an old man, life expectancy was such that he could not anticipate a long reign. The manoeuvres James undertook to advance Catholicism by means of his prerogative antagonized his most loyal supporters—the high Anglican Church with its tradition of Passive Obedience. the universities, and eventually the Catholic community. James was fatally out of touch with the general body of English Catholics. His religion was rather a 'palace' affair. His close advisers were as uninformed as he about English Catholic sentiment, and while they encouraged him to act to achieve his great objective, the English Catholics began to see that the King's plans might easily end with a rebellion of Protestants which would leave Catholics worse off than before. When William of Orange landed at Torbay on 5 November 1688 James found himself with few English Catholic supporters willing to fight for him or to go into exile with him. The Jacobite cause, as it became, commanded a deal of sentimental support in England during the next hundred years, but it was mainly the Highland Scots who were willing to fight for 'the King over the water'.

Dryden should be seen as an 'old' English Catholic, despite the fact that he was a recent convert in 1688 and moved on the periphery of the Court. It is too easily assumed that his official posts made him an 'insider' at the Courts of Charles II and James II. A letter he wrote to Sir George Etherege in 1687 gives his position more accurately, and places him among the English Catholics who looked with consternation on James's policies:

> I have made my court to the King once in seven months, have seen my Lord Chamberlain full as often. I believe, if they think of me at all, they imagine I am very proud, but I am gloriously lazy.... Oh, that our monarch would encourage noble idleness by his own example, as he of blessed memory [Charles II] did before him, for my mind misgives me that he will not much advance his affairs by stirring.

Dryden defended publicly and with vigour his belief that the Catholic Church was the true Church, but he was aware, as his King was not, that the emancipation of Catholics was a matter for patience and for an avoidance of any deed that might stampede the nervous Protestants of the Church of England. (The vital need for caution and prudence in the conduct of 'religious politics' is found in the works Dryden wrote at this time. It is reflected in both the form and the arguments of *The Hind and the Panther*.) In relation to James II, Dryden is again a moderate.

In Catholic theology, too, Dryden chose moderation. Religious writings by Catholics in Restoration England reveal that the Church, as a result of its underground existence, was severely, even violently, factional in its theological debates and was in fact the very opposite of a united and monolithic organization. When Dryden found himself studying the views of English Catholic writers on such topics as the relative importance of Scripture and tradition, he chose, as one would expect, the moderate point of view for himself. (This moderation, however, is moderation within the context of a Catholic debate, and Dryden's position in *The Hind and the Panther* on the relationship of the written to the spoken Word is very different from any Protestant position.) Having been a moderate Anglican he became a moderate Catholic. For example, in choosing in *The Hind and the Panther* (II, 80–95) between the four possible repositories of the 'infallibility' of the Catholic Church—(1) the Pope, (2) the General Councils, (3) the Pope and General Councils combined, and (4) the Pope, the General Councils and the whole wider body of the Church—Dryden rejects (1) and (2) as too narrow, and (4) as too broad. He ends with the most moderate choice, (3) Pope and General Councils combined. In setting out the arguments of the Hind, Dryden is making his own choice of conflicting Catholic doctrines, as well as indicating the distinction between Catholics and Anglicans.

Dryden's Catholicism in 'The Hind and the Panther'

The Hind and the Panther is intended for Dryden's usual audience, most members of which would inevitably be Anglicans. In important ways, the poem shows that Dryden kept this fact in mind and made it a part of his strategy. He knows he is not preaching to the converted, nor can he expect any conversions. He puts the case for his own point of view as strongly as possible without forcing his non-Catholic readers to turn away from the poem before it can affect them as he would wish. The political strategy is to show Anglicans that they have much in common with Catholics, in particular a common enemy in the ultra-Protestant 'fanatics'. In religious terms, Dryden does his best to show that his Church has the best claim, because the most reasonable one, to be the direct descendant of the apostolic fathers of the primitive Church. This matter was obviously of great importance to him, and he gives it a great deal of attention. To Anglicans, however, certain features of Catholicism were more objectionable even than the claim of 'authority'. Pre-eminent among these was 'transubstantiation', the belief of Catholics that during the Mass the bread and wine of the Eucharist are miraculously transformed or 'transubstantiated' into the body and blood, the 'real presence', of Christ, while remaining bread and wine in outward appearance. The Test Act of 1673 had made it compulsory for those taking the oaths to sign a declaration of belief 'that there is not any Transubstantiation in the sacrament of the Lord's Supper', for this doctrine had acquired enormous importance as the mark of difference between Protestants and Catholics. Transubstantiation was often treated as a self-evident absurdity by Protestant partisans, some of whom exercised even indecent wit on this 'Popish mystery'. J.P. Kenyon (in *The Popish Plot*, 1972) quotes Lord Russell in the House of Commons in 1679. 'A piece of wafer, broken betwixt a priest's fingers, to be our Saviour! And what becomes of it when eaten, and taken down, you know.' In *The Hind and the Panther* Dryden puts little or no emphasis on many features of Catholicism which customarily antagonized Protestants. He mentions the Virgin Mary, the intercession of saints, the use of Latin in worship and prayer, and other such provocative matters rarely and in ways which are non-divisive. He thus tends to present himself as a moderate Catholic having much in common with the earlier self which wrote *Religio Laici*. But he does not attempt to play down or slide over the matter of transubstantiation, and the emphasis he gives to this important doctrinal and political difference is perhaps his way of being emphatic about the change he has made. He is no half-hearted Catholic, but at the same time his conversion has been motivated by basic and important considerations, such as authority and transubstantiation, and not by less significant, though superficially more striking ones.

Transubstantiation, therefore, the doctrine accepted by English law as the most reliable 'test' of a man's Catholicism, is employed by Dryden as the manifestation of his own unqualified submission to Rome in matters of faith. As the poem unfolds, moreover, he is able to use transubstantiation for another purpose. In the 'reason or faith' debate, transubstantiation serves to show the essential reasonableness of Catholics in insisting on the 'real presence' of the body and blood of Christ during the Mass, that is in taking literally Jesus's words at the Last Supper—always a shrewd hit at Protestants, who in general were the ones to insist on the utter supremacy of the text over any 'symbolical' interpretation. Christ had said, 'This is my body', and for Catholics it was. When it comes to Church authority, however, transubstantiation exposes what Catholics saw as the shaky doctrinal compromises underpinning the Anglican position. The Hind speaks of the Church of England's efforts to try to reconcile conflicting points of view.

> In doubtful points betwixt her diff'ring friends,
> Where one for substance, one for sign contends,
> Their contradicting terms she strives to join,
> Sign shall be substance, substance shall be sign.
> A real presence all her sons allow,
> And yet 'tis flat idolatry to bow,
> Because the God-head's there they know not how.
> Her novices are taught that bread and wine
> Are but the visible and outward sign
> Received by those who in communion join.
> But th'inward grace, or the thing signified,
> His blood and body, who to save us died;
> The faithful this thing signified receive.
> What is't those faithful then partake or leave?
> For what is signified and understood,
> Is, by her own confession, flesh and blood.
> Then, by the same acknowledgement, we know
> They take the sign, and take the substance too.
> The lit'ral sense is hard to flesh and blood,
> But nonsense never can be understood.

(I, 410–19)

Dryden emphatically prefers the 'hard' mystery of Catholic teaching to the 'nonsensical' confusions of Anglican compromise. The strength of his argument depends on the reader's realization that transubstantiation was not simply denied by the Church of England. Anglicans tried to adopt a middle position between those Protestants who saw the bread and wine merely as symbols or 'signs' and Catholics who held that the bread and wine became Christ's body and blood in actual, though miraculous, fact. The Anglican catechism taught 'novices' that the bread and wine were the 'outward part or sign' of Communion, but that the 'inward part or thing signified' was 'the Body and Blood of Christ which are verily and indeed taken and received by the faithful in the Lord's Supper'. 'Verily and indeed' seemed to Dryden to insist on a miracle, yet Anglicans were not to believe in transubstantiation, nor was the sacrament to be 'reserved, carried about, lifted up, or worshipped'. When the Anglican Articles of Religion said that 'the mean whereby the Body of Christ is received and eaten in the Supper is Faith', Dryden saw shifty evasion and unwholesome compromise.

Now there can be little doubt that if Dryden had been compelled to examine and defend this part of Anglican doctrine in *Religio Laici* he would have seen it as the sensible middle way and would have solved any difficulties by pointing to God's omnipotence and mankind's feebleness of intellect. Transubstantiation would have been rejected while something like the doctrine of the real presence, though not the name, would have been kept. In *The Hind and the Panther*, such compromises are evidence of the Church of England's muddle and confusion, and Dryden makes as fine a case against that as he does for compromise as the saving middle way in *Religio Laici*. The avoidance of the transubstantiation controversy in *Religio Laici* proves nothing, though Dryden does concentrate in each poem on the strong points of each case, Anglican or Catholic, and does not regard himself as being bound in *The Hind and the Panther* to refute every point he has made in *Religio Laici*. In the Catholic poem he wishes in general to assert that the Catholic position can be defended more rationally than the Anglican, and that the Church of England, both in its doctrine and its politics, is hopelessly confused, mired in contradiction, and enmeshed in compromise. He succeeds brilliantly.

If the decision to change his Church was an anguished one, no sign of the anguish is permitted into the poetry. Had it been, Dryden might have escaped the accusation of hypocrisy, but he would not have been Dryden. In many places *The Hind and the Panther* presents opinions so exactly opposite to those in *Religio Laici* that the effect of the two treatments compared is like that produced by reading lawyers' briefs on the opposite sides of one case, which in effect is what the two poems are. Dryden had changed sides, but his skill was unimpaired, so he was able to argue very well against his earlier self.

Many students of Dryden have seen in his conversion to Catholicism a religious equivalent to his royalism and authoritarianism in politics, and it is certainly true that the emotional relief he feels at being able to acclaim the Catholic Church as the final authority in matters of faith is clearly perceptible in many passages, though he makes it clear that his acceptance of Catholicism has not turned him into the stereotype of the convert. I have already mentioned his lack of emphasis on several points of difference between Protestants and

Catholics. His attitude to the priesthood seems to have been generally unaltered by his conversion. Jesuits in particular aroused his hostility, though this was probably due in part to the poor political advice James II got from them.

The most important matter on which Dryden wished to reassure his Anglican readers, however, was that of religious persecution. Louis XIV's persecution of the French Protestants and his success on the battlefield reminded Anglicans all too vividly of an earlier Catholic foe of England—Philip II of Spain, the king who had been the husband of 'bloody Mary', and who had later despatched the Armada. Dryden, however, will in no way support a policy of persecution on grounds of religion. 'Of all the tyrannies on human kind / The worst is that which persecutes the mind' (I, 239–40). Dryden's sincerity is not to be doubted. He would always retain his suspicion of the Dissenters, whose forebears had practised religious persecution so vigorously, but he nevertheless maintained that a man willing to abide by the laws should not be persecuted for his religion. Of the passage from which the above quotation is taken, Professor Miner notes that it is 'remarkable, perhaps unique, in the seventeenth century for its plea in poetry for a toleration not achieved in England until the nineteenth century'. And one may reinforce the poetic plea with one in prose.

> We have indeed the highest probabilities for our revealed religion; arguments which will preponderate with a reasonable man, upon a long and careful disquisition; but I have always been of opinion that we can demonstrate nothing, because the subject matter is not capable of a demonstration. It is the particular grace of God that any man believes in the mysteries of our faith, which I think a conclusive argument against the doctrine of persecution in any church. And though I am absolutely convinced, as I heartily thank God I am, not only of the general principles of Christianity, but of all the truths necessary to salvation in the Roman church, yet I cannot but detest our inquisition, as it is practised in some foreign parts, particularly in Spain and in the Indies.
>
> (DRYDEN, 'Life of Lucian', written 1696, published 1711)

No one else could have defined so well the essence of Dryden's views on faith, reason, and tolerance.

6 Politics

Political topics are never long absent from Dryden's writing, and to give a complete account of the political events which touched on his work would be an impossibly painstaking task in a 'preface'. It is fortunate that, after the Restoration, Dryden's political principles were in essence permanently fixed, and that his greatest work, *Absalom and Achitophel,* and the whole body of his original satires, emerged from one well-defined political crisis which can be used to display the fundamental principles which must be understood to know him properly.

The attempt to exclude James, Duke of York, from the English throne and to replace him by a Protestant successor has been touched on already as the major political consequence or accompaniment of the Popish Plot. The events which led up to the Plot and the Exclusion attempt can be briefly set out.

The Cavalier Parliament (also known as the Pensionary Parliament or Long Parliament of the Restoration) had first assembled in 1661 and had then been a fanatically royalist body. King Charles had greeted them by saying that he could 'never hope to find better men in your places'. It had many young members, and Charles said he would keep them until they grew beards. In 1678, when Titus Oates and his fellow-liars first began to describe the Plot, the King's feelings had undergone great changes regarding that same Parliament, where beards and distrust of the monarch had grown proportionately. Dryden was lucky in that he had published *Annus Mirabilis* before the Dutch invasion of the Thames and Medway in June 1667, which marks the end of the honeymoon between King and Parliament. In response to the humiliation, the King had raised an army, but a standing army, then and later, was always to cause a large body of opinion in Parliament to feel fear and mistrust. In that view, such an army made the King a threat to his own people as well as to enemies abroad. In the 1670s the issue of the King's army greatly embittered his relations with Parliament.

Foreign affairs were another cause of discontent. King Charles's constant inclination was towards France and Louis XIV, but to many of his subjects France represented all that was worst in politics and religion: absolutism and Popery. The wars of the reign had been against Holland, a rival in commerce but a Protestant state opposed to France. To many Members of Parliament it had come to seem that France was the natural enemy of England and Holland the natural ally. As the King's differences with Parliament widened, he looked to France for help. He received money from Louis XIV in return for a secret promise to make Catholicism the religion of England. With that money, Charles hoped to become independent of Parliament whose power over his purse was thus abolished. Long prorogations of Parliament, made possible by French gold, increased suspicions that the King wished to rule without a Parliament at all. The situation before the Civil War, when Charles I had ignored his Parliament, was often recalled.

The Catholicism visible in the King's court, in addition to suspicions of secret Catholicism, added to all these fears. The Queen was a Catholic, and in 1673 the King's brother acknowledged that he too was of that faith. His second wife, whom he married in 1673, was Princess Mary of Modena, a Catholic. Charles had had two famous Catholic mistresses and his own Protestantism was very suspect. By 1678 public opinion was prepared for the plot which Titus Oates was making ready.

Shaftesbury from the first had seen the plot as the great opportunity for the opposition. Oates was carefully protected and encouraged by the anti-Court party; his accusations, and the resulting trials and executions, made him for a while one of the most powerful men in the nation and certainly the most famous. Shaftesbury and his supporters, however, intended to use Oates to alter the political composition of the English government in a fundamental way. The Cavalier Parliament was dissolved and subsequent Parliaments of Charles's calling, all shortlived and frequently prorogued, contained in each case a Commons majority of the King's opponents. These Houses of Commons, with Shaftesbury a prominent leader of the anti-Court party in the Lords, hoped to play up the dangers of Popery to a point where the King would be faced by a concerted demand by Commons, Lords, and the general public to sign into law a measure either to exclude James altogether from the throne or to allow him to succeed while treating him as a monarch with no power, like an infant or a lunatic.

The startling thing is not that Exclusion (and all the other schemes) failed, but that it came so close to success. Everyone knew that in accepting the demand for it, Charles would have been giving his assent to a basic revision of the English 'constitution'. He would be abandoning the principle of Divine Right and giving his tacit approval to a theory of government which made it possible for subjects in the last resort to cashier their ruler, the theory of Resistance. It was a non-violent development of the argument which had brought about the Civil War, and there was a real possibility that matters would come to blows again. Forty years after the Civil War the issues were alive again in a new form, and Shaftesbury, whose young manhood had been passed in those times, was in the eyes of many opponents the new King Pym. Without him there would still have been a Plot and an Exclusion crisis, but it was his leadership that nearly won the day for the opposition. It is no wonder that he became one of the most adulated and abhorred politicians in English history.

The King held out, and with the support of the Church and a majority of the House of Lords the Exclusion project was beaten back. Oates's Plot, which had supplied so much of the fuel for Exclusion, finally ran down. The Catholic 'menace' lost its power to terrify, and although the anti-Court party still had control of the Commons, Charles had received a large subsidy from Louis XIV in March 1681, and when Parliament met at Oxford later that month, a last Commons attempt to exclude James was destroyed by a dissolution. Parliament never met again the reign of Charles II.

By now, public opinion was on the King's side, and he moved swiftly to secure his position. In July 1681 Shaftesbury went to the Tower on a charge of high treason. Although the jury refused to indict him, his cause seemed lost. When he died in Holland in 1683 the succession of James II was assured, yet by 1688 Shaftesbury's ghost was presumably saying 'I told you so'. James's actions as King had alienated all the powerful support Charles had relied on to beat back Exclusion and the English had, in effect, cashiered one king and 'elected' another. The unwritten constitution was rewritten on Shaftesburian lines by the Glorious Revolution.

The Exclusion crisis is important in English constitutional history as the moment when the party system first took its embryonic shape. Those factions which gathered to strive for Exclusion soon found themselves called 'Whigs', while those who supported James's right to succeed were called 'Tories'. Dryden's intervention on the King's side was a natural step for the Poet Laureate and Historiographer Royal, and all through the years of the crisis and beyond, from 1678 to 1683, his work attempted to influence opinion in favour of what came to be called the Tory side. Our next task is to examine the political ideas which Dryden grouped together in his writings under the banners of Whig and Tory. To do so is to present a totally biased account of the party differences, but that is the way to understand Dryden's attitudes.

Name-calling : Whigs and Tories

> But how comes Pompey the Great to be a Whig? He was, indeed, a defender of the ancient, established, Roman government; but Caesar was the Whig, who took up arms unlawfully to subvert it.
>
> ('The Vindication of *The Duke of Guise*')

The word 'Whig' is derived from a Scots word, 'Whiggamore', which referred to an outlaw, particularly one who was outlawed for doctrinal reasons of religion and politics, such as a Covenanter. 'Tory' is from Ireland, and means an outlaw and robber. These names stuck because, as David Ogg expresses it, 'English civilization did not appear to provide anything suggestive of that degree of contumely which each party stigmatized in the other'. Scotland and Ireland often meant barbarism to Englishmen of the seventeenth century. 'Whig', moreover, brought to mind the part Scotland's Presbyterians had played in the Civil Wars and thus implied that the same motives lay behind the drive for Exclusion. 'Tory' brought to mind the 'wild Irish', hordes of fanatically Catholic peasants, or perhaps tribesmen, whose assistance in bringing about a Popish tyranny would be available to a Catholic monarch of England. The combined political and religious elements in these names is of great significance.

Since we can see the germ of a democratic party system in the words, we may be inclined to forget their abusive origins, and it is true that each party eventually bore its own nickname as a badge of honour. Correspondingly, however, to each party the other was for long afterwards nothing but a pack of subversive malcontents. The notion of a 'loyal Opposition' was of slow growth.

Toryism and Whiggery

The nature of kingship is a basic difference between the Whig and Tory positions. To Tories, kingship was of divine origin. Adam had been the first monarch, and after the Flood, Noah and his sons had passed the rights of kingship to their descendants. All properly constituted monarchies stemmed from these originals. A true king was, therefore, 'a religious prince...a father of his country' (Preface to *Oedipus*, 1679). When Dryden adapted Shakespeare's *Troilus and Cressida* in 1678, he found there Ulysses' famous speech on 'degree' (I. iii. 101ff), which any student of the Elizabethan age will know as the classic statement of the omnipresence of gradations of rank throughout both the physical universe and human society. The speech as it stands would seem to be all that Dryden as a propagandist for sacred monarchy could wish. Yet in his version the speech is drastically altered. Shakespeare's sixty-two lines have shrunk to nineteen; the stress on the universality of 'degree' has gone, being replaced by a single statement of the necessity of sacred monarchy.

> O when supremacy of kings is shaken,
> What can succeed? How could communities
> Or peaceful traffic from divided shores,
> Prerogative of age, crowns, sceptres, laurels,
> But by degree stand on their solid base!
> Then every thing resolves to brutal force
> And headlong force is led by hoodwinked will,
> For wild ambition, like a ravenous wolf,
> Spurred on by will and seconded by power,
> Must make an universal prey of all,
> And last devour itself.

The Shakespearean stress on a universal pattern of 'degree', which includes monarchy by implication, has been changed into a political theory which makes monarchy the principle and embodiment of all social order. Shakespeare writes of a natural principle which includes human society; Dryden writes of politics. The difference reveals the extent to which English constitutional debate had come to centre largely upon the nature of kingship. As Dryden saw it, any alternative to this kind of monarchy would lead to disaster. Whigs, therefore, were agents of Chaos.

There could be no lawful tampering with monarchy as divinely authorized. The attempt to exclude the heir to the throne struck at the great principle of kingly government.

> For the sovereign being once invested with lawful authority, the subject has irrevocably given up his power, and the dependence of a monarch is alone on God.
>
> (Postscript to the 'History of the League')

> To cabal, to write, to rail against this administration, are all endeavours to destroy the government, and to oppose the succession in any private man is a treasonable practice against the foundation of it.
>
> ('The Vindication...')

What Dryden described as the 'fundamental' of Whigs was the belief that kings were essentially created by their subjects, that their power was granted to them conditionally, and that, if the conditions were violated, the people possessed a power of revocation which could unmake the King: 'they [Whigs] take it for a maxim that the King is but an officer in trust, that the people, or their representatives, are superior to him, judges of miscarriages, and have power of revocation' ('The Vindication...'). Shaftesbury, in *The Medal*, is described as the hypocritical propounder of this doctrine.

> He preaches to the crowd, that pow'r is lent,
> But not conveyed to kingly government;
> That claims successive bear no binding force;
> That coronation oaths are things of course;
> Maintains the multitude can never err;
> And sets the people in the papal chair.
>
> (lines 82–7)

An appeal to 'the people' in this context is always regarded by Dryden as a more or less veiled desire for anarchy. He speaks a couple of times of 'the dregs of a democracy', when government falls to its lowest level of competence and responsibility. 'The people' was for Dryden synonymous with 'the rabble', and for him the archetype of a democratic action was the judicial murder of Socrates (*The Medal*, 95–6).

The motives which could propel a Shaftesbury to the head of a mob and caused him to espouse a theory which placed ultimate sovereignty in the anarchic mass of 'the people' could only be sinister. It was an easy step from this to an analogy with the oldest of rebels and rabble-rousers—Satan.

> There are not wanting malcontents amongst us, who surfeiting themselves on too much happiness, would persuade the people that they might be happier for a change. 'Twas indeed the policy of their old forefather, when himself was fallen from the station of glory, to seduce mankind into the same rebellion with him, by telling him he might yet be freer than he was: that is, more free than his nature would allow, or (if I may so say) than God could make him.
>
> (Dedication to *All for Love*, 1678).

Dryden develops this analogy skilfully, with the assistance of Milton, in *Absalom and Achitophel*.

The end result of political activity premised like Shaftesbury's would be a return to the days of the Civil War and the Commonwealth. Tories were haunted by the ghost of those days. 'The miseries of the last war are yet too fresh in all men's memories' ('The Vindication...'). A commonwealth or republic, like that which followed the Civil War, was to Dryden a system of government which made tyranny inevitable.

> Both my nature, as I am an Englishman, and my reason, as I am a man, have bred in me a loathing to that specious name of a republic. That mock-appearance of a liberty, where all who have not part in the government are slaves; and slaves they are of a viler note than such as are subjects to an absolute dominion. For no Christian monarchy is so absolute, but 'tis circumscribed with laws. But where the executive power is in the law-makers, there is no farther check upon them, and the people must suffer without a remedy, because they are oppressed by their representatives.
>
> ('The Vindication...')

In monarchy on the English pattern, Dryden saw the King as a balancing agent and an active arm of the government, but he was no tyrant. The French King had tyrannical power; England's case was different, since the King's position was midway between that of a helpless 'constitutional monarch' or 'duke of Venice', and that of a regal autocrat. The King of England submitted to the laws: 'Our liberties and our religion both are safe; they are secured to us by the laws, and those laws are executed under an established government by a lawful king. The Defender of the Faith is the defender of our common freedom' ('The Vindication...').

The Whig answer to such a view was that the King submitted to the law of his free will alone; there was nothing to prevent him from becoming a tyrant. He claimed to have acquired his kingdom by right divine; in his own view he was finally accountable only to God. What would happen when the King's conscience and his subjects' view of their interest came into conflict? The Church of England's answer, 'Passive Obedience', made the people and the country essentially the monarch's personal property.

Dryden proposed a moderate answer to this objection, trusting to the good sense of the monarch.

> Neither does it follow... that an unalterable succession supposes England to be the King's estate, and the people his goods and chattels on it. For the preservation of his right destroys not our propriety, but maintains us in it. He has tied himself by law not to invade our possessions, and we have obliged ourselves as subjects to him and all his lawful successors.
>
> ('The Vindication...')

Dryden saw no need to deal in hypotheses. Under scrutiny, his system is seen to bind the subject irrevocably, while the King is obliged to his conscience, to his interest, and to God. These checks did eventually prove insufficient. Dryden could not foresee the events of James II's reign, and many Whigs must have been startled by so swift an enactment of their hypothetical objections to the theory of sacred monarchy.

At the time of the Exclusion crisis, Dryden saw no reason for the 'innovations' in government sought by the Whigs. 'We have already all the liberty which free-born subjects can enjoy, and all beyond it is licence' (Dedication to *All for Love*). Whig claims to be reformers rather than revolutionaries could not be countenanced: 'Neither is it enough for them to answer that they only intend a reformation of the government, but not the subversion of it. On such pretences all insurrections have been founded. 'Tis striking at the root of power, which is obedience' (Dedication to *All for Love*). Dryden saw himself as one enlisted to fight with his pen 'for a lawful, established government against anarchy, innovation, and sedition'.

Religious endorsement for the Tory theory of government came from the Church of England, a Church purged of its Puritan elements by the Act of Uniformity (see page 77). The Church's support for the King in the matter of Exclusion was essential, and its belief in Passive Obedience to a bad king was, in theory, at least, a total acceptance of Divine Right. The opposition, however, could claim religious support too, but in Tory eyes such support was always disreputable. Both Roman Catholicism and the Protestant sects were held by Tories to give subversive theological countenance to Whig theories. To modern eyes one of the most startling commonplaces of anti-Whig propaganda in the reign of Charles II is the assertion that Whiggery received doctrinal support from Jesuits and Calvinists alike. An unholy alliance against true monarchy was supposed to exist between these 'extremists' in religion.

To complete this survey of Dryden's political principles and his view of his opponents, an outline sketch of the religious ideas he saw in Whiggery must be given.

Kings and Popes had often quarrelled. One English King, John, had been excommunicated by the Pope and had finally been forced to accept the status of 'vassal' in order to return himself to the favour of the Church. A later quarrel had led to Henry VIII's breach with Rome. Yet for Englishmen at the end of the seventeenth century, the most important intervention by a Pope in English affairs had come in the reign of Queen Elizabeth, the great Protestant heroine. In 1570 Pope Pius V had issued a bull formally deposing her and absolving her subjects from allegiance to her. The Pope's power to take such an action was firmly upheld by Rome, though many English Catholics were later embarrassed by it. In the Preface to his vigorously Protestant poem *Religio Laici*, Dryden himself sees the claim of this power as the major theoretical obstacle to the true loyalty of Catholics to the English crown.

> I should be glad...that [English Catholics] would join in a public act of disowning and detesting those Jesuitic principles, and subscribe to all doctrines which deny the Pope's authority of deposing kings, and releasing subjects from their oath of allegiance; to which I should think they might easily be induced, if it be true that this present Pope has condemned the doctrine of king-killing (a thesis of the Jesuits).

But Innocent XI did not condemn the theory that a Catholic subject could rightfully raise his hand against a 'heretical tyrant', and for Englishmen of intellectual interests the doctrine of 'tyrannicide' was the theoretical basis by which such actions as the Gunpowder Plot and the Popish Plot had been justified. When Dryden became a Catholic all reference to the Pope's power of deposing kings disappeared from his writings. It is not necessary to suppose, however, that he was converted to the doctrine. He regarded the exiled James II as his rightful King and William III as a usurper. No Pope had the power to depose James, but 'the people' had usurped such power and had set up a king in William. An oath of allegiance to William was therefore impossible, but that does not mean that Dryden accepted the Pope's deposing power any more than he accepted that assumed by the English Parliament.

The notion that the Jesuits were, if not the originators, then the great advocates of papal deposing power explains much of Dryden's antagonism towards them and shows how he could associate the proceedings of a vigorous anti-Catholic like Shaftesbury with the

Jesuits. Yet the sinister Society of Jesus was not the worst clerical enemy of true monarchy. The Jesuits were an open enemy; they were proscribed by law. The 'disciples of Calvin', however, were in Dryden's eyes just as opposed to kingship and more dangerous because more tolerated.

Calvinism was associated with republicanism because of its links with Geneva and because of the establishment of a Commonwealth after the victory of Puritanism in the Civil War. The 'inward light' which guided the Calvinist in religion guided him in government too. If his conscience told him he was right to rebel against his king, then nothing else existed to restrain him.

In the Preface to *Religio Laici*, Dryden gives a potted historical account of the growth of what might be called 'Protestant-sectarian-republicanism'. During the reign of Mary, many Protestants fled abroad and became infected with Calvinism. On their return to England, they set in motion a current of anti-monarchial conspiracy: 'the seeds were sown in the time of Queen Elizabeth, the bloody harvest ripened in the time of King Charles the Martyr, and because all the sheaves could not be carried off without shedding some of the loose grains, another crop is too like to follow.' The association of Calvinism with republicanism is too plain to be missed, and it leads to a situation in which Papist and ultra-Protestant alike use biblical authority against the principle of sacred monarchy.

> While we were Papists, our Holy Father rid us, by pretending authority out of the Scriptures to depose princes; when we shook off his authority, the sectaries furnished themselves with the same weapons, and out of the same magazine, the Bible. So that the Scriptures, which are in themselves the greatest security of governors, as commanding express obedience to them, are now turned to their destruction, and never since the Reformation has there wanted a text of their interpreting to authorize a rebel. And 'tis to be noted by the way, that the doctrines of king-killing and deposing, which have been taken up only by the worst party of the Papists, the most frontless [shameless] flatterers of the Pope's authority, have been espoused, defended, and are still maintained by the whole body of Non-conformists and republicans.

These last were the greatest enemy, and Dryden's manner when he deals with them frequently approaches the hysterical. In this he once again anticipates the attitudes of his 'cousin Swift'.

Dryden's main efforts of support for the royal brothers, Charles and James, in their fight against Exclusion and dominance by the House of Commons came somewhat late in the day. Incidental remarks and such things as theatrical prologues and dedications show that his support was steady for the royal side throughout the whole crisis of the Popish Plot, but *Absalom and Achitophel* and *The*

Medal were published when Shaftesbury was in decline as a political force. It might be more accurate, then, to say that Dryden's great political satires belong to the period of 'the Stuart revenge', when the King had ridden out the storm and was moving against his enemies. The abortive Rye House Plot of 1683, a conspiracy to murder the King by a number of genuine republicans and defeated Whigs, gave the King a valuable weapon to use. Dryden's moderation of principle during these years was considerably undermined by the over-zealous support he gave to the campaign against Shaftesbury's former supporters. Occasionally there is a lust for blood in Dryden's remarks, as when he rebukes Charles for his mercifulness, which is one of the few genuinely repulsive features of his career as a writer. This note of savagery helps to remind us that what to us are matters of historical interest were for Dryden and his contemporaries matters of life and death.

'Absalom and Achitophel'

Absalom and Achitophel will be, inevitably and properly, a major objective of any student of Dryden. Indeed, many who pretend to an acquaintance with Dryden's works are in fact only acquainted with this poem, which is, as a result, perhaps the best-known political poem in the English language. There can be little dispute that it is Dryden's greatest poem, the summit of his achievement; its major claim on our attention is as a work of art. Yet it is a political poem, and it is therefore necessary to understand its place among Dryden's political ideas, and to discuss it briefly, in a prefatory way, here.

The Political Utility of the Scriptures

The initial difficulty of *Absalom and Achitophel*, which is also one of the poem's greatest accomplishments and one of its principal delights, is that Dryden chooses 'fancy dress' for his fable. The contemporary political conflict is described in terms and characters derived from the Bible, from the story of Absalom's rebellion against his father, King David, as recounted in II Samuel 13–18. In encountering the poem for the first time, one has to learn that David is the counterpart of Charles II, that Absalom is the Duke of Monmouth, and that Achitophel represents Shaftesbury. One is faced at the outset, therefore, by a necessity for footnotes which for most people is associated with 'mugging up' a text for exams. The need is inescapable, yet to permit it to deter one from knowing the poem is to deny oneself countless pleasures. The utility, as well as the delight, of this allegorical framework can be indicated by showing how it serves political purposes and solves political problems for Dryden.

First, however, we should briefly consider the question of the

*ABSALOM AND
ACHITOPHEL.*

*Duke of Monmouth,
"Absalom".*

*Earl of Shaftesbury,
"Achitophel".*

originality of *Absalom and Achitophel*. In choosing the events of II Samuel for his vehicle in the poem, Dryden was drawing on what had become a conventional parallel. The identification of Charles II with King David was commonplace in the writing of the time. Dryden had made it himself in *Astraea Redux*. The use of the name 'Achitophel' (the Authorized Version has 'Ahithophel'; 'Achitophel' is the Vulgate form, and the experts say that Dryden's use of it is in no way unusual or significant) for the type of the malevolent politician was also customary. (In 1627, for example, a series of noted sermons was preached at Oxford under the title *Achitophel: or The Picture of a Wicked Politician*.) Finally, when Charles II's illegitimate son Monmouth began to be put forward as a suitable candidate for the role of Protestant successor to his father's throne, the parallel with Absalom quickly became standard. Several poems developing this allegory were known to Dryden. His originality lies, not in being the first to use the parallel, but in his unexcelled treatment of it. With his immediate audience, the choice of conventional parallels from biblical history offered advantages in that it was immediately understood how, in general, the biblical references were to be applied to the contemporary situation. Over the years this advantage has become a disadvantage. Yet to overcome it is easy once the three main identifications—David/Charles, Absalom/Monmouth, Achitophel/Shaftesbury—are grasped.

The difficulty of Dryden's task in the poem, which the Old Testament narrative helped him to solve, was that Charles II was undeniably very fond of Monmouth, who could not, therefore, be brutally denounced, and that Charles was equally firm in asserting Monmouth's illegitimacy and in refusing to countenance any claim of his to the throne, which was destined for James, Duke of York. Since Monmouth's ambitions were not those of himself alone, but were pushed by a party in Parliament and in the country, led by Shaftesbury, Dryden was able to make Achitophel, as the wicked counsellor of Absalom, the main target of his satire. Despite the rebellion, David mourned for Absalom. In the poem, this emotion for the rebellious son can be maintained, since he is tempted to rebellion by Achitophel. The parallel from II Samuel is thus, in many respects, very close. Yet if the Old Testament narrative is consulted, it can be seen that Dryden does alter it to suit his purposes.

The basic change in the story is that Dryden makes a major shift in responsibility for the rebellion from Absalom to Achitophel. In the Old Testament, Absalom's rebellion is embarked on before Ahithophel is introduced into the story. The young man is therefore wholly responsible for his own fate, and Ahithophel is not the tempter but simply a traitor in his own right. In *Absalom and Achitophel* the speeches in which Achitophel tempts Absalom to rebellion are the dramatic

Titus Oates shadows Pickering a Benedictine.

Titus Oates encounters opposition and is caught.

core of the poem. In II Samuel, the counsel of Ahithophel, which 'was as if a man had inquired at the oracle of God', is asked principally in the matter of strategy. His plan, obviously a good one, would have involved the immediate death of David without a general battle. Absalom is persuaded to reject it by the conflicting advice of David's secret ally, Hushai. 'For the Lord had appointed to defeat the good counsel of Ahithophel, to the intent that the Lord might bring evil upon Absalom.' Seeing that the rebellion will fail, Ahithophel 'saddled his ass, and arose, and gat him home to his house, and put his household in order, and hanged himself, and died'. (It is this course of action to which Dryden suavely refers in his preface 'To the Reader': 'In this poem, he is neither brought to set his house in order, nor to dispose of his person afterwards, as he in wisdom shall think fit.')

It should be clear from this summary that Ahithophel plays a significant but decidedly subservient role in the Old Testament narrative, whereas in Dryden's poem Achitophel is the most important character. Dryden's intention in making the change is to transform Absalom into the tool of Achitophel. Absalom, though a skilful orator under Achitophel's influence, is less intelligent and less self-willed than his biblical counterpart. David's love for Absalom in the poem is, therefore, more comprehensible and more justifiable than it is in the biblical story. Commentators emphasize that the lesson drawn from the story of the rebellion in II Samuel was usually highly critical of David for failing to govern his son properly. Dryden presents David as over-indulgent towards Absalom, but at this stage the poet is not sharply critical of Charles's leniency. The reason governing such attitudes concerns the role played by David in the poem.

One marked advantage of using King David as King Charles's counterpart was that David was the most eminent example of a monarch who retained God's favour despite considerable transgressions which would have ensured the destruction of any person less important to God's plans. At the beginning of his poem, Dryden is clearly aware that by the close he must transform David/Charles into a credible, dramatic representative of God on earth, God's vicegerent, so the famous opening of *Absalom and Achitophel*–the best of all Dryden's splendid openings—presents David/Charles as a sexual transgressor who is really no transgressor at all. Charles II's bastards are the result of his Davidic sympathy with 'Heaven's own heart'. Simultaneously, therefore, Charles's sexual lapses are condoned and the illegitimacy of Monmouth is underlined. The mood of pleasant indulgence which the reader is persuaded to extend to David/Charles leaves the way open for this same figure to speak in God's accents and with God's express approval in the poem's last lines.

David is one of the great figures of the Old Testament, but in a sense the grandeur of David/Charles in *Absalom and Achitophel* is more emphasized and made more systematic, since Dryden holds to a consciously elaborated theory of the Divine Right of Kings. At no time is the biblical David exalted as David/Charles is at the end of the poem. The biblical narrative serves as a base on which to build an account of a modern conflict and a modern theory of kingship. (That the theory claimed to have an ancient pedigree made the biblical narrative all the more appropriate.)

The alterations and changes of emphasis Dryden made in his version of the story tended, therefore, to bring the account of Absalom's rebellion into conformity with a Tory theory of government. The new role given to Achitophel in the poem served this end, too, by aligning him with an even greater tempter whose machinations pointed an important political moral. When Achitophel sets out to persuade Absalom of the inequities of David's rule and of the miseries of what is in obvious reality a political paradise, he undeniably becomes a Satan-figure tempting an Adam-figure and even Satan tempting Christ or a wouldbe Christ, since Absalom is persuaded to give himself a Messianic role. Dryden reinforces the Achitophel–Satan analogy by several echoes of *Paradise Lost*, though we must be wary of seeing Milton's poem as a 'source' or specific inspiration for Dryden. Achitophel is Satan because Satan is the greatest and most evil of tempters. He is a Miltonic Satan because *Paradise Lost* was the greatest of all interpretations of the story of the Fall. (There is some pleasure to be had in trying to imagine what Milton would have said if he had been able to see *Paradise Lost* used to buttress Dryden's theory of sacred kingship.) Most of all, Shaftesbury is Achitophel who is Satan because Dryden saw political events in England in the year 1681 as a repetition of a rebellion which had occurred again and again in history. Its first occurrence was with Adam; another instance was Absalom's rebellion. Hundreds of other analogies could have been discovered. For Dryden and many others in his day, history repeated itself because history re-enacted time after time certain basic events. Those events were shaped by human nature, which in turn was shaped by Adam's initial act of disobedience. ('Shaped' but not 'determined'; man was inclined to act this way, but his will was free to choose a better course of action.) In reaching into the past for his fable, Dryden was affirming his belief in this theory of re-enactment. The rebellion of Absalom is not, therefore, a disguise for the events of the Exclusion crisis, but a forerunner of them.

Political Prophecy: 'The Hind and the Panther', Part III

After *The Medal*, Dryden's poetic involvement with political events on a large scale decreased, simply because the controversies themselves died down or followed courses which did not suggest his intervention. His last substantial piece of political poetry is the Third Part of *The Hind and the Panther* (1687) which is concerned with the politics of religion in the reign of James II. The accession of a Catholic king presented English Catholics with a number of problems concerning their future conduct. Dryden, as we have seen, belonged to that group of Catholics which watched with consternation the King's hasty and injudicious attempts to free his Catholic subjects from the restrictions on their lives imposed by the Test Acts and other measures against religious non-conformity. The first of the two prophetic fables of Part III of *The Hind and the Panther* dramatizes this consternation and predicts the outcome if foolish counsels are followed.

The Panther (III, 420–638) tells the story of the Swallows (the English Catholics) who, instead of migrating at the onset of winter, preferred to listen to the advice of the Martin (representing James's adviser, Father Petre, and all those Catholics who supported the King's unwise measures) who said there was no need to make the difficult flight over the sea. The Swallows did not cross the water, and the Martin became a person of great importance. The birds were deluded by a 'St Martin's Summer', and were then destroyed by the harsh climate of winter. The lesson is clear, and serves to strike both at the over-optimistic Catholics and at the Church of England, since the Panther tells the tale and it is obviously persecution by the Anglican establishment which will 'freeze' the Swallows in the end.

The Hind's fable is more elaborate and involves secular politics much more. James II assumed that the Church of England would support, or at least would not actively oppose, his measures to relieve his Roman Catholic subjects. There were, however, three parties to be accounted for in any arrangements: the Anglicans, the Catholics, and the Dissenters. James began by regarding the Anglicans as his natural allies, but he soon perceived that an alliance of Catholics and Dissenters might prove more effective. These two groups, though at opposite ends of the religious spectrum, were alike in both being denied, as 'nonconformists', the social and political rights available to Anglicans. Both principle and expediency, therefore, came to suggest that any extension of rights to the Catholics should be matched by a similar extension to Protestant Dissenters. The Hind's fable of the Pigeons (III, 906–1288) is a warning to those Anglicans who, to prevent the nullification of the Test Acts, were willing to abandon the principle of 'passive obedience' and to flirt with the idea of intervention by William of Orange. In particular, it is aimed at those Church of England clergymen, like the famous Gilbert Burnet, who were so anti-Catholic as to favour an Anglican alliance with the Dissenters. Dryden always distrusted the Dissenters; he favoured the Anglican–Catholic alliance, and the fable of the Pigeons (the Anglicans) tells how those birds, pampered and cosseted though they were, became jealous of the 'poor domestic poultry' (the English Catholics) kept by their honest master (James II). The irrational jealousy of the Pigeons leads them to invite the Buzzard (a figure combining features of the Whiggish Burnet and of William of Orange) to become their leader, since he is the avowed enemy of poultry. At this point the owner (James) intervenes and declares that the Pigeons shall keep all their rights except that of persecuting other birds (the Test Acts) and that all birds shall be entitled to exist on their own limited territories. This intervention represents James's Declaration for Liberty of Conscience, or Indulgence, proclaimed in April 1687.

The Declaration came, apparently, as Dryden was finishing his poem, and it caused him difficulties which are visible in the text. The obvious ending of the fable—that the Pigeons will be eaten up by the Buzzard—is left undeveloped, rather like the story of Absalom. As long as James lives, peace and justice between the groups of birds will be preserved. But at this stage James had no son, and at the end of the poem Dryden is worried that the next reign will allow the Buzzard in to devour both the Pigeons and the 'domestic poultry'. *The Hind and the Panther* thus ends on a note vaguely ominous, pointing to a future which was, in fact, just as turbulent as Dryden imagined it to be.

The later events of James's reign led to an invasion of England by William of Orange, to the joint sovereignty of William and Mary, and to a limited degree of enfranchisement for Dissenters with a continuing repression of Catholics. Dryden's prophetic fables, therefore, proved largely true. Though the Church of England was never 'devoured' by the Buzzard, the Revolution of 1688 did mark the beginning of its slow decline as a great political force. The future of Catholicism in England was blighted for nearly two hundred years by the consequences of James's politics.

In exile at home: Dryden's 'Augustan' experience

Here is a field of satire opened to me; but, since the Revolution, I have wholly renounced that talent: for who would give physic to the great, when he is uncalled—to do his patient no good, and indanger himself for his prescription?

(DRYDEN, *Virgil*, 'Postscript to the Reader',)

After the Revolution of 1688 Dryden's career as a political poet was, for obvious reasons, at an end. He lost his Court posts, for he could not take the oath of allegiance to William and Mary demanded of all office-holders. The thought of going into exile with James must have been particularly painful for him. There is no record of his ever having travelled beyond the seas, he was ever a francophobe, and his roots in England were so deep that it seems likely that, had he brought himself to take the step into exile, he would not have long survived the transplanting. So he stayed in England, and, it seems, was allowed to stay in London, despite a law which expelled Catholics from the city. He continued until his death to be a 'Jacobite', a supporter of James's right to the throne. Writing to the Earl of Chesterfield, a fellow-Jacobite, in 1697, he said he had delayed publication of his *Virgil* 'in hopes of his [James's] return, for whom, and for my conscience, I have suffered, that I might have laid my author at his feet'.

This assertion of Jacobite faith, however, must be examined with care if we are to understand Dryden's political position during the last twelve years of his life. One thing is at once clear and is easily documented. Dryden regarded with aversion the general direction of the political and social changes which had taken place in England since 1660. *Annus Mirabilis* (1667) is virtually unique in his work as an expression of content and optimism regarding the state of England and the relationships between King and people, City and Court. It is particularly striking that the poem is dedicated to the City of London, 'which has set a pattern to all others of true loyalty, invincible courage and unshaken constancy', and that it celebrates a war of commerce against Holland. The commercial classes of London in the next twenty years came to represent everything Dryden regarded as unwholesome in politics, religion, and society. They were Whiggish (if not actually republican); they were often Dissenters in religion and almost universally anti-Catholic; they repudiated the values of the Court and implicitly the hierarchic, ordered society which Dryden had come to revere; their wealth was derived from trade, not from land. In *The Medal* (1682) Dryden does his best to maintain that London is not wholly corrupt, but it is clear that virtue there will not long survive.

> Sedition has not wholly seized on thee;
> Thy nobler parts are from infection free.
> Of Israel's tribes thou hast a numerous band;
> But still the Canaanite is in the land.
>
> (lines 175–8)

There follows a curse on those fools and knaves who represent for Dryden the modern enemy, commercially rapacious, religiously unorthodox, and politically anarchic.

Those let me curse; what vengeance will they urge,
Whose ordures neither plague nor fire can purge;
Nor sharp experience can to duty bring,
Nor angry heav'n, nor a forgiving king!

(lines 187–90)

The aesthetic sensibility, or lack of it, manifested by such persons is the groundwork of *Mac Flecknoe*. Nor is this a trivial matter, for in supporting such bad writers as Shadwell, the City of London, representative of all the forces of anarchy, is abandoning an entire culture and a philosophy of man.

After 1688 Dryden found himself having to live in a world in which, to his way of thinking, these principles had triumphed with the 'capture' of the monarchy. The Revolution of 1688 was social and moral, as well as political; Dryden's life from then on followed a pattern of 'exile', alienation from the governing principles of society, which was to be the experience of Swift and Pope, the experience which defines the useful meaning of the term 'Augustan'. It cannot be applied properly to everyone living in the period; Bunyan, Locke, Defoe and many others are not really Augustan writers. The term is best kept for those, like Dryden in his later years, who found little to admire in the world around them and who had to look back in time to find a society governed by principles of virtue. Dryden's reaction to this experience was less vehement and bitter than that of Swift or Pope, a fact due in large measure to his personality and in some part to his faith that the Jacobite cause could and should triumph. Swift and Pope could not have clung unquestioningly to that faith, even if it had been viable for them; their reaction was inevitably less restrained than Dryden's.

The knowledge that Dryden was seriously at odds with the post-Revolution world has led to many attempts to discover in his writings after 1688 criticism of the new establishment, and in particular attacks on William of Orange and his supporters. Such criticism certainly exists, but if it is investigated in too simple a manner on the assumption that he was always seeking to express hostility to William III by means of cryptograms, or concealed implications in his works, then misunderstanding will be the result. It is important to examine carefully the kinds of criticism of William and the Williamites which Dryden did permit himself. In doing so, we can begin to understand his politics in the last years of his life.

Had he been an Anglican clergyman, Dryden could have been described as a non-juror. Since he did refuse to take the oath to William and Mary, he might be called a 'secular non-juror'; he adopted for himself the doctrine of 'passive obedience' and 'non-resistance' which had been for years the political doctrine of the Church of England. This meant that Dryden could not hold office under William and Mary; he would not ask for favour from the new regime by dedicating his *Virgil* to King William or by writing a funeral elegy for Queen Mary—concessions asked of him. When an analogy between the current situation in England and past history occurred to him in his writing, he drew it. In all these senses, there is plenty of criticism of the Revolution of 1688 in Dryden's work and we should pause to take note of it.

For reasons already explained, Dryden after the Revolution was principally a translator and a dramatist. In the theatre, two of his plays illustrate the fact that public life was always apt to be reflected in his work. He was always passionately interested in what, for want of a broader term, has to be called 'politics'. *Don Sebastian* (published 1690) is frequently concerned with topics related to the events of 1688, and *Cleomenes* (1692) was banned from the stage for a while, perhaps because the topic of the Spartan hero in exile in Egypt seemed too close to the situation then existing in England and France. But it is in the translations that most of Dryden's commentary on the Revolution is to be found.

The practice always followed in trying to separate a translator from his author is to pay particular attention to passages omitted from the translation and to those added by the translator. (The logic of this process is far from infallible, but in Dryden's case it holds up well in general.) Take, for example, Dryden's 'The Character of a Good Parson; Imitated from Chaucer, and Enlarged'. This was written in 1699 at the suggestion of Samuel Pepys, who said that this good parson would make him some amends 'for the hourly offence I bear with from the sight of so many lewd originals'. (Pepys, though an unwavering Protestant, had been a loyal servant of King James, had lost his Admiralty position after the Revolution, and had been briefly imprisoned in the Tower on suspicion of Jacobitism; he always maintained in public a strict line of moral conduct and religious observance.) The 'enlargement' of Chaucer's 'character', to which Dryden calls attention, lies in making it a portrait, disguised in historical terms, of a non-juror. (The specific model was Bishop Thomas Ken.)

> The tempter saw him too, with envious eye;
> And, as on Job, demanded leave to try.
> He took the time when Richard was deposed:
> And high and low, with happy Harry closed.
> This prince, though great in arms, the priest withstood:
> Near though he was, yet not the next of blood.
> Had Richard unconstrained, resigned the throne:
> A king can give no more than is his own:
> The title stood entailed, had Richard had a son.
>   Conquest, an odious name, was laid aside,
> Where all submitted; none the battle tried.

The senseless plea of right by providence,
Was, by a flatt'ring priest, invented since:
And lasts no longer than the present sway;
But justifies the next who comes in play.

The people's right remains; let those who dare
Dispute their pow'r, when they the judges are.
He joined not in their choice; because he knew
Worse might, and often did from change ensue.
Much to himself he thought; but little spoke:
And, undeprived, his benefice forsook.

(lines 106–26)

Quite obviously, Richard II here stands for James II and William III is represented by 'happy Harry' Bolingbroke (Henry IV). Dryden's sly irony is delightful. Unlike Richard II, James II *did* have a son. The Revolution of 1688 was not one of 'conquest', since no one dared resist. The good parson sees no way of accommodating his principles to this usurpation. He leaves the Church establishment and becomes a wandering priest, 'And like a primitive Apostle preached'. Yet he does nothing actively to oppose the interloper now in possession of the throne. Dryden is praising the principles which he himself tried to follow.

Total poetic silence, however, was no part of the tacit 'agreement' to which Dryden adhered. His wit persisted in seeing analogies which found their way into his translations. When he was working on the Fourth Book of Virgil's *Georgics*, he came to the passage describing the two wouldbe kings of the bees. (Queen bees were long thought to be 'kings'.) Dryden added greatly to a passage distinguishing the true king from the false claimant.

With ease distinguished is the regal race:
One monarch wears an honest, open face;
Shaped to his size, and godlike to behold,
His royal body shines with specks of gold,
And ruddy scales; for empire he designed,
Is better born, and of a nobler kind.
That other looks like nature in disgrace:
Gaunt are his sides and sullen is his face;
And like their grisly prince appears his gloomy race.

(lines 137–45)

(A plain translation of what Virgil wrote would read: 'There are two kinds. One is the better, noble in bearing and covered with shining scales; the other squalid with sloth, ignobly dragging a large belly. As the features of the kings are distinct, so are the bodies of the subjects...') James II certainly had an advantage in appearance over his Dutch son-in-law, though the difference was hardly so striking as this passage suggests. William's lean face was much disfigured by illness, and Jacobites enjoyed hearing that William's followers, especially his fellow Dutchmen, were a 'gloomy race'. Dryden could not resist this kind of thing, but it should be remembered that he thought of it as within the terms of his 'bargain'. It is not a manifesto for an uprising.

The work in which Dryden's interpolated political comments cause most difficulty of interpretation is his translation of *The Aeneid*. Virgil's epic had long been used as a 'mirror for magistrates', a prince's guide to proper conduct in all spheres of his duty, especially the political. It was impossible for Dryden to translate the poem without an awareness of this reputation, and any reader taking it up would know that it was to teach him political lessons.

Unfortunately Dryden's version has yet to undergo a searching examination by critics competent to judge his political intentions and to evaluate the effects he achieved in the work. Certain limited studies have been made, but their overall tendency is to contradict each other and to leave the non-specialist confused. Certain passages of Dryden's translation have been isolated to show his 'modifications' of Virgil, but quite contrary interpretations of the text have followed.

Certain matters, however, are clear. The idea of a political role for the 'mob', for instance, was always abhorrent to Dryden, especially after the Revolution of 1688 began to be defended as 'the people's choice'. Thus, in translating a famous simile in the first book of *The Aeneid*, Dryden heightens the anti-democratic element.

> As, when in tumults rise th'ignoble crowd,
> Mad are their motions, and their tongues are loud;
> And stones and brands in ratt'ling vollies fly,
> And all the rustic arms that fury can supply;
> If then some grave and pious man appear,
> They hush their noise, and lend a list'ning ear;
> He soothes with sober words their angry mood,
> And quenches their innate desire of blood.
>
> (I, 213–20)

This mob is a more rabid creature than Virgil's and Dryden's vehemence is augmented by certain additions, especially the last line.

This type of modified translation and this order of sentiment were common to many seventeenth-century translations of Virgil. Dryden's own particular attitude to the Revolution of 1688, however, presents more vexed questions. A famous passage from Book VI will illustrate the difficulties. An unadorned prose translation (by L. Proudfoot) reads:

Here those are imprisoned who whilst they lived hated their brothers, who turned out a parent or cheated their followers; those who found treasure and hoarded it privately, giving no share of it to their own folk (great is the number of these); those who were murdered for adultery; and those who took up arms in an accursed cause, not doubting they would evade the right arm of their rulers; trapped they await their punishment.

Dryden's translation reads:

> Then they, who brothers' better claim disown,
> Expel their parents, and usurp the throne;
> Defraud their clients, and, to lucre sold,
> Sit brooding on unprofitable gold;
> Who dare not give, and ev'n refuse to lend
> To their poor kindred, or a wanting friend,
> Vast is the throng of these; nor less the train
> Of lustful youths, for foul adult'ry slain:
> Hosts of deserters, who their honour sold,
> And basely broke their faith for bribes of gold.
> All these within the dungeon's depth remain,
> Despairing pardon, and expecting pain.
>
> (VI, 824–35)

Dryden, quite clearly, has made Virgil's general terms very much more specific. Moreover, his editors seem quite reasonable in their suggestion that Dryden's very 'interpretive' rendering of the first couplet directs it at William III. The deserters who sold their honour may be a stroke at John Churchill, the future Duke of Marlborough, and the passage may contain other allusions to specific persons involved in the events of 1688 and later.

This is certainly Dryden expressing Jacobite sentiment, yet there is a difference of opinion as to the exact uses to which such a passage was to be put. Some would see it as evidence of simple intransigence and anticipation of counter-revolution, a sort of literature of the Jacobite *maquis*, but W. J. Cameron has pointed out that there could be another explanation. These characters, after all, are being punished in hell. It would square exactly with 'passive obedience' and 'non-resistance' for Dryden to be encouraging his fellow-Jacobites with a vision of future torments for the usurper and the deserters while at the same time telling them to leave vengeance to the Lord.

In trying to establish the political orientation of Dryden's *Virgil*, one inevitably turns to the rambling and lengthy Dedication of the poem in which, among other topics, Dryden discusses Virgil's own political motives in writing. Here again no authoritative study exists to guide us. Dryden picks out a path for himself with such care that it is always possible to lose his trail. His general position, however, seems to be that he assumes the freedom to point out that William III has acquired power by violence, but that his rule has in practice proved stable and non-tyrannical and is not to be opposed openly. It is hard, indeed, to avoid the suspicion that the Dedication to *The Aeneid* contains something for every political persuasion. Aeneas is clearly presented as an elective monarch, as William could claim to be. But 'Aeneas, though he married the heiress of the crown, yet claimed no title to it during the life of his father-in-law'.

The only certainties one can cling to in starting an examination of Dryden's *Aeneid* as a political document are that it presents a very complex situation and that the work is not simply an anti-Williamite or pro-Jacobite tract. The nearest Dryden comes to expressing himself directly is in his discussion of the customary weaknesses of elective monarchies, where he says: 'I meddle not with others, being, for my own opinion, of Montaigne's principles, that an honest man ought to be contented with that form of government, and with those fundamental constitutions of it, which he received from his ancestors, and under which himself was born.' The conservative tendency of Montaigne's advice is clear, but if we ask, 'Would Montaigne there-fore counsel acceptance of the 1688 Revolution or resistance to it?' then things are less clear. Dryden does not say whether he thought the Revolution had tampered with the 'fundamental constitutions' of the English government, though one supposes he did think so. Yet Montaigne's advice is built on tacit acceptance of the view that any stability is better than any turmoil: 'Common quiet is mankind's concern.' Dryden is living with a dilemma; his basic allegiance is to James, yet every day of William's rule builds up a body of social stability which was worth a great deal to the poet. He steers his way, with a skill we are only beginning to appreciate, between the many hazards of this difficult position.

In his Postscript to *The Aeneid*, Dryden makes an open statement of his debt to several noble supporters of King William. These Williamite patrons have 'not only distinguished me from others of the same party, by a particular exception of grace, but, without considering the man, have been bountiful to the poet'. Dryden was well aware that he was in receipt of a kind of political favour which allowed him the liberty of conscience in his political views as long as he accepted a voluntary limitation on their expression. That limitation, as we have seen, was not rigorously enforced by Dryden on himself, but in recent years a small but significant piece of evidence has been discovered which shows that he and his friends took great care to maintain a perfect balance in his relations to the government after 1688.

In 1691 Dryden published his opera *King Arthur*. In the dedication he mentioned that he had made some cuts, beginning the account with these significant words:

But not to offend the present times, nor a government which has hitherto protected me (and by a particular favour would have continued me what I was, if I could have complied with the terms which were offered me) I have been obliged so much to alter my first design . . .

The exact details of this offer will perhaps never be known, but obviously Dryden would have received special treatment and maybe the return of his Laureateship had he been able to do what was asked. He could not agree, but he felt grateful for the offer and expressed his gratitude. Yet when *King Arthur* was being printed, either Dryden or his friends thought better and arrangements were made to suppress the phrase which would perhaps have embarrassed the government. A new leaf, omitting the matter in parentheses, was printed and was substituted for the cancelled leaf. In 1953 Professor Fredson Bowers found a unique copy of the original leaf and thus illuminated for us a small but valuable incident in Dryden's delicate relationship with the administration of William III. Dryden knew he was a special case, and both he and the government behaved with considerable tact to preserve the 'bargain' they had struck.

The twentieth century has seen such a destruction of legends attached to Dryden's name that a point has been reached at which a new Dryden legend is being silently created. Now that we know that his religious conversion did not come about for mercenary reasons and that he was not an unprincipled turncoat, his critics stress the sincerity and simplicity of his politics with a zeal which inadvertently denigrates his political astuteness and subtlety. When and if the full story of Dryden's attitudes towards the 1688 Revolution and the Jacobite cause is fully known, it may well be revealed that he conducted himself during those years, in his life and in his writings, with consummate skill. In the meantime one might speculate on what would have happened had there been a successful restoration of James II in, say, 1698. It seems very possible that Dryden would have been restored to the Laureateship and acclaimed, both then and later, for his loyalty to James. One can only admire the ease with which he was able to uphold that loyalty under William without suffering, despite his protestations, too painfully for it. His translation of Virgil may, when fully understood, tell the story of his personal accommodation to the difficult times in which he lived.

Part Three
Dryden's Craftsmanship and his Audience

7   Establishing an Idiom:
The Foundations of Augustan Style

Restoration Literary Standards

> And though the fury of a civil war, and power, for twenty years together, abandoned to a barbarous race of men, enemies of all good learning, had buried the muses under the ruins of monarchy, yet with the restoration of our happiness, we see revived poesy lifting up its head, and already shaking off the rubbish which lay so heavy upon it.
>
> *An Essay of Dramatic Poesy*

The great events which men recognize as the turning points of history are often accompanied by major shifts of literary taste. Thus the French Revolution is felt, however obscurely, to have had important influence on literature, just as the complex of attitudes which can be grouped under the heading of 'Romanticism' is thought to have helped bring about that Revolution. Scholars will argue for ever about the difficulties which in reality adhere to such simplifications of history and literary history, for simplifications are simultaneously essential and deceptive. Yet it is important to recognize that the simplified view of what happened in literary history is always in the first instance the creation of the men involved in the events. Dryden's view of his place and that of his contemporaries in the development of English literature now strikes us as a great simplification, but to know what he thought his generation had done is indispensable.

There is what might be called an 'authorized version' of the development of English literature in the middle years of the seventeenth century. According to this account, the literature which Dryden's generation inherited from the generation of Donne stood greatly in need of 'reformation' and 'refinement'. These terms should be carefully considered. The reformers and refiners found nothing radically wrong with their literary inheritance, but they felt a strong need to bring order into literature, to restrain excesses, to set limits, and to get rid of elements which were felt to be discordant or beneath the true dignity of literature. In verse, the great reformers were held to be Sir John Denham and Edmund Waller. In his 'Preface to *The Rival Ladies*' (1664), Dryden accepts the authorized version.

> But the excellence and dignity of [rhyme] were never fully known till Mr Waller taught it; he first made writing easily an art.... This sweetness of Mr Waller's lyric poesy was afterwards followed in the epic by Sir John Denham, in his *Cooper's Hill*, a poem which...for

the majesty of the style is, and ever will be, the exact standard of good writing.

Denham and Waller, however, are undeniably a pair of lightweights whose reputations are largely upheld by the respect given them by Dryden and his followers. Dr Johnson well understood, when he came to sum up Dryden's achievements, that the authorized version had to give him pride of place.

> The veneration with which [Dryden's] name is pronounced by every cultivator of English literature, is paid him as he refined the language, improved the sentiments, and tuned the numbers of English poetry.
>
> After about half a century of forced thoughts, and rugged metre, some advances towards nature and harmony had already been made by Waller and Denham. . . .
>
> But though they did much, who can deny that they left much to do? Their works were not many, nor were their minds of very ample comprehension. More examples of more modes of composition were necessary for the establishment of regularity, and the introduction of propriety in word and thought.

Johnson thus gives Dryden a place in the movement of literary reform which Dryden undoubtedly assumed would be his. A successful literary movement needs a leading figure, a 'big name', and though Waller and Denham were always paid their tribute, it was Dryden who took the credit for doing something important with the style they had refined. Moreover, Dryden's prose displayed such marked differences from that written previously that he could obviously take credit for extending the reform in that direction, while the critical ideas expressed in that prose showed him to be—albeit unsystematically and sometimes self-contradictorily—the theoretician of whom all such movements stand in need. Much of his theory was developed in the service of the drama, where again Dryden took a leading position among the reformers, though his achievements there are less easy to isolate since most of the Restoration dramatists worked on broadly similar 'reformist' lines.

The assumption made in these accounts by Dryden and Johnson is, of course, that the art of writing could be improved by the conscious application of principles. As a mere statement this idea may seem innocuous enough to us, but when it is applied to real poets, then the historical relativism which we prize is outraged. Dryden, for instance, greatly admired Shakespeare as an author, finding him, as we all agree, the most naturally gifted of all the English poets. Yet Dryden adapted three of Shakespeare's plays for the Restoration stage, and he leaves us in no doubt that by adaptation he means 'improvement'. Of his version of *Troilus and Cressida*, he says: 'Yet after all, because the play was Shakespeare's, and that there appeared in some places of it the admirable genius of the author, I undertook to remove that heap of rubbish under which so many excellent thoughts lay buried.' Today this is heresy, but Dryden was confident that he could bring his readers to agree with his assumptions, which were that English social life had been greatly refined since Shakespeare's day, and that the increase in knowledge of the sciences was accompanied by a proportionate improvement of the arts, 'for if natural causes be more known now than in the time of Aristotle, because more studied, it follows that poesy and other arts may with the same pains arrive still nearer to perfection'. Dryden gives these words to Eugenius in the *Essay of Dramatic Poesy*, and there is no doubt that he supported the idea of such progress himself. Dryden does not denigrate Shakespeare's natural genius, but Shakespeare was unfortunate in living before the Restoration, when various kinds of 'refinement' had taken place which would have enabled him to weed out of his work many bad elements.

Some idea of the nature of these refinements will have been gathered from the terms used above by Dryden and Johnson—dignity, sweetness, majesty, exact standard, advances towards nature and harmony, regularity, propriety in word and thought—but a more comprehensive impression of the advantages Dryden saw for writers in his own society can be obtained by looking at his essays, particularly at the 'Defence of the Epilogue [to the Second Part of *The Conquest of Granada*], or An Essay on the Dramatic Poetry of the Last Age' (?1672). In this work, Dryden claims that the supremacy of his own age as an environment for writing is due simply to the general progress which has taken place with the passage of time. He defends himself against disrespect towards the 'ancients', using the authority of Horace to buttress his assertion that 'antiquity alone is no plea for the excellency of a poem; but that, one age learning from another, the last (if we can suppose an equality of wit in the writers) has the advantage of knowing more and better than the former'. The Restoration, compared with the previous, antebellum age is 'refined' and Dryden defines 'refinement' as 'an improvement of our wit, language, and conversation; or, an alteration in them for the better'. He then proceeds by taking up each of these aspects in turn, first language, then wit, and finally conversation.

The state of the English language was an important and perpetual concern of Dryden's. In the 'Defence of the Epilogue' he first defends his opinion that the language *has* improved rather than declined since Ben Jonson's day by saying that the refinement of language consists 'either in rejecting such old words or phrases which are ill sounding, or improper, or in admitting new, which are more proper, more sounding, and more significant'. He leaves undefined the meanings of 'proper', 'sounding', and 'significant', assuming that his readers will understand. 'Proper' referred to 'decorum', the rightness of the word for its context, 'sounding' to what Dryden calls the 'well placing of words for the sweetness of pronunciation', and 'significant' to consistency of sense. When Dryden (after a digression on the 'lameness' of some plots used by Shakespeare and Fletcher) turns to a close examination of the language of Jonson's *Catiline*, he points out instances of what he sees as the failure of the language to be proper, sounding, and significant. His criticisms seem unjustifiably picayune, but he has committed himself to finding such faults in the style of the great writers of the previous era and does so to his own satisfaction. Had they lived in the Restoration period, Shakespeare, Fletcher, and Jonson 'had doubtless written more correctly'. 'The times were ignorant in which they lived.'

The superiority of Restoration wit to that often displayed by Shakespeare is again a matter of refinement. Dryden expects writing to be witty; his point is that Shakespeare often employs the wrong means to that end. Dryden's own definitions of the notoriously difficult term 'wit' have often been found inadequate. In the 'Account of *Annus Mirabilis*' (1667) he says:

> The composition of all poems is or ought to be of wit, and wit in the poet, or wit writing...is no other than the faculty of imagination in the writer...which searches over all the memory for the species or ideas of those things which it designs to represent. Wit written, is that which is well defined, the happy result of thought, or product of that imagination.

The failure of such a definition is that it seems too general, as does his later definition: 'a propriety of thoughts and words; or, in other terms, thought and words elegantly adapted to the subject.' But 'wit' was certainly for Dryden a much more comprehensive term than we are likely to think it, and if we add to his definitions certain of those found in the *Oxford English Dictionary*, then we should have a good enough idea of what was meant.

Wit 5: Good or great mental capacity; intellectual ability; genius, talent, cleverness; mental quickness or sharpness, acumen.

Wit 7: Quickness of intellect or liveliness of fancy, with capacity of apt expression; talent for saying brilliant or sparkling things, especially in an amusing way.

Wit 8: That quality of speech or writing which consists in the apt association of thought and expression, calculated to surprise and delight by its unexpectedness.

Addison's *Spectator* papers on wit, numbers 58 to 63, are also of use.

Pre-Restoration wit, Shakespeare's for example, is often undignified ('low') or is obtained by tasteless means, such as puns—'the lowest and most grovelling kind of wit, which we call clenches'. Outside the drama, and therefore outside the scope of the 'Defence of the Epilogue', Dryden found much that needed correcting and regulating in the poetry of the writers who—Dryden gave Dr Johnson the name for them—are now called the 'Metaphysicals': Donne and his fellows. Here again, the wit often depended on puns. One of the anonymous poets described by Lisideus in the *Essay of Dramatic Poesy* is clearly one of these degenerates. 'I ask you if one of them does not perpetually pay us with clenches upon words and a certain clownish kind of raillery? If now and then he does not offer at a catachresis [improper use of a word] or a Clevelandism, wresting and torturing a word into another meaning.'

The introduction of the name of John Cleveland is significant, for his work displays, besides puns, many outlandish versions of the famous Metaphysical conceits, those poetical comparisons in which the similarities brought out by the poet's ingenuity fight a battle with the reader's perception of the dissimilarities of the situation. Dryden does not condemn the conceit out of hand, but he deplores the excesses which Donne's example gave rise to in the work of lesser poets like Cleveland. Eugenius says: 'We cannot read a verse of Cleveland's without making a face at it, as if every word were a pill to swallow. He gives us many times a hard nut to break our teeth, without a kernel for our pains.' Dryden was too sensible to reject Donne completely; he later called him 'the greatest wit, though not the best poet of our nation'. The distinction between 'wit' and 'poet' concerned the style of Donne's poetry. Dryden paid homage to the power of intellect so evident in Donne's work, but he felt that the manner of expression was often ill-chosen. In his flattery of the Earl of Dorset in 1693, Dryden says, absurdly:

> Donne alone, of all our countrymen, had your talent; but he was not happy enough to arrive at your versification; and were he translated into numbers [correct metre], and English, he would yet be wanting in the dignity of expression. . . . He affects the metaphysics, not only in his satires, but in his amorous verses, where nature only should reign; and perplexes the minds of the fair sex with nice speculations of philosophy, when he should engage their hearts, and entertain them with the softnesses of love. In this (if I may be pardoned for so bold a truth) Mr Cowley has copied him to a fault.

Donne's wit, in other words, is given play in quite inappropriate contexts, and in a style which is not 'natural', a term Dryden uses to mean unexaggerated or realistic.

Wit, then, was essential to poetry, but pre-Restoration wit was undisciplined and extravagant, both in its excesses of ideas—the wildest of conceits—and in its expression. Dryden's own pre-Restoration verses 'On the Death of the Lord Hastings' provide us with good examples of the excessive conceits he later rejected (see pp. 164–6) and the 'Defence of the Epilogue' explains why the poets of the early seventeenth century were at a disadvantage in their style.

'The wit of this age is much more courtly,' says Dryden. Shakespeare, Jonson, and their contemporaries often amused their audiences with depictions of vulgar characters in 'low' situations. Mercutio is the best Shakespeare could do in the way of 'courtly' wit, and Dryden thinks little of him.

> I have always acknowledged the wit of our predecessors with all the veneration which becomes me, but, I am sure, their wit was not that of gentlemen; there was ever somewhat that was ill-bred and clownish in it, and this confessed the conversation of the authors.
>
> And this leads me to the last and greatest advantage of our writing, which proceeds from conversation.

Dryden believed that the disappearance of social barriers between gentlemen and playwrights had led to the purging from Restoration drama of vulgar characters and incidents (a belief which is sustainable as long as one remembers that 'vulgar' means 'plebeian' or 'lower-class'), and that it had made available to the stage a kind of dialogue which was 'easy and pliant', courtly and polished, without affectation or 'vulgarity'. But this improvement came about not simply because of the fraternization of playwrights and courtiers. The conversation of the courtiers themselves had improved, and this Dryden attributed to King Charles's influence. His exile had served to educate him.

> His own misfortunes, and the nation's, afforded him an opportunity which is rarely allowed to sovereign princes, I mean of travelling and being conversant in the most polished courts of Europe.... At his return, he found a nation lost as much in barbarism as rebellion. And as the excellency of his nature forgave the one, so the excellency of his manners reformed the other. The desire of imitating so great a pattern first weakened the dull and heavy spirits of the English from their natural reservedness, and made them easy and pliant to each other in discourse. Thus, insensibly, our way of living became more free: and the fire of the English wit, which was before stifled under a constrained, melancholy way of breeding, began first to display its force, by mixing the solidity of our nation with the air and gaiety of our neighbours.

Dryden does not define the characteristics of this 'conversational' style in the 'Defence of the Epilogue'. His own prose at its best is the best example that could be given, and elements of a definition can be gathered from others of his works. Thus, in the Preface to *The Rival Ladies* he says: 'I have endeavoured to write English, as near as

I could distinguish it from the tongue of pedants, and that of affected travellers.' The desired style, therefore, is to be 'unspecialized', the language of educated gentlemen but not of those gentlemen who have been drawn aside, by learning or travel, from the broad, main road of urbane conversation. The proper simplicity of this style prevents obscurity. Eugenius says, 'wit is best conveyed to us in the most easy language; and it is most to be admired when a great thought comes dressed in words so commonly received that it is understood by the meanest apprehensions'. The acquisition of such a style, however, is not to be encompassed simply by conversing with the right people, though that is indispensable.

> There are many who understand Greek and Latin, and yet are ignorant of their mother tongue. The proprieties and delicacies of the English are known to few; 'tis impossible even for a good wit to understand the practice of them without the help of a liberal education, long reading, and digesting of those few good authors we have amongst us, the knowledge of men and manners, the freedom of habitudes and conversations with the best company of both sexes; and in short, without wearing off the rust which he contracted, while he was laying in a stock of learning.
>
> (Preface to *Sylvae*, 1685)

One was to work and study, therefore, to achieve in writing the unlaboured and apparently unstudied ease, clarity, and politeness of genteel conversation. This applied as much to verse as to prose. Each was to avoid the pedantry, obscurity, and harshness which were now felt to be incompatible with refined conversation. (John Evelyn: 'Such as have lived long in universities do greatly affect words and expressions no where in use besides, as may be observed in Cleveland's poems for Cambridge.') Literary English was to be brought into alignment with the best spoken English, and it is interesting to note that the change being made was, in theory at least, close to Wordsworth's revolution in literary style at the end of the eighteenth century. Literary English was in each case 'refined' by measuring it against a selection of the language really used by men. (The men chosen in each case were, of course, at the opposite ends of society, and while Wordsworth treasured spontaneity, Dryden wanted an easy, polished formality.) In both cases, the reformers insisted that 'a large portion of the language of every good poem can in no respect differ from that of good prose'. If one thinks of a later 'reformation', that of Ezra Pound, with its stress on the vernacular and the declaration that 'poetry should be at least as well written as prose', it begins to seem that some realignment of written English with spoken English, and of poetry with prose, faces great poets every hundred years or so.

Dryden's assessment of the achievements of his age in reshaping English literature and in perfecting the Augustan style is a simplification. It distorts the history of a major shift in literary taste by implicitly and explicitly comparing it to political events of the time—the chaos of the Civil War followed by the resumed authority of the Restoration. We know, for instance, that a reaction against the Metaphysical style in poetry had been evolving for many years, and that men had decided much earlier that a consciously difficult style was ungentlemanly and that the standard should be 'the phrase of the Court, and...the speech used among the noble and among the better sort in London' (Edmund Bolton, *Hypercritica*, c. 1618). No harm is done as long as we remember that Dryden is presenting a simplified account, for what is most important is that his criteria for good style in verse and prose were accepted for most of the eighteenth century.

It was believed, as Dr Johnson believed, that with Dryden English verse had reached a 'steady state' of near perfection, that properly regulated wit was the essence of poetry, and that genteel conversation provided a standard of style in both prose and verse. The Augustan writers are so impressively united in their tastes and ambitions because for many decades men were able to agree on the proper foundations of style. Even a writer like Defoe, who dissented from most of the social ideals upheld by his Augustan contemporaries, could daydream, as Swift did, of an English Academy whose function would be chiefly stylistic, to bring 'our gentlemen to a capacity of writing like themselves'. Dryden frequently violates the laws he helped to codify (an always encouraging sign of human fallibility), but it remains one of his great achievements that he helped create a style whose stability was an important feature of English life for a hundred years. Eventually it received the tribute paid to all successful revolutions, the tribute of a rising against it.

Fixing the Language

> But who can hope his line should long
> Last in a daily changing tongue?...
>
> Poets that lasting marble seek
> Must carve in Latin or in Greek;
> We write in sand, our language grows,
> And, like the tide, our work o'erflows.
>
> WALLER, 'Of English Verse'

One idea which accompanied the well and widely received notion of the 'refinement' and progress of culture in the Restoration was the dismaying realization that as time passed so language changed. Men observed that the English writers who had lived in earlier centuries were antiquated and hard to understand. The Restoration was the stage in our literature at which it may be said that there was for the first time a general commitment to English as the language for all kinds of writing. Many continued to write in Latin; French became the language of diplomacy. But no poet after Milton was really faced with the problem of deciding whether Latin or English was the right medium. English had grown to full adult status, yet the difficulty of understanding the poetry of a Chaucer and the awareness of how much English had changed even since the days of Charles I were enough to make men worry. Swift expressed the fear that English did not have the permanence of Latin.

> The rude Latin of the monks is still very intelligible; whereas, had their records been delivered down only in the vulgar tongue, so barren and so barbarous, so subject to continual succeeding changes; they could not now be understood, unless by antiquaries.
>
> (*A Proposal for Correcting . . . the English Tongue*)

Early in his career, Dryden began to agitate for an English Academy to 'fix' or stabilize the language. In his Preface to *The Rival Ladies* in 1664, he wrote: 'I am sorry that (speaking so noble a language as we do) we have not a more certain measure of it, as they have in France, where they have an Academy erected for that purpose.' Dryden's is thus one of the earliest proposals for an Academy, and he maintained his enthusiasm for it throughout his life. In dedicating *Troilus and Cressida* to the Earl of Sunderland in 1679, Dryden repeats his advocacy and encourages Sunderland to become the English Richelieu, who had founded the French Academy in 1635. By 1693, when he wrote the 'Discourse of Satire', Dryden still saw the need for an Academy, but was justifiably pessimistic.

> Our language is in a manner barbarous [since it has no dictionary or grammar]; and what government will encourage any one, or more, who are capable of refining it, I know not; but nothing under a public expense can go through with it. And I rather fear a declination of the language, than hopes of an advancement of it in the present age.

This last fear, however, was unfounded, for the authority of Dryden's own writings in verse and prose helped provide the 'certain measure' for several generations of English writers. When Dr Johnson wrote the Preface to his *Dictionary* in 1755 he saw no need for an Academy, and in effect his work brought to completion a hundred years of writing which determined the course of English written style, especially in prose, to the present day.

The desire for an Academy, as expressed by Dryden and Swift, can be explained simply as another instance of the Augustan wish for authorized stability, but actually a variety of impulses urged these men to support the idea—the 'impermanence' of the language, its function as an instrument of social cohesion, and the need for prose, especially, to be a useful and easy means of communication. In respect of this last factor, Dryden's membership of the Royal Society provides an interesting episode in his history of concern for the English language.

In December of 1664 the Royal Society established a committee.

It being suggested that there were persons of the Society whose genius was very proper and inclined to improve the English tongue, and particularly for philosophical [scientific] purposes, it was voted that there should be a committee for improving the English language.

It was to meet once or twice a month, and its twenty-two members included Dryden, Edmund Waller, and John Evelyn.

Nothing much came of the committee. Its meetings ceased when plague and fire interrupted London life; no minutes have survived. A letter written by John Evelyn in 1665 tells us what one member thought about the committee's task. Evelyn could not attend one meeting, so wrote down some ideas and sent them to the chairman. He gives no special consideration to the language of science, and calls for such 'authoritarian' tools as a grammar, dictionaries, a system of punctuation, and collections of elegant expressions as examples of good style. He concludes: 'There must be a stock of reputation gained by some public writings and compositions of the members of this assembly, so that others may not think it dishonour to come under the test, and accept them for judges and approbators.' Reputations were gained by members of the Royal Society, but it is interesting to note that Dryden's own status as a 'judge and approbator' has little to do with his membership.

Thomas Sprat, another member of the language committee, published in 1667 a *History of the Royal Society* (begun in 1664) in which he too called for the establishment of an Academy. In another and famous passage in the *History*, Sprat set out the stylistic qualities avoided and desired by the Society.

They took [he says] a constant resolution to reject all the amplifications, digressions, and swellings of style; to return back to the primitive purity, and shortness, when men delivered so many *things* almost in an equal number of *words*. They have exacted from all their members a close, naked, natural way of speaking, positive expressions, clear senses, a native easiness; bringing all things as near the mathematical plainness as they can, and preferring the language of artisans, countrymen, and merchants before that of wits or scholars.

This passage has long been a cause of dispute among experts on the prose of the Restoration, and the reader should be warned that, here again, the whole question of prose style, especially as it is connected with the history of the Royal Society, is a terrain over which battles are still being fought. The account given here relies heavily on the work of the latest historian of the Royal Society's origins, Margery Purver (*The Royal Society: concept and creation*, 1967).

Miss Purver denies that Sprat in this passage is recommending a style of English for each and every purpose. He is describing the style recommended for scientific purposes only.

> It was not a literary form, and the Royal Society knew this. . . . Sprat himself in the Royal Society's *History* did not employ the style which he had recommended to scientists, for the obvious reason that he was writing history, not science.

To amplify these remarks of Miss Purver's, one may point out that Sprat had 'apologised' earlier for having 'written of philosophers without any ornament of eloquence', but his reader perceives that Sprat's work *is* eloquent, though not ostentatiously so; he rejects 'this vicious abundance of phrase, this trick of metaphors [though not all metaphors], this volubility of tongue' without bringing his work near to 'mathematical plainness'.

Dryden's prose style is similarly 'unmathematical'; it is far from the language of science. Yet like Sprat's prose in the *History*, it is unaffected and unostentatious. All these styles, including the scientific, start from the same general position: prose should be 'conversational', flexible, easy to follow, and (to a greater or less degree) polished. But from this starting place they diverged towards the 'two cultures'. The achievement of Restoration prose writing was that it did permit such a new beginning and that it said a clear farewell to the great but non-utilitarian prose of the earlier seventeenth century.

The episode of Dryden and the language committee is a reminder of his interest in science (an interest Wordsworth shared) and also of the early nature of the Society, which had broader aims and a greater range of membership than at present. Dryden's own concern for the language, however, both antedated his membership and survived his expulsion for not paying his dues. If the Society's stylistic criteria had no apparent effect on Dryden's own style, that is not because he did not share the general premises governing those criteria. He realized that the business of a poet was different from that of a scientist, and demanded, within the limits agreed, a more eloquent manner.

Confidence of Metre

> I learned versification wholly from Dryden. . . who had improved it much beyond any of our former poets; and would, probably, have brought it to its perfection, had he not been unhappily obliged to write so often in haste.
>
> ALEXANDER POPE

Prosody, the study of the forms of versification, has become the dismal science of literature. Having inherited the Romantic tenet that poetry is 'grown' rather than 'made', we regard with impatience any suggestion that a poet's work should be corrected or brought into conformity with rules or laws of versification. While we may be tolerant of descriptive prosody, which shows us how versification has helped bring about a poet's effects, prescriptive versification, which lays down the law for poems yet unwritten, is entirely out of favour. The idea of a verse form which has to be 'filled' like a glass bottle and which does not change its shape to conform to internal pressure often seems today an unjustifiable and unnatural imposition on a poet, though this is less true in the opinions of poets themselves than in the assumptions of many readers. (Robert Frost said, apropos free verse, that he preferred to play tennis with a net.) It is in some ways unfortunate that the only major poet thought of as modern who has made a prominent fuss about prosody is Gerard Manley Hopkins. The stress marks in his poems and his elaborate notes about sprung rhythm (which is in essence a matter of charming simplicity) have contributed to the assumption that prosody is a disagreeably technical business of horrid complexity, the sort of thing which only a Jesuit could love. (The term 'sprung rhythm' itself suggests, to the technologically unsophisticated, something akin to 'four-wheel independent suspension'.) Moreover, educational systems until lately have worked to ensure that there should be little contact between students of the classics, who were expected to 'make' verses, and students of modern literature, who have generally resented being 'forced' to write poems, since spontaneity is the essence of poetry—isn't it?

There is now plenty of evidence that the classicists' view of verse-making simply as a pedagogical exercise according to rule is disappearing. It would be pleasant to know that the modernists' detestation or ignorance of prosody was similarly giving way to a more reasonable appreciation of its place in the art of poetry. As a freshman, I once went to a lecture on Milton's Prosody under the assumption that I was to be told about Milton's prose. If today's undergraduates are less ignorant, I still see no evidence that most of them would not share the assumption I made on learning the true subject of the lecture, that prosody was a subject both nugatory and rebarbative.

The attitude of Dryden and his contemporaries in the matter of versification separates them clearly from the twentieth century, but to appreciate Dryden as the founder of Augustan poetry it is necessary to understand what he achieved as a verse technician. Some technicalities will, therefore, be unavoidable, but the heart of this business is not machinery.

A twentieth-century reader, asked to specify the greatest pleasure of poetry would, in all likelihood, answer 'imagery'. Dryden's answer to the same question is given in the 'Discourse concerning Satire'

(1693). 'But versification, and numbers, are the greatest pleasures of poetry.' (He was, it must be admitted, apt to say that the most *important* element of poetry was whatever he happened to be interested in at any given moment.) For Dryden, the purposes of poetry were —it was the classical answer—delight and instruction, but delight came first, since instruction could be in prose, but poetry could only instruct so long as it gave delight. The chief means for delight was formal versification, for this was what separated poetry from prose. (No definition of poetry which omitted a formal verse pattern would have satisifed him.)

Dryden's interest in the theory and practice of prosody was life-long. In the 'Discourse concerning Satire' he saw the need of a *prosodia*, a body of rules for English versification which would provide for the language the same kind of authority and stability as would a grammar and a dictionary. In the Dedication to his *Virgil*, he wrote: 'I have long had by me the materials of an English *prosodia*, containing all the mechanical rules of versification, wherein I have treated with some exactness of the feet, the quantities, and the pauses.' Dryden gives several reasons why these materials have not been worked up into a book. 'Since I have not strictly observed those rules myself which I can teach others; since I pretend to no dictatorship among my fellow poets; . . . and above all since your lordship [Mulgrave] has advised me not to publish that little which I know.' The lack of the *prosodia*, however, does not prevent us from knowing the outlines of Dryden's opinions on matters of versification, for throughout his critical writings he scattered occasional remarks on the topic and these have been collected. It seems clear that if Dryden's finished *prosodia* had been published, the prestige of his name would have given it an authority of beneficial effect on the development of English literary theory. One respects Dryden's wish not to become a literary dictator, but in this case his withdrawal meant that others, eminently less fitted, were chosen as arbiters of correct prosody in the eighteenth century.

The desire for rule and order, in prosody as in everything else, may be seen as another manifestation of the dominant trait of the Augustan frame of mind. Yet it may possibly be thought that prosody is too slight a matter to bear the weight of such social and political theory. Can the choice of verse form tell anything about the non-poetical beliefs of the poet? Dryden would have affirmed that it could, but the most impressive (or depressing) display of the assumption that a form of verse could guarantee orthodoxy of social and political beliefs came at the end of the eighteenth century, when the versification of Dryden and Pope had become established in many minds as the historically perfected and 'only' way to write English poetry. The hostile reaction of many early reviewers of the verse of Leigh Hunt, Scott, Coleridge and Keats can in large part be explained as a reaction to the political beliefs which were assumed to accompany such unorthodox verse forms. 'A literary generation terrified by the French Revolution and its repercussions on the British political scene instinctively saw in the rise of a more free and varied prosody a lurking and sinister Jacobinism' (Paul Fussell). 'Jacobinism' was, of course, a fearful exaggeration on the part of the critics, but many of the Romantic poets themselves certainly shared the view that new political beliefs demanded a break with old poetical forms. And the association of radical politics with 'innovations' in poetics is one which Dryden would himself have made.

In seeking precedents on which to base the 'laws' of a new English prosody, Dryden's contemporaries looked to three sources: the native English tradition, the classical tradition (particularly Latin poetry), and modern French verse. The versification of Latin poems is 'quantitative', that is based on the pronunciation of long and short syllables. Various men had, in Elizabethan times, experimented with quantitative metres in English, but it was generally agreed that these experiments were failures. (Dryden may not have agreed with the general agreement.) The most important idea to be carried over from Latin verse into English was, therefore, that the verse of a great people at the height of its political authority should be regulated, measured, carefully made according to rule. If English poetry was to become truly Augustan, then obviously it must have an Augustan prosody.

French prosody became in many ways more influential on English verse than classical precedent. France had harboured large numbers of English refugees during the interregnum, French civilization was the model for the rest of Europe, and French literature had undergone the 'refining' which was now to be effected for English literature. Boileau's L'Art Poétique, which Dryden knew well and had helped to translate in 1680, had been published in 1674, and was a work of great prescriptive authority, equal to that of the often translated Ars Poetica of Horace. French verse rhymed, but it had no quantitative basis, no 'long' or 'short', and the measure of its lines was simply the number of syllables—twelve in the Alexandrine, the most important line form. The Restoration poets in England adopted the view that an exact number of syllables was required of 'correct' verse, and to this end they employed and marked in their verse contractions of individual words and the running together, in order to eliminate syllables, of pairs of words ('An ancient fabric, rais'd t'inform the sight'). Rigid 'syllabism', as it is called, was adopted with enthusiasm by many of the 'authorities' on prosody who wrote in the eighteenth century and it was emphasized so much that for many people it became the only factor which determined whether a line was 'correct'.

From the prosodic point of view, the great difference between French and English is stress. The syllables of a French word are given equal stress, while an English polysyllabic word usually has one dominant, heavily stressed syllable. The arrangement of these stresses within a line of verse is one of the English poet's main tasks. The commonest of all English metres is an iambic pattern of alternative unstressed and stressed syllables making up a line of ten syllables, an iambic pentameter: 'Mў wárbliñg lúte, thĕ lúte Ĭ whĭlŏm strúng'. To orthodox prosodists of the eighteenth century, the establishment of a pattern of iambic metre in a ten-syllable line was all that was desired of a poet's form and it was often thought proper to 'correct' lines which did not conform to the pattern. So widespread was the belief in the correctness of this line that, as Paul Fussell shows, orthodox prosodists often became incapable of hearing anything else. In 1799, for example, one Joseph Robertson, assuming that Milton wrote always to a regular iambic pattern, said that 'Milton frequently lays an accent [stress] on insignificant particles [syllables]', and cites several individual lines to prove his point, with 'stressed' syllables in italics.

> Thus Belial *with* words cloth'd in reason's garb.
>
> Thy ling'ring, *or* with one stroke *of* this dart.
>
> Yet fell. Remember, *and* fear *to* transgress.
>
> And dust shalt eat all *the* days *of* thy life.

Such readings show that by the end of the eighteenth century the 'new prosody' of the Restoration had become for many readers a rigid frame into which lines of poetry were to be forced, even if a nonsensical result was obtained. One of the greatest beauties of English verse occurs when the poet, having established a basic rhythm of, say, iambic metre, then varies it in individual lines, so that the reader is able to hear a kind of 'counterpoint' as the expected iambic rhythm is overlaid by the variations. Dryden and Pope in their practice made stress variation an important effect of their verse, and had Dryden devoted his full powers to producing his *prosodia* he might have been able to bring home to readers the propriety and desirability of such variation. As it was, the main stream of English eighteenth-century prosody soon came to regard stress variation as a blemish. Thus the first line of *Mac Flecknoe* 'Aĺl húmăne thíngs ăře súbjĕct tŏ dĕcáy', where the first 'foot' of two stressed syllables (a spondee) is 'balanced' later in the line by a pyrrhic foot of two unstressed syllables, would have been read by many later prosodists as 'Aĺl húmăne thíngs ăře súbjĕct tó dĕcáy', with a loss of stress variation and a violation of sense.

The reason for the near-total triumph of the combination of ten syllables and invariable iambic metre was that, when this simplistic prosody was being formulated, the poets of the day were writing verse which could be adequately analysed in these terms. The English metrical tradition, which, despite the fuss made about French and classical models, had the greatest influence on what the Restoration poets did, had long been evolving towards ten syllables and iambics. The Restoration poets settled on the ten-syllable line as the English 'heroic' measure because, from Chaucer to their own day, it had been the line used, whether in rhyme or blank verse, by most poets for most purposes. The French and the ancients were useful as authorities to justify the formal acceptance of English past practice as the rule for the future. In the earlier part of the seventeenth century the octosyllabic line had been very popular with such poets as Donne and Marvell. The decasyllable finally triumphed as the 'heroic' measure partly because Samuel Butler used the eight-syllable line with great success for comic purposes, a tradition maintained by Swift. Practice became fixed as precept.

Dryden's employment of stress variation has been mentioned as a feature of his prosody displaying more sense than the rules of most eighteenth-century prosodists. Other statements of his can be used to support the suggestion that his *prosodia* would have been better than many which were actually published. Dryden was a strict syllabist, 'The English verse, which we call heroic, consists of no more than ten syllables', but he also recognized that English poetry was written in feet, deriving their origin from the long and short of classical metres. Dryden denied that a metrical foot could be trisyllabic (no anapaests uu/or dactyls/uu, despite the evidence of his own songs, 'Till oŭr lóve wăs lŏv'd óut iñ ŭs bóth'), but his insistence on the fact of the disyllabic foot shows that, had he brooded over his ideas and worked them up into a finished system, he might have come to see and to give authority to the vital place of the foot and of scansion (learning to mark the feet) in English verse. The matter of 'quantity', a system of length and shortness of syllable, also crops up in Dryden's prosodic remarks—'the feet, the quantities, and the pauses'—and though discussed too briefly to be clear, it is interesting that this problem of quantity should have led Dryden to differ, perhaps, from virtually all the orthodox eighteenth-century prosodists in seeing English as a language in which quantitative versification was possible. Dryden's sense of literary history would have been of great help in a full study of prosody, as would have been his awareness of what he called the 'genius of the English tongue', the qualities inherent in the language and found in no others. Finally, his *prosodia* would have led him to analyse his own practice with care, and that alone would have made the effort worthwhile for later generations.

Yet though we may reasonably lament the loss of Dryden's *prosodia*, his poetry gives us his prosody in practice. In the Critical Survey (pp. 195–200) an attempt is made to analyse one passage of Dryden's verse as a step towards appreciation of his *prosodia de facto*.

8　Making an Audience: Dryden's Criticism

Criticism, as it was first instituted by Aristotle, was meant a standard of judging well; the chiefest part of which is to observe those excellencies which should delight a reasonable reader.

'The Author's Apology for Heroic Poetry and Poetic Licence'.

Those who try to sum up Dryden as a critic often face a dilemma. On one hand, it seems impossible not to agree, with Johnson and the historians of literature, that Dryden is 'the father of English criticism', but, on the other, a study of his critical writings shows them to be quite often derivative, self-contradictory, rambling, inexact, at times over-specialized and at others too sweeping. 'Fatherhood' should surely carry more sense of paternal authority and unquestionable achievement. This reaction, coming from an age which has put into criticism of all kinds most of the energy that used to be devoted to theology, is mainly that of a thriving business discovering its small beginnings in a corner shop. Dryden knew quite well that he was getting into something new in English writing—'I was drawing the outlines of an art without any living master to instruct me in it. . . before the use of the loadstone, or knowledge of the compass, I was sailing in a vast ocean'—and he expected praise for the voyage he had managed to make. It would be churlish to withhold it just because we can go farther and faster.

But the historical importance of Dryden's criticism is not alone sufficient to earn it a place in this preface. The criticism deserves some attention here because of what might be called its overriding but undeclared purpose: to shape and educate an audience for Dryden's plays, poems and translations. He wanted his works to be read the right way, so set about teaching his readers how to read. In a sense, he was creating his readers, and if we attend to the nature of that 'creation' we can confirm many intuitions about Dryden as a writer and critic.

The nature of Dryden's prose style relates intimately to his critical objectives. Its 'conversational' base indicates that he expected a 'polite' audience, one which belonged or aspired to belong to a cultivated society. Such an audience was not to be bullied nor to be blinded by the science of university learning. Dryden could assume that his readers knew who the major writers of antiquity and of modern times were. He could assume, that is, the ordinary information of educated persons. But technicalities were to be avoided. (He was by no means always able to keep from technicalities, since in writing his prefaces he often defends himself from attack by critics and fellow-playwrights, as in his argument with Sir Robert Howard. As a general rule, however, he avoids 'terms of art', and even when involved in controversy manages to keep the dispute open to the judgment of non-specialists.) The tone of critical debate, as Dryden ideally conceived it, is to be found in *An Essay of Dramatic Poesy*, where, though the speakers disagree, they do so urbanely with no loss of temper, no acrimony. The tone in which Restoration literary critics often delivered their remarks—a mixture of impertinence, arrogance, and long-windedness, as found in the work of Thomas Rymer and John Dennis—was something Dryden tried, not always successfully, to avoid. Abrasiveness was the manner of embattled specialists, quarrelling pedants, and though Dryden as a specialist could understand such debates perfectly well, he tried not to let his published writings take on that form. He would have applauded the choice of style made by his Royal Society colleague, Robert Boyle, for his work in dialogue form, *The Sceptical Chemist* (1661):

> To keep a due decorum in the discourses it was fit that in a book written by a gentleman, and wherein only gentlemen are introduced as speakers, the language should be more smooth and the expressions more civil than is usual in the more scholastic way of writing.

Modern literary criticism is nothing if not scholastic. The kind of discussion of literature which Dryden helped bring into being is now largely despised by academic specialists as chat, review journalism, or—worst of all—belle-lettrism. One striking development of modern critical practice has been explication, 'close analysis', 'practical criticism'. Dryden's own 'examen' of Jonson's *The Silent Woman (Epicoene)* in *An Essay of Dramatic Poesy* has been described twice in recent years as 'barely pass work' for a modern undergraduate, and the supposition has thereby been let loose that, while Dryden was good at 'chat', he was not much good at rigorous and minute critical examination of a text, that his criticism lacked 'practicality'.

We might, therefore, examine a passage from one of Dryden's letters to William Walsh, who had sent Dryden an epigram for his inspection. It ended with the lines,

> Blend'em together, Fate, ease both their pain;
> And of two wretches make one happy man.

Dryden felt some correction was needed.

> The word 'blend' includes the sense of *together*. 'ease both their pain': 'pain' is singular, 'both' is plural. But indeed 'pain' may

have a collective and plural signification. Then the rhyme is not full, of 'pain' and 'man'. An half rhyme is not always a fault; but in the close of any paper of verses, 'tis to be avoided. And after all, tell me truly, if those words 'ease both their pain', were not superfluous in the sense, and only put, for the sake of the rhyme, and filling up the verse. It came into my head to alter them, and I am afraid for the worse.

> Kind Fate, or Fortune, blend them if you can:
> And, of two wretches, make one happy man.

'Kind Fate' looks a little harsh; 'fate' without an epithet, is always taken in the ill sense. 'Kind' added changes that signification. (Fata valet hora benigni.) The words, 'if you can', have almost the same fault I taxed in your ending of the line: but being better considered, that is, whether Fortune or Fate can alter a man's temper, who is already so tempered, and leaving it doubtful, I think does not prejudice the thought in the last line.

(Walsh accepted all Dryden's emendations when the poem was printed.)

Dryden is here putting the work of a fellow-poet to close scrutiny, considering the suitability of every word, and the example helps one to see that twentieth-century close reading is in effect the same kind of treatment. Every word must earn its keep, and there must be no inconsistencies of logic. But Dryden never uses this technique of criticism to any important extent in his published writings. Clearly he could do it but chose not to.

His reason, I believe, was that this was 'professionalism', and as such inappropriate for the public he was cultivating. To a modern way of thinking, accounts of poets bringing their work from first thoughts to final perfection are fascinating. The drafts of Yeats's poems, for example, have been published and scrutinized as a means of studying his sensibility and his poetic skills. Dryden, I think we may say, would have been startled to see his own drafts published and would probably have tried to prevent it. We have a romantic interest in the nature of the creative mind, which perhaps overshadows the idea of the poem as a made and completed object. Dryden wanted his readers to focus on the object, not on the making of it. Thus the kind of criticism he will not supply is that which the twentieth century most admires.

Dryden's prose at its best has one striking quality which also generally informs his criticism. It is a prose which is markedly considerate of its reader. By placing his level of style at that of urbane conversation (though it is always conversation raised and polished one degree above the realism of actual speech) he accepted the conversational obligation to be immediately understood. The great baroque prose of Sir Thomas Browne, to name an older contemporary of Dryden, is willing to make the reader read again to be sure of the sense conveyed in those superbly ornate sentences. Although gorgeous to the ear, the prose of Browne relies on the reader's eye to maintain the thread of argument. In reading Dryden's prose one can use the ear as the main instrument. His prose can be read aloud and understood first time. The avoidance of suspended constructions, such as the periodic sentence, where the main clause is held suspended till the end, is marked in Dryden's prose. He writes essentially to be heard, and his sentences are typically accretive in form, conveying first the main idea, then attaching modifications and additions. It was his achievement to make such prose elegant. 'The clauses are never balanced, nor the periods modelled; every word seems to drop by chance, though it falls into its proper place' (Johnson).

This consideration for the reader governs the nature of Dryden's criticism. The style of his many prefaces, for example, is often admired while their ideas are denigrated. If we remember for whom Dryden was writing, then the style and the ideas are brought into agreement (see Critical Survey, pp. 200–03).

All Dryden's criticism repays reading, for in the most specialized of his theatrical prefaces one encounters fine summary judgments and witty epigrams. He could be far too deferential to men who were his obvious inferiors as critics, and it is irritating to see how he respects the opinions of a Thomas Rymer. Yet in a letter to John Dennis, Dryden says all that is needed about Rymer's criticisms of Shakespeare.

> You see what success this learned critic has found in the world, after his blaspheming Shakespeare. Almost all the faults he has discovered are truly there; yet who will read Mr Rymer or not read Shakespeare? For my own part I reverence Mr Rymer's learning, but I detest his ill nature and his arrogance. I indeed, and such as I, have reason to be afraid of him, but Shakespeare has not.

As Dryden grew older, and as his prefaces became more and more concerned with the authors he was translating rather than with defence of his own plays, so his criticism became more rambling, more anecdotal—and better! He obviously knew, in the Preface to *Fables*, for example, that his readers enjoyed his digressions and personal comments; his apologies for them come too often to be serious. Such writing is not criticism as we now love it. In the hands of many of Dryden's successors such a style of literary discussion did become 'chat'. Yet the greatest of those successors was Samuel Johnson, and it may be said that Johnson's *Lives*, especially those of Dryden and Pope, represent the beneficial effects of Dryden's type of criticism. Near the end of his 'Life of Pope', Johnson summed up the two great poets in a series of figures that owe much to Dryden's 'characters' of Homer and Virgil, Horace and Juvenal, Chaucer and Boccaccio, Shakespeare and Jonson.

> Dryden's page is a natural field, rising into inequalities, and diversified by the varied exuberance of abundant vegetation; Pope's is a velvet lawn, shaven by the scythe and levelled by the roller.... If the flights of Dryden therefore are higher, Pope continues longer on the wing. If of Dryden's fire the blaze is brighter, of Pope's the heat is more regular and constant. Dryden often surpasses expectation, and Pope never falls below it. Dryden is read with frequent astonishment, and Pope with perpetual delight.

9 The Kindred Arts

Dryden's status as the greatest literary figure of his day is well displayed in his relationships with the other arts and their practitioners at the Court and in the wider world of London. The precedents set by Ben Jonson and Davenant made the Poet Laureate a collaborator in the production of Court entertainments, but Dryden's involvement with music and painting went beyond anything the often aggrieved Jonson experienced in his collaborations on masques with Inigo Jones. The later Stuarts had less taste for that kind of thing, and it is significant that Dryden wrote nothing for the Court's entertainment which was not transferable to the 'reformed' public theatres of London. The actual Court circle in Restoration London tended to blend easily with the larger, though still genteel, public which patronized the arts outside the Court. It should be no surprise, therefore, that when Dryden lost his Laureateship the theatre was still available to him and still occasionally provided him with a royal audience. Likewise, his friendships with painters and musicians continued, and when a group such as the Stewards of the St Cecilia's Day Feast twice needed poems to be set to music for their celebrations they turned to Dryden. In the last two decades of his life especially, Dryden was a sought-after collaborator in many artistic enterprises. He was, in effect, the Poet Laureate of all London. His quite extensive involvement in the other arts, while he practised only literature, is unique in English history, and it was the occasion for some of his best poetry.

This subject, however, must again be broached with a caution. Dryden refers to the 'sister-arts', but there was never any doubt in his mind that painting, music, and sculpture were lesser kindred of literature—not, perhaps, 'poor relations', but certainly unequal to poetry, the head of the family. While we are apt to admire a Da Ponte because he is hitched to the star of Mozart, Dryden saw Purcell as fortunate to work with Dryden. The material of poetry was the word, the mirror of reason. Poetry was the greatest art because the epic was the highest kind of poetry and 'a heroic poem, truly such, is undoubtedly the greatest work which the soul of man is capable to perform'. Dryden was generous in acknowledging the powers of the other arts, but none of them could rise to this. In upholding the supremacy of poetry, he was aware that he had not produced his own epic, but it was the dignity of his art and of his artistic forebears that he defended. Moreover, he defended it with a blithe confidence that indicates that he expected general assent to his declaration that an epic poem was 'the greatest work of human nature'. If asked now to name the 'greatest work of human nature' produced in England between 1660 and 1700, one could give a number of reasonable answers—St Paul's Cathedral, Purcell's music, Newton's *Principia*, or Locke's *Of Human Understanding*. *Paradise Lost* would have its advocates, as would Dryden's poetry, but they would have no certain predominance. Yet Dryden assumed at the time that poetry would be granted unquestioned supremacy as the greatest of the arts, and he was surely right. This assumption is found everywhere in his dealings with 'the kindred arts'.

Painting

When on 15 June 1694 Dryden signed his contract with Tonson for the translation of Virgil's *Works*, it was stipulated that he would 'not write, translate, or publish...any other book' except 'a little French book of painting which he hath engaged to perform for some gentlemen virtuosos [connoisseurs] and painters'. This book, for which Virgil could be laid aside, was Fresnoy's Latin poem *De Arte Graphica*, accompanied by the notes in French of Roger de Piles. Dryden's translation was published in 1695 and had as preface his own 'Parallel of Poetry and Painting'.

Dryden obviously considered his commitment to the 'gentlemen virtuosos and painters' a very serious one, and they in turn must have thought him to be well qualified, by interest and expertise, to make the translation. It is therefore a disappointment that Dryden's original contribution to the book, the 'Parallel', is a very pedestrian performance, marred by frequently admitted haste and by a peculiar superficiality of approach. The work is of some use to experts, but to most readers its main interest will always be its moments of autobiographical revelation rather than the parallels Dryden was able to discover between poetry and painting. These are remarkably unenlightening, and give the impression that Dryden is racking his brains to find them.

> To avoid absurdities and incongruities, is the same law established for both arts. The painter is not to paint a cloud at the bottom of a picture, but in the uppermost parts; nor the poet to place what is proper to the end or middle, in the beginning of a poem.

Even when the parallels are less trivial than this extreme example, the effect still tends to be of an analogy discovered and then abandoned, the parallel being the end in itself.

> As in a picture, besides the principal figures which compose it, and are placed in the midst of it, there are less groups or knots of figures disposed at proper distances, which are parts of the piece, and seem to carry on the same design in a more inferior manner; so, in

epic poetry there are episodes, and a chorus in tragedy, which are members of the action, as growing out of it, not inserted into it.

He goes on to discuss, as an instance, his favourite episode of Niṣus and Euryalus in *Aeneid* IX.

With the best of good will, it is hard not to see the 'Parallel of Poetry and Painting' as evidence that Dryden had acquired an inflated reputation as a student of painting. Yet painting does play a part in his poetry and perhaps the fairest thing to say is that the 'Parallel' is an unfortunate attempt to systematize something which otherwise was useful and productive in Dryden's thinking about poetry. Horace's famous phrase, *Ut pictura poesis erit*, was usually interpreted in Dryden's day to mean 'A poem will be like a painting', but in practice Dryden seems to have reversed its terms. For him, a painting was often like a poem, and it seems reasonable to conclude that the art of painting was most useful to him as a source of metaphor and analogy when discussing poems or when writing them.

Dryden is rarely a poet of the vivid, graphic detail. Painting seems to have had no influence over him towards making his descriptions realistically pictorial. Yet it should be realized that descriptions which are 'unrealistic' could easily be analogous to what was done in painting. In *Annus Mirabilis*, for instance, Dryden 'describes' the fire near the river.

231

A quay of fire ran all along the shore,
    And lightened all the river with the blaze:
The wakened tides began again to roar,
    And wond'ring fish in shining waters gaze.

232

Old Father Thames raised up his reverend head,
    But feared the fate of Simoeis would return:
Deep in his ooze he sought his sedgy bed,
    And shrunk his waters back into his urn.

There is very little here one would wish to call realistic, yet it is quite easy to imagine a painting of the time including such elements as the 'wond'ring fish' and Father Thames. Before concluding that Dryden was not pictorial in his poetry, it is sensible to recall that the painting of the time was often elaborately 'poetic' in employing mythological figures and personifications.

Dryden's normal practice was to draw on the analogy between poetry and painting for illuminating simile, without delving deeply into the 'philosophy' of the relationship. In *Astraea Redux*, for example, he employs a simile to suggest the gradual change from Commonwealth to restored monarchy.

Charles II depicted as nautical victor.

Yet as wise artists mix their colours so
That by degrees they from each other go,
Black steals unheeded from the neighb'ring white
Without offending the well cous'ned sight:
So on us stole our blessed change; while we
Th'effect did feel but scarce the manner see.

(lines 125–30)

This is ingenious and apt, the kind of analogy which helped Dryden get the reputation of a man well informed about painting. It represents in itself nothing profound, but it must have earned Dryden much goodwill among painters and patrons.

Yet there was a profound element in Dryden's employment of the analogy between poetry and painting. Quite typically, the effect of the analogy as he drew it was to confer on painting something of the special power of poetry. The predominance of epic among the literary kinds, and of poetry among the arts, was due to their ability to combine the highest pleasure with the most serious moral instruction. 'Heroic poetry has always been sacred to princes, and to heroes', and therefore 'that kind of poesy, which excites to virtue the greatest men, is of the greatest use to human kind'. The equivalent of the epic in painting was the 'history' picture, a work depicting real or mythological events in which the treatment was on a 'heroic' scale. In his poem 'To Sir Godfrey Kneller' (1694), Dryden says, 'Or, what a play [compared] to Virgil's work would be, / Such is a single piece [e.g. a portrait] to History'. The type of painting most worthy of admiration was, however, in short supply among his contemporaries. Sir Godfrey Kneller, who was apparently quite close to Dryden, built his fortune and his reputation on his portraits. In the poem, Dryden makes the claim that Kneller is akin to himself in finding that the age in which he lives cramps his genius. It was the fault of the time that Kneller had not become a great history painter.

Thy genius bounded by the times like mine,
Drudges on petty draughts, nor dare design
A more exalted work, and more divine.

(Kneller did not see his own career in this light. He was a well-rewarded adherent of William III and was made a baronet by George I. He never showed more than the faintest yearning to become a 'history painter'.) The scarceness of history painting may have been one of the reasons that led Dryden to make the assertion in the 'Parallel' that 'at this time, or lately, in many countries, poetry is better practised than her sister art'. He clearly thought that his own country was one such, and was willing to extend to Kneller the excuse he himself made for not being a greater poet. 'Thus in a stupid military state. / The pen and pencil [i.e. brush] find an equal fate.' The

145

Sir Godfrey Kneller, royal painter.

146

unartistic 'iron age' of William and Mary hampered poet and painter alike. Yet even so, poetry is the elder sister, and Dryden jocularly (but with underlying seriousness) upholds her claims even when addressing Kneller.

> Our arts are sisters; though not twins in birth:
> For hymns were sung in Eden's happy earth,
> By the first pair; while Eve was yet a saint;
> Before she fell with pride, and learned to paint.
> Forgive th'allusion; 'twas not meant to bite;
> But satire will have room, where e'er I write.

(The last four lines were omitted from the edition of 1701.)

The advantages Dryden concedes to painting are its international 'language'—'Thy pencil speaks the tongue of every land'—and its ability to convey something of the Platonic ideal of beauty while being true to the earthly reality.

> Likeness appears in every lineament;
> But likeness in thy work is eloquent:
> Though Nature, there, her true resemblance bears,
> A nobler beauty in thy piece appears.

Yet earlier, in expressing the same idea, Dryden employs very significant terms. 'Likeness is ever there; but still the best, / Like proper thoughts in lofty language drest.' Painting, at times, can approach the heights of poetry, and the terminology of poetry comes readiest to Dryden's mind when he wishes to praise the 'sister art'.

These ideas about the relationship of poetry and painting come together very conveniently in one of Dryden's greatest poems, his ode 'To the Pious Memory of the Accomplished Young Lady Mrs Anne Killigrew, Excellent in the Two Sister Arts of Poesy and Painting' (1686). The poem as a whole is a complex work, which has occasioned much commentary. Here, however, the discussion can be restricted to the sixth and seventh stanzas, which describe Anne Killigrew as a painter.

In stanza VI Dryden opens with an elaborate metaphor drawn from contemporary international politics.

> Born to the spacious empire of the Nine,
> One would have thought, she should have been content
> To manage well that mighty government:
> But what can young ambitious souls confine?
> To the next realm she stretcht her sway,
> For painture near adjoining lay,
> A plenteous province, and alluring prey.
> A Chamber of Dependences was framed,
> (As conquerors will never want pretence,
> When armed, to justify the offence)
> And the whole fief, in right of poetry she claimed.

The allusions here ('Chamber of Dependences' and so on) are to the methods employed by Louis XIV in extending his territories in Europe, but in terms of the 'sister arts' it is remarkable that the subservience of painting to poetry is so clearly set out. Anne Killigrew is by birth the ruler of the empire of 'the Nine' muses (which does not include painting) and she extends her power over painting with something of the arrogance and ruthlessness employed by Louis XIV in his conquests. She conquers painting 'in right of poetry', and there is little doubt that poetry's is the greater kingdom, as France was greater than the territories annexed. The rest of the stanza celebrates —appropriately since territory is the motif—Anne Killigrew's abilities as a landscape painter, and shows that Dryden was familiar with the schools of landscape in the French style popular in his day.

> The sylvan scenes of herds and flocks,
> The fruitful plains of barren rocks,
> Of shallow brooks that flowed so clear,
> The bottom did the top appear...

The notable 'smoothness', or perhaps the somewhat facile nature of this description is Dryden's commentary on this type of painting. One can surmise that to him it was pleasing, maybe 'pretty', but has nothing of the human importance he sought in art. When he describes a rather different type of landscape (the style of Claude Lorraine or Poussin perhaps) later in the stanza, a picking up of interest can be felt.

> The ruins too of some majestic piece,
> Boasting the power of ancient Rome or Greece,
> Whose statues, friezes, columns broken lie,
> And though defaced, the wonder of the eye,
> What Nature, Art, bold Fiction e'er durst frame,
> Her forming hand gave feature to the name.

When, in stanza VII, Dryden turns to Anne Killigrew's work in the English school of portraiture, particularly to a portrait (still at Windsor) which she made of James II, he finds there one of the highest abilities of painting, that of bringing forth the inner truth.

> For not content t'express his outward part,
> Her hand called out the image of his heart,
> His warlike mind, his soul devoid of fear,
> His high-designing thoughts were figured there,
> As when, by magic, ghosts are made appear.

James II depicted by Anne Killigrew.

Kneller's portraits, too, have this power, and it is the greatest achievement Dryden is able to find in the painters around him. Since history painting is hardly practised at all, poetic epic is left alone as the greatest of the arts.

Dryden's explicit use of painting thus generally serves to reinforce the pre-eminence of poetry. There may be, however, a concealed pictorial element in the overall structure of *Absalom and Achitophel*. Several critics have followed up the apparent hint given by Dryden's motto for the poem, *Si proprius stes, Te capiet magis* ('The nearer you stand, the more it strikes your fancy', from Horace's *Ars Poetica*, immediately following the famous '*Ut pictura poesis*'), and have concluded that 'the poem, taken as a whole, should be viewed as a painting' (Jean Hagstrum). Ian Jack has formulated the argument:

> The poem as a whole may be compared to a masterpiece of 'historical painting': it is written with the same purpose, that of pleasing its patron; and the canvas, which is a very large one, is crowded with figures, clearly divided into two opposing groups and painted in varying perspective. Above the head of the King hovers his 'Guardian Angel', while a serpent is hinted at by the feet of Shaftesbury. Each character is brilliantly portrayed in some suitable pose, as if on a canvas by Kneller. But the whole work is more static than dynamic: action is rather implied than portrayed.

The 'anti-climactic' structure of the poem can thus be explained by the analogy with painting.

The real value of applying the analogy with painting to Dryden's poetry (and the value of it extends far beyond *Absalom and Achitophel*) is that it draws attention to spatial structure and organization in the poems and that is an important part of some of them. Dryden is excellent at depicting action and movement across a wide landscape (see 'To the Duchess of Ormonde', Critical Survey, pp. 185–9) and some of his poems do recall the placing of figures on broad canvases.

Yet in the case of *Absalom and Achitophel* the analogy must be used with care. It is not, as Ian Jack seems to suggest, a static work (for that matter, baroque history painting is hardly static either), and the analogy with painting tends to make the groups opposing and supporting the King too important in the poem's economy. The core of the poem is the seduction of Absalom, leading to King David's intervention at the end. The body of the poem is thus akin to drama. The analogy with painting helps to explain Dryden's arrangement of characters around the central events, but painting is not the underlying structural principle of the work. (Music, too, has an important role to play in *Absalom and Achitophel*, but, like that of painting, a supporting rather than a principal one.)

Music: song, opera, ode

The concept of music provided the Renaissance poet and his Restoration successor with a body of ideas of the greatest utility and variety. Music was a universal principle, since the invisible spheres of the Ptolemaic cosmos produced in their movement the greatest of all harmonies—the music of the spheres. Music had mysterious powers over man and other living creatures, and classical mythology and biblical history supplied a fund of persons and incidents which could exemplify those powers: Orpheus, Amphion, Arion, Terpander, the Sirens, Jubal, Saul, and David. Ideas drawn from music could be applied, especially in metaphor, to most aspects of life. Thus the King as the agent of political harmony within the state was figured as David, the harpist. When Achitophel sarcastically suggests that David's legacy to Absalom will be 'Perhaps th'old harp, on which he thrums his lays: / Or some dull Hebrew ballad in your praise', the reader sees at once that Achitophel scorns the sacred principle of harmony symbolized by the harp and the civilization made emblematic in the song. Chaos was cacophony, musical and political. Though such ideas were by the late seventeenth century often no more than the stage properties of verse, it is characteristic of Dryden to give them life and validity once more in his work.

Above all, poets were accustomed to thinking of themselves as musicians. The poet as singer was such a stock analogy that it could be used automatically. Dryden's proof in his poem to Kneller that poetry was older than painting because 'hymns were sung in Eden's happy earth' is also 'proof' of the antiquity of music, but conventionally Dryden assumes the two arts to be one and, typically, subsumes music into poetry. It was, of course, a fact that poetry and music had long been separate arts, but the poets' feeling that, in some essential and irreducible way, theirs was the true music remained unshaken long past Dryden's time.

Thus the feeling of superiority which the poet could entertain when he compared himself to the painter was carried over and even magnified when he compared himself to the musician. This state of affairs is well reflected in what may at first sight seem a curious antipathy against Italian opera shared by a whole generation of writers, from Addison and Steele to Swift and Pope. (Addison wrote an opera of his own to show how it should be done.) The intellectual basis for this opposition (as distinct from the basis in simple xenophobia) was the belief, traceable back to the 'musical humanists' of the Renaissance, that music by itself was unable to be 'significant'. Autonomous music was believed by men who came to wield great influence to be simply a sensuous experience, unable to communicate anything to the reasoning mind. Much effort was therefore devoted to the problem of providing music with significance. The musical humanists had pointed back to classical times, when 'music' meant the accompaniment of song. The answer to the problem, therefore, seemed to be the relegation of music to the role of poetry's handmaid.

The Royal Society asked one of its distinguished members, Dr John Wallis, to find out why ancient music enjoyed such esteem and to decide what should be done to improve modern music. His conclusion was that music should abandon the 'senseless' polyphony of several voices in harmony and subordinate itself to poetry. This opinion became 'authorized'. Dryden's colleague, John Dennis, wrote in his essay on opera,

> Music may be made profitable as well as delightful, if it is subordinate to some nobler art, and subservient to reason; but...if it presumes to set up for itself, and to grow independent...it becomes a mere sensual delight, utterly incapable of informing the understanding.

Italian opera, as introduced into England early in the eighteenth century, violated these canons by emphasizing music to the detriment of words—and the words, moreover, in Italian!

Dryden had a great admiration for the Italian language as a poetic instrument, and he said that he admired Italian opera. It is unlikely, therefore, that he would have supported his Augustan successors in the most extreme of their denunciations of this 'mindless' art. Yet his own comments on the relationship of music and poetry show that he accepted that music in itself was unintelligible and needed the support of words if it was to reach the mind. Even when he wrote a dedication (not published until 1935) for Purcell to use before his opera *Dioclesian* in 1691, Dryden unconsciously made music subservient. His intention was to praise music as the equal of poetry. 'Both of them may excel apart, but sure they are most excellent when they are joined, because nothing is wanting to either of their perfections: for thus they appear like wit and beauty in the same person.' But for Dryden, wit and beauty were not equals.

The circumstances of Dryden's career often involved him with music, and a full account of that involvement, in terms of events and ideas, would make a small book in itself. Here there is space only to sketch an outline of his collaborations. The opponents of the Italian opera held up as the desirable alternative the 'English' tradition of Purcell. Since Dryden's career interlocks with Purcell's at several points, and since their collaboration included one English opera, it is worth asking what this tradition was and how Dryden interpreted it.

He interpreted it, first of all, somewhat from the outside, for he seems to have been no amateur of music. But as a man of the theatre he could not avoid some contact with musicians. Most of his plays incorporate songs, and Dryden's texts for these form a considerable body. It is at once noticeable, however, that his songs are very self-sufficient (see Critical Survey, pp. 173–5). It could never be said of one of them that 'it is nothing without the music'. One guesses from reading them that Dryden wrote his text without reference to any musician, and left it to be set as one might take a picture to be framed. This attitude can be clearly seen to exist in his mind when he comes to more considerable collaborations, and by the lowly standing of musician suggested by the advice Flecknoe gives Shadwell: 'Or if thou wouldst thy diff'rent talents suit, / Set thy own songs, and sing them to thy lute.'

Dryden's *Works* include four so-called operas. There was an operatic version of the Davenant–Dryden *Tempest*. Dryden's adaptation of *Paradise Lost*, called *The State of Innocence*, is an 'opera', though no music seems to have been written for it and no composer is mentioned, facts which illustrate something of Dryden's assumptions concerning the respective roles of author and composer. (*The State of Innocence* was performed once, as a puppet-show in 1712, though whether it was an operatic puppet-show is uncertain.) *Albion and Albanius: an opera* was performed in 1685, and *King Arthur: a dramatic opera* in 1691. It is with these two last that we shall be concerned.

Two theatrical traditions led Dryden towards opera. The masques, which had been the great entertainments at the Courts of James I and Charles I, and which were the principal responsibilities of the Poets Laureate, were less frequent after the Restoration but they still occurred on some occasions, and the tradition of the royal entertainment, centred on some regal or patriotic theme, with a slight text of poetry supported by and in many cases buried under all the resources of scene painting, spectacular effects, music, and dancing continued as a real influence on the development of opera in England. Under the Commonwealth, private theatrical performances which included a large element of music had been less frowned upon than simple plays. It is from one such work, Davenant's *The Siege of Rhodes* (1656), 'a representation by the art of perspective in scenes and the story sung in recitative music', that the new beginning of the English stage after the Civil War is dated. After the Restoration, according to Dryden, Davenant 'reviewed his *Siege of Rhodes*, and caused it to be acted as a just drama'. Dryden thus saw Davenant's work as the origin of the heroic play, with the music as a ruse to get it past the censorship, which may indeed have been the truth. Yet it was no accident that the heroic play should have had operatic beginnings, for the chief characteristic of such a work was thought to be 'elevation'. It dealt in a grand manner with great figures, rent by great conflicts, facing great issues. Dryden saw the heroic play as a sort of theatrical epic, and said that its convention gave the dramatist the liberty 'of drawing all things as far above the ordinary proportion of the stage as that is beyond the common words and actions of human life'. To make the great still greater, if such were desired, the only further recourse was music.

The heroic play as Dryden wrote it managed to be elevated enough without becoming actual opera. (Its decline came about because elevation turned so easily to inflation and subsequent bathos, and it is sometimes hard to refrain from using 'operatic' as a pejorative epithet for this species of play.) Yet the beginnings of the heroic play in *The Siege of Rhodes* fixed firmly the idea that operatic music was the proper concomitant of the grandest stage entertainments, an idea which the masque had already set afoot.

Albion and Albanius shows clearly the influence of masque and heroic play, but its parentage is French. The composer was Louis Grabu, a Frenchman who had become Master of the King's Music, and it followed the French model in being a true opera: recitative, aria, or chorus throughout. It describes in a heavily allegorical manner the political events of the Exclusion Crisis. Albion is Charles II, Albanius is James, Duke of York, and the other characters include Democracy, Zelota (or Feigned Zeal), Tyranny, and Asebia (Atheism or Ungodliness). The work was planned as a one-act prologue to what eventually became *King Arthur*. The death of Charles forced Dryden to recast it, and he made it into three acts. When finally produced it was a failure, attributed by the musical historians largely to Grabu's dull music. (The contempt expressed for Grabu's work is so universal and so impassioned that it makes one want to hear this terrible stuff.)

Dryden's ideas on opera and on his part in *Albion and Albanius* are found, of course, in his Preface. One can conclude from it that the experience was somewhat jarring to his self-esteem as a poet, and that he decided that in any future collaboration his own role would be dominant.

The Preface has been described as 'a contribution of real importance to the theory of English opera' (E.J. Dent), and this is an interesting remark precisely because *Albion and Albanius* is so clearly modelled on the French opera of the time. Those places where Dryden expresses some discontent with the work all point to adaptations which will bring about the English school, of which *King Arthur* is one representative.

This is especially so when Dryden discusses the relationship of poet and composer. His basic argument is that the libretto of a wholly sung opera will be so hampered by the necessity of making words conform to music that it cannot help being rather stupid: 'I have therefore no need to make excuses for meanness of thought in many places.' He reveals, by a remark to which we shall return shortly, that he believes he knows how to avoid such 'meanness', and goes on to express his discontent at the measures he was sometimes forced to adopt in finding words for Grabu's music,

...as if I had not served out my time in poetry, but was bound 'prentice to some doggerel rhymer, who makes songs to tunes, and sings them for a livelihood. 'Tis true, I have not been often put to this drudgery; but where I have, the words will sufficiently show that I was then a slave to the composition, which I will never be again. 'Tis my part to invent, and the musician's to humour that invention.

This declaration of poetic superiority is clearly a move by Dryden towards the position of those who held, and were to hold, that musical significance could only be achieved by allowing words to be dominant. Other remarks in the Preface confirm this, and show that Dryden, quite typically, had found scholarly support for his opinion. Had he possessed his freedom in writing *Albion and Albanius*, he would, he says, have avoided 'meanness of thought' by applying the doctrine of *rhythmus* as understood by the ancients, and which he defines as 'the choice of words', not 'elegancy of expression, but propriety of sound, to be varied according to the subject'. This idea he had picked up from reading a book published in 1673 by Isaac Vossius, *De poematum cantu et viribus rhythmi*. Vossius argued that the way for music to obtain 'significance' was for it to imitate in its rhythms the 'motions' which the passions and affections produced in the mind. The poet, supported by the musician, should do this in such a way that the mind of the hearer could perceive the shapes of these motions in the poetry as set to music and could thus appreciate intellectually their significance. Crudely put, this meant that the poet, employing the rhythmical devices descended from the metres of classical poetry, should 'imitate' emotions in his verse structure, and music should be used to emphasize them. A monodic, rather than polyphonic, musical line was called for, since the single line could be more easily followed as it communicated ideas and emotion.

Dryden makes the most important use of Vossius's doctrine of *rhythmus* in his two St Cecilia odes, but before considering them, the story of his collaborations in opera should be completed. Henry Purcell first wrote for Dryden in 1690, when he contributed music for the comedy *Amphitryon*. Dryden, who had expressed his admiration for Grabu, now wrote that in Purcell 'we have at length found an Englishman equal with the best abroad'. Purcell went on to write music for several more of Dryden's plays, both new ones and revivals, but his major collaboration was *King Arthur*. Dryden, in labelling this a 'dramatic opera', was pointing to a feature which differentiated it from *Albion and Albanius*. *King Arthur* is a spoken play, heavily embellished with music, now often called a 'semi-opera'. The English operatic tradition demanded that music should make no contribution to the plot. Purcell's music, therefore, was forced to exist as 'merely aggrandized incidental music' (R.E. Moore), a limitation reinforced by the fact that only one of the main characters is a singer. This English tradition of opera accords well with the idea that the poet was to be the dominant partner, and one can see why this kind of opera should have appealed to those who disliked the 'senseless', wholly sung, Italian variety. The music in *King Arthur* functions to emphasise emotions already conveyed in the spoken scenes or to create atmosphere. The significant words are kept separate from the music.

Yet Dryden, by his own account, did not have it all his own way. Apparently Purcell refused total submission of music to verse.

> But the numbers of poetry and vocal music are sometimes so contrary that in many places I have been obliged to cramp my verses and make them rugged to the reader that they might be harmonious to the hearer. Of which I have no reason to repent me, because these sorts of entertainment are principally designed for the ear and eye, and therefore in reason my art, on this occasion, ought to be subservient to his.

Dryden can appear complacently resigned to this situation because the conventions of English opera inevitably gave him the master hand, whatever small concessions he might make in the songs. In other ways, too, *King Arthur* reveals its literary and theatrical origins. Its plot and characters are akin to those of the magniloquent heroic play, and it contains a number of full-scale masques.

Yet finally it is Purcell's music which is the best thing about *King Arthur*, and there is a sort of justice in the fate of the work in the modern opera house. The English Opera Group's recent production at Sadler's Wells made the work more 'operatic' by 'importing' music from elsewhere in Purcell's *oeuvre*, by giving singing roles to the principal characters, and by treating Dryden's plot largely as a joke. Strictly speaking, such tampering is deplorable, but it might have cheered Purcell.

The last thing Dryden wrote for Purcell was set to music by John Blow, for it was 'An Ode on the Death of Mr Henry Purcell' (1695).

> Ye brethren of the lyre, and tuneful voice,
> Lament his lot: but at your own rejoice.
> Now live secure and linger out your days,
> The gods are pleased alone with Purcell's lays,
>   Nor know to mend their choice.

Dryden's two odes for the celebration of the feast of St Cecilia, patroness of music, were written in 1687 and 1697. Both are acknowledged as masterpieces, though the later one, *Alexander's Feast*, is usually preferred. Both show the marked influence of the doctrine of *rhythmus,* but the earlier work, *A Song for St Cecilia's Day, 1687,* is the more interesting as an embodiment of musical theory. The poem consists of seven stanzas and a 'Grand Chorus'. In the opening stanza and the final chorus, Dryden is clearly presenting a view of music which we recognize as the traditional one. It has been called 'speculative music', and it presents music as the universal principle of harmony, an aural image of benevolent creativity and ordained destruction, which latter, paradoxically, is just as 'harmonious' since the end of the world is as much a part of God's plan as the beginning.

Grand Chorus

As from the power of sacred lays
  The spheres began to move,
And sung the great Creator's praise
  To all the bless'd above;
So when the last and dreadful hour
This crumbling pageant shall devour,
The trumpet shall be heard on high,
The dead shall live, the living die,
And music shall untune the sky.

(God will signal the end of the earth-centred cosmos with the 'last trump', so that music will be the means to 'untune' by destruction the 'harmonious' universe with its music of the spheres.) This is one of the greatest stanzas Dryden ever wrote. The final, witty paradox is given great splendour by the triplet, and what a superb epithet and metaphor Dryden finds for the collapsing universe: 'this crumbling pageant'.

These ideas, of course, were hackneyed well before Dryden ever wrote a line, and by the end of the seventeenth century they were 'unscientific' as well. Yet here they are fresh and vital. One can make out a good case for Dryden as a Renaissance poet.

In the middle stanzas, II to VII, on the other hand, he is just as certainly the believer in *rhythmus* and the follower of Vossius. These stanzas are a demonstration of what *rhythmus* meant. It is the 'affective' power of music that is dramatized here, its ability to move men's emotions by joining with words to reproduce and thus stimulate 'motions' of the mind: 'What passion cannot music raise and quell!'

IV

The soft complaining flute
In dying notes discovers
The woes of hopeless lovers,
Whose dirge is whispered by the warbling lute.

V

> Sharp violins proclaim
> Their jealous pangs, and desperation,
>   Fury, frantic indignation,
> Depths of pains, and heights of passion,
>   For the fair, disdainful dame.

In *Alexander's Feast*, the 'speculative music' makes only a token appearance with St Cecilia at the end, and the rest of the poem is one great demonstration of *rhythmus*. Timotheus puts on a display of music's affective power by moving Alexander's emotions whichever way he wishes by the sole means of his lyre. Each stanza, which describes and creates an emotion, is followed by a chorus, which functions like an aria to embody the emotional significance of the preceding 'scene'. (The pattern is naturally reminiscent of the method of proceeding in 'English' semi-opera.) In this poem, Dryden delights in the extremes of violent emotion, and his verse is very ambitious, and very successful, in its daring rhythmical effects.

> Revenge, revenge, Timotheus cries,
>   See the Furies arise!
>   See the snakes that they rear,
>   How they hiss in their hair,
> And the sparkles that flash from their eyes!
>   Behold a ghastly band,
>   Each a torch in his hand!
> Those are Grecian ghosts, that in battle were slain,
>   And unburied remain
>   Inglorious on the plain.
>   Give the vengeance due
>   To the valiant crew.

Such virtuosity, however, poses an interesting question. What was the composer to do? In *Alexander's Feast* it is clear that Dryden is virtually functioning as his own composer. The rhythmical effects and the arrangement of the lines mean that the composer must either follow doggedly and slavishly, or must act independently of the text. Handel, who by common consent has done best with *Alexander's Feast*, tries to have it both ways and his setting has had a mixed reception. The experts must be allowed to discuss this point.

Alexander's Feast, however 'musical' by Vossius's standards, was a hopeless challenge to contemporary music, and it symbolizes the antagonism which then existed between actual music and the 'music' of the word. The complex *rhythmi* of the poem, the very basis of its form, were confusing to contemporary composers, none of whom, including Handel, knew always what to do with them.

Although one modern reader of the poem [R.M. Myers] has argued that Dryden took great care in this second ode to adapt his text to the requirements of actual music, I find this not everywhere obvious in the poem. No late seventeenth-century poet, with any knowledge of or experience with music would offer verses with the metrical subtleties of Timotheus's revenge stanza, and at the same time fancy he was co-operating with a composer. Moreover, the Alexander-Timotheus subject in itself suggests that Dryden's intention was less to please contemporary composers than to remind them of the inadequacies of their 'harmonious' art.

(D.T. MACE)

Alexander's Feast, one might say, is Dryden's answer to his difficulties of collaboration with composers. It is the ultimate in 'significant' verbal music, and it subordinates the composer so firmly as to handicap him, or even eliminate him. The poem has been called Dryden's greatest libretto, but it also goes a long way towards having its own 'score'. There is a disturbing remark in the Preface to *Albion and Albanius* which may throw light on Dryden's real attitude: "Tis no easy matter in our language to make words so smooth and numbers so harmonious, *that they shall almost set themselves*' (my italics). He would probably have approved of Horace Walpole's remark: 'Though I like Handel, I am not bigoted. I thought Dryden's *Ode* more harmonious before he set it than after.'

We find therefore, despite Dryden's not unimportant place in the history of English music, that he could not countenance its claim to equality with poetry. Nothing could stand with poetry, and that confident assurance in the importance of his art helps make him so interesting a figure. Few poets since his time have been able to be so certain of the importance of their work, and his confidence has in large part been justified.

Part Four
Critical Survey

A Poetry of Allusion

Dryden's kind of poetry is made distant from us in important ways by its frequent allusions to men, ideas, and events now vanished from common knowledge. This is, of course, inevitable with the passage of time, but in the case of Dryden and the poetry of his day, more is involved than the simple obscurity produced by age. The nature of successful poetry then was that it should be public both in manner and in subject, treating the life of its time directly. Such topicality natural-ly requires a deal of explanation, but the public nature of Dryden's verse is not the only reason for its wealth of allusion.

Reference to topics of shared knowledge can create a feeling of complicity and community, a sense that the poet and his audience are members of a special group. The greatest verse of Dryden and his successors is satirical, and the element of hostility towards certain men and certain values which is at the heart of satire depends for success on the skill with which the poet is able to take his reader along with him in establishing shared, if vague, positive values by which to measure the negative qualities the poet attacks. The poet brings his reader to agree that 'we' are on the side of the angels in opposition to clearly defined and sharply described devils. Allusion, skilfully managed, is one way of reinforcing this sense of the shared identity of poet and reader. Moreover, a poetry which sets high value on wit and the epigrammatic expression of truth needs a large source of materials which can be drawn upon without lengthy explanation.

Dryden's skill in allusion is similar to his mastery of tone. The familiarity or strangeness of allusions varies with the audience he is addressing. Sometimes he stumbles, but usually he gauges his audience's capacity perfectly. This is for a playhouse audience.

Epilogue from *Amboyna*

> A poet once the Spartans led to fight,
> And made 'em conquer in the Muse's right:
> So would our poet lead you on this day,
> Showing your tortured fathers in his play.
> 5   To one well born, th'affront is worse and more,
> When he's abused and baffled by a boor;
> With an ill grace the Dutch their mischiefs do,
> They've both ill nature and ill manners too.
> Well may they boast themselves an ancient nation,
> 10   For they were bred e'er manners were in fashion;
> And their new Common-wealth has set 'em free,
> Only from honour and civility.

Venetians do not more uncouthly ride,
Than did their lubber-state mankind bestride.
15   Their sway became 'em with as ill a mien,
As their own paunches swell above their chin;
Yet is their empire no true growth but humour,
And only two kings' touch can cure the tumour.
As Cato did his Afric fruits display,
20   So we before your eyes their Indies lay;
All Loyal English will like him conclude,
Let Caesar live, and Carthage be subdued.

OCCASION. *Amboyna* was written rapidly in 1672 or 1673 to whip up feeling against the enemy during the third Anglo-Dutch War (1672–4). In 1623 English merchants at Amboyna in the East Indies had been abused and massacred by the Dutch. The story was well known and often reappeared at times of Anglo-Dutch hostility. The play is Dryden's first assignment as Historiographer-Royal.

ALLUSIONS. The epilogue begins with an allusion to Greek history and ends with a reference to Rome, yet the knowledge demanded of the audience is minimal. The poet referred to in the opening lines is Tyrtaeus, who was sent, as a sign of contempt, by the Athenians to the Spartans, who had asked for a general to lead them. His songs, however, inspired the Spartans to victory over the Messenians. But to learn this from the commentary adds nothing to Dryden's essential point. He has told us all we need to know, since he can rely even now on a general knowledge of the martial character of Sparta. His own function as propagandist for Charles II's foreign policy is ennobled by association with the poet, whose specific identity is not required. Similarly, the last four lines draw on a well-known incident from Roman history. Cato the Censor displayed fine figs in the Senate, to show that Carthage was worth invading and easily reached. England and Holland thus appear as Rome and Carthage respectively, the victor and the vanquished in a war to secure absolute supremacy of the known world. Too careful a study of the parallel would show a number of significant differences, but Dryden merely plays the well-known card which has England-as-Rome defeating Holland-as-Carthage and he concludes with an echo of one of the most famous of Latin tags, Cato's *Carthago delenda est*, 'Carthage must be destroyed'.

These are classical allusions, but the former explains itself and the latter is near-proverbial even now. Between them, Dryden fills his epilogue with allusions even more immediately comprehensible to an audience of 1673. He flatters his English hearers by alluding to the popular mythology of the day in which the national characteristics of the Dutch were taken to be the bad manners and lack of refinement associated with republicanism. The Dutch commonwealth, like that of the English Parliamentarians a generation before, is an ill-manner-ed, barbaric, and unnatural form of government. The individual Dutchman is a total materialist, living on beer and butter. Holland's Protestantism and her struggles against French hegemony in Europe, which often made her seem a natural ally of England, are quite understandably suppressed. (Andrew Marvell's *The Character of Holland* gives a much fuller picture of the Dutch seen in this distorting light.) That Venetians were poor riders (line 13), sailors on horseback, was another commonplace of the day, and Venice, like Holland, was a republic, famous for the powerlessness of its head of state.

The one genuine piece of wit in the poem comes in lines 17 and 18 and depends on allusion, this time a politico-medical one. Holland is a power large and menacing, but her size is not true growth but a diseased swelling, 'humour'. The 'two kings' are Charles II and Louis XIV, allies against the Dutch, and their 'touch' is the power thought to be possessed by true monarchs of curing scrofula, 'the king's evil', by touching the victim. (Queen Anne kept up the practice as evidence of her Stuart birthright. She touched the young Samuel Johnson.) By ironic reversal, the 'touch' in this case will be the destructive impact of English and French arms on Holland's tumour. The disease of republicanism is cured by monarchy.

Spread out like this, the allusions may seem complex, but the fact that they would have given no trouble at all to their first audience should encourage us. Any real difficulty can easily be overcome. It is worth unfolding the meaning of these allusions because to do so puts the modern reader on a par of knowledge with his seventeenth-century counterpart, and allows him to appreciate the poet's manipulation of the audience. He sees how he is being flattered and how he is being spurred. Dryden, thanks to a footnote or two, is freed to exercise one of his greatest talents, that of persuasion.

The 'Metaphysical' Dryden

Dryden's first published poem, 'Upon the Death of the Lord Hastings' (1649), has achieved notoriety because of its description of the smallpox which killed the young lord.

> Was there no milder way but the small pox,
> The very filth'ness of Pandora's box?
> 55 So many spots, like *naeves*, our Venus soil?
> One jewel set off with so many a foil?
> Blisters with pride swelled; which through's flesh did sprout
> Like rose-buds, stuck i'th'lily skin about.
> Each little pimple had a tear in it,
> 60 To wail the fault its rising did commit:
> Who, rebel-like, with their own lord at strife,
> Thus made an insurrection 'gainst his life.

METAPHYSICAL ELEMENTS. Dryden's lack of taste in confronting the disease head-on in his poem is what usually offends the modern reader. We may deplore his taste, but it was undoubtedly the taste of his time, and to the student of poetry the style of the passage as an instance of the transition from Metaphysical to Augustan is most interesting.

The poem is taken to be highly representative of its period. The middle of the seventeenth century saw the style perfected by Donne—simultaneously cerebral and passionate, witty and yet serious—become something of a lifeless mechanism in the hands of lesser poets. They tended to rely on extravagance of idea and mere ingenuity of 'conceit', and often the resulting poetry was a matter of literary outrageousness and excess.

The conceit, the poetical figure in which the ingenuity of the comparison attracts attention to itself even as the elements compared are illuminated by it, is particularly open to abuse. The ingenuity can become self-defeating and a substitute for real poetic sensibility. In the hands of Donne the conceit can hold in balance conflicting aspects of a situation, producing a fascinating irony. In the work of Cleveland, usually thought of as the epitome of the decadent 'conceited' style, ingenuity can be a mere elaboration of trivialities. 'I am no poet here; my pen's the spout / Where the rain-water of my eyes runs out' ('Upon the Death of Mr King').

Turning to Dryden's lines, it becomes possible to separate those elements which he will later reject totally from those which he will 'refine' and retain. Line 55 contains an anagrammatic pun; *naeves* (Latin, 'spot, blemish') can be rearranged (nearly) to make 'Venus'. Later Dryden came to despise the pun. This one, being both anagrammatic and all too clearly the work of a schoolboy proud of his Latin, would be highly repugnant to him later.

Lines 57–8 attempt to 'beautify' the pustules of smallpox by applying the language of amorous poetry. The result is discordant, but Dryden learned something from this kind of blunder. Flecknoe praises his 'son' Shadwell in terms of clashing and blithe incongruity: 'Shadwell alone my perfect image bears. / Mature in dullness from his tender years.' (Likewise Pope: 'And the fresh vomit run for ever green'.)

Lines 59–62 are in some ways the most interesting. Dryden's seizure of the 'tears' of fluid in the pustules as expressions of regret might be too extravagant for his later poetry, but the use of 'rising' to mean 'swelling' and 'political uprising' and the strongly implied admiration for political stability—these are features prophetic of the mature verse.

VERSE FORM. The poem is in decasyllabic couplets, and it should be noted that much of the impression of callowness it makes is traceable to the incompetence Dryden shows in the form. In the poem as a whole there is an unwillingness to 'trust' the couplet. Dryden uses much enjambement, and shows little appreciation of the balanced effects possible. His word order is often unnatural, with a number of parentheses: 'Is death (sin's wages) grace's now? Shall art / Make us more learned, only to depart?' To get a true count of syllables, a great deal of contraction is sometimes necessary, as in lines 57–8 here. The metre, as in line 53, often strays so far from the iambic as to be inexcusable on grounds of deliberate variation.

LATER USES OF THE CONCEIT. The comparison of extravagant ingenuity does not disappear from Dryden's work after 1649. He 'refined' it and used it often, especially in poems of compliment and panegyric, and in the 'heightened' language of his tragedies and heroic plays.

'Heroic Stanzas': succeeding and faltering

'Heroic Stanzas' is written in the four-line stanza which Davenant had used for his epic *Gondibert* in 1651. (Dryden used it again for his ambitious *Annus Mirabilis* in 1667.) It is a panegyric, a poem of heroic praise, rather than an elegy, or lament for the dead, and Dryden concentrates on Cromwell as an example of heroic virtue and achievement. It has frequently been pointed out that there is an element of restraint or of prudence in the poem, in that it in no way reflects on the Stuarts, on the origins of the Civil War, or on those aspects of Cromwell's rise to power most likely to kindle disagreement. Yet Dryden's commitment to Cromwell seems wholehearted. Praise is bestowed in particular on the improvement of England's reputation abroad and on Cromwell the peacemaker, but though Dryden approves of Cromwell's rejection of the crown, he does not seem to reject the idea itself.

> Nor was his virtue poisoned soon as born
> With the too early thoughts of being king.

Technically, the poem improves both on Dryden's earlier, one might say his 'schoolboy', poems and on Davenant's own versification in this stanza form. In places one hears the authentic note of Dryden's great verse.

13

> Swift and resistless through the land he passed
> Like that bold Greek who did the East subdue;
> And made to battles such heroic haste
> As if on wings of victory he flew.

But Dryden is not yet wholly in command of his resources of wit and allusion. Cromwell's victories come thick and fast,

> Till he, pressed down by his own weighty name,
> Did, like the vestal, under spoils decease.

The allusion is to Tarpeia, a maiden who betrayed Rome to the Sabines and who asked as payment for 'that which they wore on their left arms', meaning their gold bracelets. The Sabines, despising her treachery, deliberately misinterpreted her words to mean their shields, and hurled them upon her, killing her. Dryden, aware that 'spoils' is from the Latin 'spolia', trophies of battle, has Cromwell crushed beneath the emblems of his victories. But other associations override that one, for there is an unavoidable moral difference between Dryden's Cromwell and Tarpeia. She is the type of a greedy traitor, and the Tarpeian Rock was a place of execution in ancient Rome. If the reader takes Dryden's allusion, the lack of relevance is likely to strike him first, since the only valid point of comparison is the idea of a person crushed beneath a pile of shields. The other elements which come to mind, treason and greed, to say nothing of the Lord Protector as a 'vestal', are antithetical to the idea of Cromwell's glory Dryden strives to uphold. He is too eager to display allusive wit to make sure of its effective functioning.

Yet, on the whole, 'Heroic Stanzas' is an impressive poem, the earliest announcement of one of Dryden's great themes—the value of peace and stability in the kingdom of England.

36
> No civil broils have since his death arose,
> But faction now by habit does obey:
> And wars have that respect for his repose,
> As winds for halcyons when they breed at sea.

37
> His ashes in a peaceful urn shall rest,
> His name a great example stands to show
> How strangely high endeavours may be bless'd,
> Where piety and valour jointly go.

NOTE. The halcyon or kingfisher was reputed to breed in a nest on the waves of the sea at the winter solstice. The weather was legendarily calm at this time to aid the halcyon.

The Prologues and Epilogues

A play in the Restoration theatre began with a prologue and ended with an epilogue. An actor or actress, often speaking in the person of the author, addressed the audience directly to introduce or conclude the entertainment. The prologues and epilogues written for the English stage after 1660 became indispensable, virtually every play had them, and they became a form of literature in their own right, detachable from the plays on which they apparently depended for their existence. Although Shakespeare wrote a sonnet to be spoken as prologue to *Romeo and Juliet*, it belongs wholly to the play and is never collected as one of 'Shakespeare's Sonnets'. Yet whenever Dryden contributed to a volume of miscellaneous poems he included prologues and epilogues, for he saw them as poems to be appreciated for themselves as much as for their association with plays.

The subject matter of Restoration prologues and epilogues is the clearest indication of their often independent status as poems. Some reference to the play or playwright was usually made, to preserve a sort of propriety, but the prologue writer—the playwright himself or an ally such as Dryden—was then free to discuss matters of literary criticism, current politics, playhouse manners, or social gossip. He might abuse his critics or beg their applause. Sexual innuendo was a favourite topic. The personalities of well-known actors were exploited, as well as the sexual reputations of even better-known actresses. Dryden's epilogue to *Tyrannic Love* shows Nell Gwynn, who played St Catherine and who was martyred at the end of the play, rising like a ghost and abusing the bearers trying to remove her 'corpse'.

> Hold, are you mad? you damned confounded dog,
> I am to rise, and speak the epilogue.

The only indispensable element was wit, or the attempt at it. Many playwrights found this additional burden a strain, and complained besides, in prologues and epilogues of course, that the rage for the things was an implicit denigration of the play itself.

> Our next new play, if this mode hold in vogue,
> Shall be half Prologue, and half Epilogue.

For Dryden, however, whose wit increased with age, prologues and epilogues were an invaluable means of communication with his audiences as well as a source of income. He wrote over a hundred in all, nearly a third of them for other men's plays. It is a form which he practised throughout his career and at which he excelled.

The prologue and epilogue had perceptible functions when the writer was asking for applause or instructing his audience how to understand his play. One can understand flattery or the desire to 'warm up' an audience even by abusing them. But a larger reason than these must exist for the importance of prologues and epilogues, and the fact that these devices flourished to such an extent only in the Restoration theatre suggests that theatrical conditions, and particularly the nature of the audience, may have had a lot to do with it.

The Restoration theatre drew its audience from a restricted group which can be crudely described as the Court and its hangers on. The audience might include a King and a footman, and usually included prostitutes looking for custom, but it was never a cross-section of the community. In the fifty years since the death of Shakespeare the class of people from which he sprang and for which, in the main, he wrote, had become a largely Puritan class, especially in London. The capital was geographically and morally polarized into Court, at Westminster, and City—of London. The theatre for which Dryden wrote was the class-entertainment of the Court.

This is a gross simplification, but it is one which Restoration playwrights and audiences loved and fostered. The simplification, especially in the prologues and epilogues, was elaborated into a myth. The theatrical audience was supposedly the world of wit and wickedness, beauty and courage. It embodied the social standards and almost always the politics of the Court. Those who disapproved and stayed away from the theatre were the 'cits'—the merchants of the City of London. In the theatrical myth these became puritanical kill-joys, wealthy but tightfisted, opponents of the Court in politics, Low Churchmen at best, but usually Dissenters, and, most of all, cuckolds. Their wives were supposed never able to resist the glamorous gentlemen of the Court, and consequently, in the oldest joke of all, the cits wore horns.

Prologues and epilogues give an account of theatrical conditions in the Restoration which, if swallowed whole, would defy belief. We read of a theatre used as a place of rendezvous, of noisy audiences, sword-fights in the pit, and frequent interruptions of a less violent nature. The conclusion seems to be that the last thing Restoration audiences were interested in was the play.

It is true that audiences were small, and that even a moderately successful play ran only a few nights. Yet audiences kept coming, plays were worth printing, and criticism of the drama was published and discussed. What we read in the prologues and epilogues, which seem so often to provide proof of the impossible conditions under which plays were performed, is really evidence of one element which helped keep the theatre going—the sense of common identity of actors, playwrights, and audiences. References to the critics of the pit, appeals for their clemency or defiance of their scorn, are intended to acknowledge publicly the role which a certain element of the audience wished to assume. In exactly the same way, the prologue or epilogue was a declaration by the playwright, or a declaration on his behalf by another poet, that he was subscribing to the myth, assuming the role of the playwright as it had become stylized in the Restoration theatre. It is not too extravagant to say that in its psychological essence the Restoration prologue or epilogue is a kind of courtship display by the author for his audience, in which he presents himself as one of them and assures them, by his parade of wit, that his play issued from a mind and sensibility akin to theirs.

Seen in this way, certain bewildering features of prologues and epilogues make more sense. One is always struck by the way in which a comical or even lewd prologue or epilogue can precede or follow a solemn tragedy. The apparent shattering of the mood and destruction of illusion would seem intolerable today, but in the Restoration theatre it was evidently more important for the author to establish a special *rapport* with the audience than to preserve what we would call dramatic propriety. Similarly, many prologues and epilogues are, in the topics they discuss, quite irrelevant to the plays with which they are associated. The apparent irrelevance can be understood if we see that the writer's real purpose is to indicate that he accepts the role given him in the theatrical myth. He did not need to stick to the subject of his work to display himself in that role; indeed, there were advantages in appearing as man of the world rather than as man of the theatre. The numerical smallness of the only potential audience and their homogeneity of belief made them into something like a club—and the playwright had to establish his membership by means of prologue and epilogue.

Prologue to *Oedipus*, 1679

When Athens all the Grecian state did guide,
And Greece gave laws to all the world beside,
Then Sophocles with Socrates did sit,
Supreme in wisdom one, and one in wit:
5 And wit from wisdom differed not in those,
But as 'twas sung in verse, or said in prose.
Then *Oedipus* on crowded theatres
Drew all admiring eyes and list'ning ears;
The pleased spectator shouted every line,
10 The noblest, manliest, and the best design!
And every critic of each learned age
By this just model has reformed the stage.
Now, should it fail, (as Heav'n avert our fear!)
Damn it in silence, lest the world should hear.
15 For were it known this poem did not please,
You might set up for perfect salvages:
Your neighbours would not look on you as men,
But think the nation all turned Picts again.
Faith, as you manage matters, 'tis not fit
20 You should suspect yourselves of too much wit.
Drive not the jest too far, but spare this piece;
And, for this once, be not more wise than Greece.
See twice! Do not pell-mell to damning fall,
Like true-born Britons, who ne'er think at all:
25 Pray be advised; and though at Mons you won,
On pointed cannon do not always run.

With some respect to ancient wit proceed;
You take the first four councils for your creed.
But when you lay tradition wholly by,⎫
30   And on the private spirit alone rely, ⎬
You turn fanatics in your poetry.   ⎭
If, notwithstanding all that we can say,   ⎫
You needs will have your penn'orths of the play,⎬
And come resolved to damn because you pay, ⎭
35   Record it, in memorial of the fact,
          The first play buried since the Woollen Act.

NOTES. Line 16: 'salvages' savages, at that time an acceptable variant form.

Line 25: English and Scottish troops in the army of William of Orange had performed bravely at Mons against the French on 17 August 1678. In fact, a peace had been signed the day before, and it was alleged that William suppressed the news in order to be able to fight. Dryden may be implying that the English were, though brave, dupes.

Line 28: the first four General Councils of the ancient Church, from 325 to 451 AD., were accepted by the Church of England as standards of doctrine equal in authority to canonical scriptures. Dryden alludes to the fact as an example of English willingness to submit to ancient authority.

Lines 29–31: 'Fanatics' in the language of the time were members of the Protestant sects outside the Church of England, notably the Presbyterians. It was claimed that one of their characteristics was a refusal to rely on any religious authority except that of their own private and direct communication with God's spirit, which, being imaginary in the eyes of their enemies, meant that the fanatics simply followed their own inclinations. See Dryden's *Religio Laici*, lines 398–426, and the character of Jack in Swift's *A Tale of a Tub*.

Line 36: the Woollen Act of 1 August 1678 was a somewhat gruesome measure, famous in the literature of the time, designed to promote the consumption of woollen material, a very important English product, by making it obligatory for the dead to be buried in woollen shrouds.

PERSUASIVE METHOD. The basic procedure of this prologue is the ancient one of the *plaudite*, the appeal for applause. Dryden's variation is to combine it with a threat. The *Oedipus* of Sophocles is a master-work of the Greek theatre and to boo the Dryden and Lee version would be to reveal a shameful ignorance. (The gap in the logic is given no time to appear.) Dryden is trading openly on the audience's feeling that theirs is a refined age, a time in which civilization has risen to a new level of excellence. To abuse *Oedipus* would expose them, and the nation in general, as 'perfect salvages' in the eyes of foreigners. National honour demands, humorously, a good reception for the play.

It is entirely typical of Dryden's prologues and epilogues that in summing up his 'threat' (lines 19–22) he should make it more open, add an element of abuse of his audience, and show himself dominant. Dryden's theatrical *persona* is that of a lordly, commanding playwright, never prepared to cringe for long. But the cleverness of his stance in relation to the public can be appreciated from lines 22 to 26. He has accused his audience of being wiser than Greece, but in these lines the audience's wrong judgment is presented as the result of an excess of courage. As 'true-born Britons' they may never think much, but that is because of their impetuous courage in charging into action. The British at Mons are an example, and the 'pointed cannon' may be the metaphorical 'canons' of classical judgment as well as real guns. Dryden is building up a sort of 'John Bull' picture, in which their faults are real but not really contemptible.

He then adds religion to his pattern of allusions (lines 27–31) to suggest that a contempt for literary tradition would make his audience the theatrical equivalent of 'fanatics'. Again, the threat is that by damning the play the audience would show itself to belong to an undesirable group. The analogy drawn between literary tradition and religion is witty rather than valid, but something of the respect for tradition present in many aspects of Dryden's thinking underlies his allusion.

Finally, Dryden's prologue speaker makes his exit on a topical piece of wit. If the play is 'buried' by its audience, it will be the first one to be interred in accordance with the new law.

THE PLAY. For all Dryden's appeal to classical tradition, the Dryden–Lee *Oedipus* is very different from that of Sophocles. It is, in fact, a bloody melodrama, very unclassical. And it was a great success, running for ten nights. The audience had the mingled pleasure, therefore, of being encouraged by the prologue to demonstrate their classical taste by liking the play, which was not really classical at all in its conventions.

VERSE AND TONE. This prologue demonstrates well the convenience of the heroic couplet in permitting rapid movement from topic to topic. An allusion can be made in two lines and once the couplet is 'filled' the poet can go on to another matter. Conversely, long verse paragraphs on single topics can be built up from couplets.

The use of two triplets together at the end (lines 29–34) gives a sense of build-up and anticipation which is exploited by the quick wit of the last couplet. (Note that neither of the triplets includes an alexandrine, which would give a sense of finality rather than anticipation.)

The greatest achievement of Dryden's prologues and epilogues is their tone. All his critics agree that the 'voice' he so often assumes, that of a witty, slightly libertine member of the courtly world, recurs again and again in his satires and, suitably modified, in his ratiocinative poems. The essence of this tone is its ability to promote a sense of equality between reader and poet. Dryden's verse is usually rhetorical; its function is often to bring the reader to conspire in praise or censure of someone or something. The tone is conversational, that of a 'man speaking to men', but speaking in public, with the manners due to equals and gentlemen and the frankness which comes from certainty of shared beliefs in all basic matters. It can be dignified or familiar, but never anything to excess. It brings poet and reader face to face on terms of equality, and it might be said that the style which Dryden founded and which Pope perfected had its beginnings in the prologues and epilogues of the Restoration theatre.

Dryden's songs

Dryden's songs are in many styles and moods, for they were usually part of his plays and had to conform to their context, though that was never a rigid obligation. The songs were very popular in the eighteenth century. Here, to illustrate something of Dryden's range in the form, are three of them.

From *An Evening's Love* (1668)

After the pangs of a desperate lover,
When day and night I have sighed all in vain,
Ah what a pleasure it is to discover
In her eyes pity, who causes my pain!

5   When with unkindness our love at a stand is,
And both have punished ourselves with the pain,
Ah what a pleasure the touch of her hand is,
Ah what a pleasure to press it again!

When the denial comes fainter and fainter,
10   And her eyes give what her tongue does deny,
Ah what a trembling I feel when I venture,
Ah what a trembling does usher my joy!

When, with a sigh, she accords me the blessing,
And her eyes twinkle 'twixt pleasure and pain;
15   Ah what a joy 'tis beyond all expressing,
Ah what a joy to hear, shall we again!

This song, like so many, employs the pastoral convention, but, in a typical Restoration fashion, infuses into it a libertine element. The song is personal only in that it involves the emotions of the participants. It is utterly impersonal as far as Dryden is concerned. As Professor Miner says, Dryden's love poems 'never tempt one to use the author's name to designate the speaker of the poems'. Dryden treats his speakers as actors, performing a drama of love, and the obvious but detached interest he takes in the psychology of sex is sometimes disturbing. The metre is unusual—basically anapaestic, but with many variations (Whén with ă sígh, shĕ accórds mĕ the bléssǐng). Professor Miner notes the strangeness of the fact that 'the closer an affair comes to its sexual climax the more lilting the measure is apt to be'.

From *The Kind Keeper* (1680)

'Gainst keepers we petition,
Who would enclose the common:
'Tis enough to raise sedition
In the free-born subject woman.
5   Because for his gold
I my body have sold,
He thinks I'm a slave for my life;
He rants, domineers,
He swaggers and swears,
10   And would keep me as bare as his wife.

NOTE. Sung by the characters Mrs Tricksy ('a termagant kept mistress') and Judith, her maid. 'Keepers' were men who 'kept' their mistresses, in one sense by providing homes for them, in another for their own exclusive pleasure. Line 2 refers to the enclosure of rural common land by the richer landowners, frequently a cause of social strife and hardship.

IMAGERY. The ladies, wishing to be free to 'play the field', make witty use of political metaphors to carry their complaints. This, of course, is a comic song, worthy of W.S. Gilbert, who would have liked the metre, if not the subject.

The Lady's Song (1704)

I

A choir of bright beauties in spring did appear,
To choose a May-lady to govern the year:
All the nymphs were in white, and the shepherds in green,
The garland was given, and Phyllis was queen:
5   But Phyllis refused it, and sighing did say,
'I'll not wear a garland while Pan is away.

While Pan, and fair Syrinx, are fled from our shore,
The graces are banished, and love is no more:
The soft God of Pleasure that warmed our desires,
10   Has broken his bow, and extinguished his fires;
And vows that himself, and his mother, will mourn,
Till Pan and fair Syrinx in triumph return.

Forbear your addresses, and court us no more,
For we will perform what the deity swore:
15   But if you dare think of deserving our charms,
Away with your sheephooks, and take to your arms;
Then laurels and myrtles your brows shall adorn,
When Pan, and his son, and fair Syrinx return.'

NOTE. The 'deity' of stanza III is Cupid of stanza II.

This was published after Dryden's death, for it is a Jacobite song. The pastoral convention dresses James II as Pan, Mary of Modena as Syrinx, and Dryden is careful to include the 'pretended Prince of Wales' in the last line. The call to arms in line 16 is probably the only line that could have caused trouble, for the choice of such a form for such a sentiment would tend to make anyone censuring the song on political grounds feel a little foolish.

'Absalom and Achitophel': The characters

The writing of 'characters' in the seventeenth century was a strong literary fashion, rather as that of sonnets had been earlier. Anyone with pretensions to wit would try. In the form in which they became popular, characters were word portraits of types. They were often used as school exercises and one schoolmaster defined the character as 'a witty and facetious description of the nature and qualities of some person, or sort of person'. The classical precedent was the character as written by Theophrastus, and the basic method was to note deviations from the Aristotelian middle way. Most characters, therefore, were denunciations, though there was a complementary school of exemplary characters. Both types are represented in *Absalom and Achitophel*.

By the end of the seventeenth century, the character of the pure type—a Squire, a Pedant, a Lawyer, a Fop, a Miser—was giving way to the polemical character, whereby the principles of a group or party could be described and satirized—a Puritan, a Jesuit, a Bishop, a Dissenter, a Tory, a Whig. A further development was the approximation of the character to the portrait of an individual, a brief biography or character sketch. As a further refinement, an individual's individuality could be described in character terms, to suggest that his faults or virtues were those of a whole class.

The most famous character in *Absalom and Achitophel* is Zimri (543–68). The advantages of giving it here include the insight it gives to the true originality of the Augustan poet.

Dryden's first description of Buckingham comes in a letter to the Earl of Rochester in 1673.

> I hope your lordship will not omit the occasion of laughing at the great Duke of Buckingham, who is so uneasy to himself by pursuing the honour of Lieutenant-General which flies him, that he can enjoy nothing he possesses. Though at the same time, he is so unfit to command an army that he is the only man in the three nations who does not know it. Yet he...thinks this disappointment an injury to him which is indeed a favour, and will not be satisfied but with his own ruin and with ours. 'Tis a strange quality in a man to love idleness so well as to destroy his estate by it, and yet at the same time to pursue so violently the most toilsome and most unpleasant part of business. These observations would easily run into lampoon, if I had not forsworn that dangerous part of wit.

Thus Buckingham, nearly ten years before *Absalom and Achitophel*, was already notorious for his unstable personality and impulsive enthusiasms. When Samuel Butler, the poet of *Hudibras*, wrote a collection of prose characters between 1667 and 1669, he included 'A Duke of Bucks'.

> His appetite to his pleasures is diseased and crazy, like the pica in a woman, that longs to eat that which was never made for food, or a girl in the green-sickness that eats chalk and mortar....His mind entertains all things very freely that come and go; but, like guests and strangers, they are not welcome if they stay long. This lays him open to all cheats, quacks, and imposters....

And so on.

Buckingham as Zimri is one of the anti-Court party.

> Some of their chiefs were princes of the land:
> In the first rank of these did Zimri stand:
> 545 A man so various that he seemed to be
> Not one, but all mankind's epitome.
> Stiff in opinions, always in the wrong;
> Was everything by starts, and nothing long:
> But in the course of one revolving moon,
> 550 Was chemist, fiddler, statesman, and buffoon:
> Then all for women, painting, rhyming, drinking;
> Besides ten thousand freaks that died in thinking.
> Blest madman, who could every hour employ,
> With something new to wish, or to enjoy!

555   Railing and praising were his usual themes;
           And both (to show his judgment) in extremes:
           So over-violent, or over-civil,
           That every man with him was God or Devil.
           In squandering wealth was his peculiar art:
560   Nothing went unrewarded, but desert.
           Beggared by fools, whom still he found too late:
           He had his jest, and they had his estate.
           He laughed himself from court, then sought relief
           By forming parties, but could ne'er be chief.

NOTES. Line 552: 'freaks', whims, vagaries; line 561: 'whom still he found', whom he always found out.

ORIGINALITY. Dryden would claim no credit for being the first to discern Buckingham's character; that was public property. The brilliance of his achievement lies in his use of the epigrammatic qualities of the heroic couplet to fix forever the image of that unbalanced mind. In lines 547–8, for example, the strong caesuras which break the lines give us four staccato sense units, so that the form of the statement imitates the grasshopper leaps taken by Buckingham's mind. There is a lapidary, inscription-like quality about this great 'character', for in effect it is Dryden's epitaph on an old enemy.

IN CONTEXT. As a supporter of Achitophel/Shaftesbury, Zimri is obviously no asset. His political involvement (lines 563–4) is a result of pique, not principle, and its only object is to assuage his vanity. Is the portrait, then, merely lampoon?

By drawing on the character style, Dryden suggests that Zimri's qualities are shared by a vaguely shadowed body of Achitophel's party, and the implication is clear. Could any sane man wish his country to be ruled by such people? Notice the placement of the word 'statesman' in line 550, a technique Pope was to employ in his character of the vain Belinda, 'Puffs, powders, patches, bibles, billet-doux'. Buckingham did have a keen interest in chemistry (and alchemy) and was an accomplished violinist. In the hands of an apologist for him, these lines could emerge as characteristics of a 'well-rounded' man. Dryden uses them contemptuously ('fiddler') to suggest a mind incapable of steady application. The word 'moon' in the previous line gives hints of 'lunacy' and applies to Zimri the proverbial inconstancy of the ever-changing moon.

An instance of the eulogistic 'character' is provided by the portrait of Amiel, chief of the Sanhedrin, by which Dryden means Speaker of the House of Commons.

Indulge one labour more, my weary Muse,
For Amiel, who can Amiel's praise refuse?
900 Of ancient race by birth, but nobler yet
In his own worth, and without title great:
The Sanhedrin long time as chief he ruled,
Their reason guided and their passion cooled;
So dexterous was he in the crown's defence,
905 So formed to speak a loyal nation's sense,
That as their band was Israel's tribes in small,
So fit was he to represent them all.
Now rasher charioteers the seat ascend,
Whose loose careers his steady skill commend:
910 They like th'unequal ruler of the day,
Misguide the seasons and mistake the way;
While he withdrawn at their mad labour smiles,
And safe enjoys the sabbath of his toils.

NOTES. 'Israel' (line 906) represents England. Line 909 could be paraphrased 'Whose uncontrolled dashes ('careers') pay tribute to his steady skill'. The 'unequal ruler of the day' (line 910) is Phaethon, son of Helios, who persuaded his father to let him drive the chariot of the sun for one day. His failure to control it imperilled the world, upset the proper sequence of time (hence, perhaps, 'unequal', although Phaethon was also 'unequal' to the task), and caused Zeus to slay him with a thunderbolt.

AMIEL. 'Amiel' is Dryden's name for Edward Seymour (1633–1708), Speaker of the Commons from 1673 to 1678. He was a Devon man, a Western grandee, proud of his ancestry and fierce in his prejudices. Dryden praises him for his handling of the House of Commons during his period of office as Speaker, when, as is strongly indicated, he did all he could to serve the interests of the Court. Gilbert Burnet, the Whig bishop and historian (the Buzzard of *The Hind and the Panther*) gives an interesting account of Seymour's parliamentary skill as seen from the opposition benches.

He was the most assuming Speaker that ever sat in the chair. He knew the House and every man in it so well that by looking about he could tell the fate of any question. So if any thing was put when the Court party were not well gathered together, he would have held the House from doing anything by a wilful mistaking or misstating the question, so he gave time to those who were appointed for that mercenary work, to go about and gather in all their party. And he would discern when they had got the majority, and then he would very fairly state the question, when he saw he was sure to carry it.

Seymour's place among David's friends in *Absalom and Achitophel* is due to his opposition to Exclusion, but since the strongest of his prejudices was against Catholicism it is significant that he opposed Exclusion on practical grounds only. Moreover, Seymour, despite Dryden's implication in lines 912–13, had not retired voluntarily as Speaker. In 1679 Charles II had refused to accept him for a second term. These facts are confirmed as omens when we learn that Seymour was an opponent of James II and went over conspicuously early to the side of William of Orange. He became a firm Tory in the reign of Queen Anne, but was always an anti-Jacobite.

PRAISE BY BLAME. Dryden selects for his 'band of angels' the only Speaker in recent times to be sympathetic to the Court. The first ten lines of this character are insipid, with an opening couplet which is rather desperate. This flatness testifies to the peculiar difficulty facing the eulogist. Human nature and the nature of literature make virtue far less interesting than vice. The portraits of the King's friends in the poem are generally shorter and less inspired than those of Absalom's faction; good men are often necessary in satire, but they cannot be its main topic. Thus the character of Amiel comes momentarily to life only when Dryden uses the example of Seymour as an excuse to inveigh against his successors in the Speaker's chair (lines 908–911). The poet employs the stock figure of misgovernment, Phaethon, to imply that the chaos threatened by Shaftesbury and Monmouth would be a catastrophe in nature, not merely in Parliament or in England. Like his Augustan successors, Dryden often uses a pinch of satire to spice his eulogy and employs instances of eulogy in satire to turn back the criticism that nothing positive is shown or offered to counteract all the satiric denunciation. Often, as here, a eulogy will be found to have most vigour when the poet contrasts his model of virtue with the immoral reality of the world all around. He praises Amiel most convincingly by blaming Amiel's successors.

'Mac Flecknoe': the threat of dulness

Mac Flecknoe is Dryden's most delightful poem. It seems to have been the product of a literary and personal quarrel between Dryden and Thomas Shadwell, the utterly silent, largely inactive, and nearly anonymous 'hero' of the poem. Shadwell, a dramatist who saw himself as the continuer of Ben Jonson's 'humours' type of comedy, resented Dryden's carefully qualified criticism of Jonson and set out to disparage Dryden's own comic method of witty repartee. The beautiful instrument of Dryden's final solution to his Shadwell problem was Mac Flecknoe, which circulated in manuscript for several years before being printed.

The 'fiction' of the poem is indicated by its title. Dryden pretends that Richard Flecknoe, a poetaster of a slightly earlier generation (perhaps recently dead when the poem was written) has selected Shadwell to be his successor and heir as emperor of dulness. Hence the title, 'Son of Flecknoe'. The poem is, therefore, both a proclamation of the new ruler and his coronation ceremony. It is packed with allusions, parodies, and quotations, yet it is light and graceful and very funny.

Flecknoe, whose speeches are the main body of the poem, does not pretend that his dulness is wit; he asserts that dulness is itself virtue. He is a praiser of folly. The passage below describes the coronation of Shadwell.

> Now Empress Fame had published the renown
> 95 Of Sh—'s coronation through the town.
> Roused by report of Fame, the nations meet,
> From near Bun-Hill and distant Watling Street.
> No Persian carpets spread th'imperial way,
> But scattered limbs of mangled poets lay:
> 100 From dusty shops neglected authors come,
> Martyrs of pies, and relics of the bum.
> Much Heywood, Shirley, Ogilby there lay,
> But loads of Sh— almost choked the way.
> Bilked stationers for yeomen stood prepared,
> 105 And H— was captain of the guard.
> The hoary prince in majesty appeared,
> High on a throne of his own labours reared.
> At his right hand our young Ascanius sate,
> Rome's other hope, and pillar of the state,
> 110 His brows thick fogs, instead of glories, grace,
> And lambent dulness played around his face.
> As Hannibal did to the altars come,
> Sworn by his sire a mortal foe to Rome;
> So Sh— swore, nor should his vow be vain,
> 115 That he till death true dulness would maintain;
> And in his father's right, and realm's defence,
> Ne'er to have peace with wit, nor truce with sense.

NOTES. Line 95: Dryden pretends to follow the usual practice in satires, especially those circulated in manuscript, of not naming living persons in full. His comic exploitation of the suggestive abbreviation 'Sh—' can be seen in line 103.

Lines 96–7: an important device in the poem is the coupling of the great with the paltry to create the essential bathetic plunge of the mock heroic. In this case the 'nations' inhabit the regions around the City of London. Dryden's placing of the action in the mercantile centre of London indicates the important and truly dangerous natural alliance he saw between Whigs, the mercantile middle classes, sedition, and bad art. The ceremony of the Lord Mayor's pageant can be glimpsed amid the trappings of coronation.

Lines 98–103: the 'scattered limbs' of the 'mangled poets' are the torn leaves of their volumes of verse. The proverbial fate of unsold books of bad poetry was that they should be made into pie-dishes and, of course, toilet paper (line 101). 'Martyrs' and 'relics' indicate the pseudo-religious aspect of this mock coronation. Besides being crowned, Shadwell is anointed, and Flecknoe is both emperor and prophet. Heywood and Shirley are older playwrights who represent the tradition of theatre to which, in Dryden's view, Ogilby and Shadwell currently belonged.

Lines 104–5: the 'stationers' (booksellers) are 'bilked' because they publish the awful, unsaleable stuff written by the poets of dulness. 'H—' is Herringman, for many years Dryden's own publisher; his inclusion here may indicate an unpleasant termination of their relationship in 1678. He was Shadwell's publisher, too, until that year.

Line 107: recalls Satan on his throne in Pandemonium (*Paradise Lost*, Book II). There may be a hint of the famous 'darkness visible' in 'lambent dulness' (line 111).

Line 108: Ascanius was the son of Aeneas, but Shadwell's identification with this great imperial heir is undercut at once (lines 112–13) by an identification of him with Hannibal, Rome's greatest enemy.

SHADWELL. The memory of Shadwell is kept alive by *Mac Flecknoe*. Dryden has branded him forever as a dullard and has made him a manifestation of cultural anarchy. Yet it is perhaps worth noting that as a writer of comedies Shadwell is hardly inferior to Dryden. The notoriety Dryden has bestowed has really very little to do with exact truth, nor does this fact in any way alter the value of the poem. The relationship between Shadwell and the 'Sh—' of the poem is as complex as that between life and art.

When Dryden lost his Laureateship in 1688, Shadwell was chosen to replace him. The situation has many obvious ironic possibilities, but Dryden could have pointed out that there was a natural appropriateness in it. In his view, the new regime had got the Laureate it deserved.

THE DUNCIAD. Pope was pleased to acknowledge that the basic plan of his great work on the power of Dulness came from *Mac Flecknoe*. Dryden's poem could hardly be improved on; it is masterly in form and detail. To Pope, however, the threat of Dulness seemed greater and grimmer than it had to Dryden. Pope treats Dulness in epic terms, despite his mock epic approach, and with sardonic laughter. To Dryden, the threat could still be handled as an episode (*Mac Flecknoe* has 217 lines) and in terms less bitter though fundamentally as serious.

Thomas Shadwell.

182

'Religio Laici': Anglican arguments

The following fragment is from the second half of *Religio Laici*, in which Dryden is arguing against the Roman Catholic claim for 'tradition'. In matters where the Scriptures are unclear and must be interpreted, the Catholic Church claims the right to be the interpreter because it has been the 'hander down' of the Scriptures.

360   yet grant they were
       The handers down, can they from thence infer
       A right t'interpret? or would they alone
       Who brought the present, claim it for their own?
       The Book's a common largess to mankind;
365   Not more for them, than every man designed:
       The welcome news is in the letter found;
       The carrier's not commissioned to expound.
       It speaks itself, and what it does contain,
       In all things needful to be known, is plain.

In dealing with the subtle arguments of the Catholics, Dryden adopts a blunt, commonsense unsophistication, a sort of Anglican peasant shrewdness. By making the Scriptures analogous to a letter and the Catholic Church to a postman, he scores a debating point whose wit is set precisely at that level. One of his most emphasized arguments is that 'the things we *must* believe are few and plain', and that 'points not clearly known, / Without much hazard may be let alone'. In a passage which occurs a few lines earlier than the above, Dryden relies on the proverbial English impatience with too much subtlety.

       Shall I speak plain, and in a nation free
       Assume an honest layman's liberty?
       I think (according to my little skill,
       To my own mother-church submitting still:)
320   That many have been saved, and many may,
       Who never heard this question brought in play.
       Th'unlettered Christian, who believes in gross,
       Plods on to heaven; and ne'er is at a loss:
       For the strait gate would be made straiter yet,
325   Were none admitted there but men of wit.

Basic sincerity, common sense, and a humble confidence in God— all emotionally recreated by such words as 'plods'—are enough for salvation. This is Dryden's version of the Anglican middle way, and we should not underestimate the art he brings to the creation of a mood and tone that let him put aside as 'over-sophisticated' so many arguments.

However, in countering the deist, a rather simple-minded adversary, in the first half of the poem, Dryden as speaker takes on a very different and more varied character. There he is by turns confident, subtle, assertive, contemptuous, and polite. His own nature as a disputant changes in response to the nature of his adversary. In the following passage he begins by defending the divine authorship of the Bible.

> Then for the style; majestic and divine,
> It speaks no less than God in every line:
> Commanding words; whose force is still the same
> 155   As the first *fiat* that produced our frame.

Even as an Anglican, Dryden seems to have read the Bible in the Vulgate version, and his response to the style is probably a response to the Latin words. He knows as well as anyone, of course, that the style of the Scriptures is not uniform, but he wishes to remind his reader of the grandeur of the early verses of Genesis. The deist, it is implied, argues that the Bible is simply a human document. Dryden's style responds by suggesting a majesty beyond the reach of a merely human author.

The passage then turns to the unlikeliness of the triumph of Christianity.

> All faiths beside, or did by arms ascend;
> Or sense indulged has made mankind their friend:
> This only doctrine does our lusts oppose:
> Unfed by nature's soil, in which it grows;
> 160   Cross to our interests, curbing sense, and sin;
> Oppressed without, and undermined within,
> It thrives through pain; its own tormentors tires;
> And with a stubborn patience still aspires.
> To what can reason such effects assign
> 165   Transcending nature, but to laws divine?
> Which in that sacred volume are contained;
> Sufficient, clear, and for that use ordained.

NOTES. Lines 157 and 160: 'sense' refers to those pleasures obtained by gratifying the senses. Lines 159 and 165: 'nature' is *human* nature.

These are by no means unanswerable arguments. (The deist, were he permitted to rebut, might point out that Dryden's knowledge of comparative religion is not extensive, and that his definition of human nature as inherently sensual and sinful is a matter of basic disagreement between Christian and deist, not something both sides would concede.) Yet the effectiveness of the passage is undeniable. The paradox Dryden establishes, whereby Christianity is the religion least likely to succeed on rational, deistic grounds, and yet succeeds, is brilliant debating. The speed and compactness of the presentation sweep the reader along, yet without any feeling that rational argument is being abandoned to emotional fervour. It is the art of Dryden's ratiocinative verse to use the emotional resources of poetry to produce the effects of reasoned argument.

Baroque praise: 'To the Duchess of Ormonde'

Dryden's last, and perhaps his finest, poem of compliment was published as part of the dedication to his *Fables* in 1700. So finely wrought is it, that it seems impertinent to think of it in the context of the flattering dedications, yet, initially at least, it is flattery and may have brought a flattering reward—Dr Johnson records a tradition that Dryden was given a present of £500 for it.

Since it is a poem and not a prose dedication, Dryden's poetic resources, which serve him as a form of conscience, are called on to put the flattery into a structure of ideas and images which will enable him to lift his eyes from the realities of the situation and concentrate on what, as poet, he can make of them. From the very start, the Duchess is an ideal figure, and Dryden idealizes her by his favourite device of associating her with poetry. The Duke and Duchess of Ormonde are reincarnations of the noble couple who served as models for Chaucer's Palamon and Emily. (The first poem in *Fables* is a 'translation' of Chaucer's *Knight's Tale*.) The Duchess's first visit to Ireland in 1697 is described with a wealth of exuberant detail which makes it sound like instructions given to a painter for a picture to commemorate the journey.

> When westward, like the sun, you took your way,
> And from benighted Britain bore the day,
> Blue Triton gave the signal from the shore,
> 45   The ready Nereids heard, and swam before
> To smoothe the seas; a soft Etesian gale
> But just inspired and gently swelled the sail;
> Portunus took his turn, whose ample Hand
> Heaved up the lightened keel and sunk the sand,
> 50   And steered the sacred vessel safe to land.
> The land, if not restrained, had met your way,
> Projected out a neck, and jutted to the sea.
> Hibernia, prostrate at your feet, adored
> In you, the pledge of her expected lord;
> 55   Due to her isle; a venerable name;
> His father and his grandsire known to fame:
> Awed by that house, accustomed to command,
> The sturdy kerns in due subjection stand;
> Nor hear the reins in any foreign hand.

At your approach, they crowded to the port;
And scarcely landed, you create a court:
As Ormonde's harbinger, to you they run,
For Venus is the promise of the sun.
The waste of civil wars, their towns destroyed,
65 Pales unhonoured, Ceres unemployed,
Were all forgot; and one triumphant day
Wiped all the tears of three campaigns away.
Blood, rapines, massacres, were cheaply bought,
So mighty recompense your beauty brought.

NOTES. *Portunus* (line 48), Roman god of harbours, was invoked to ensure safe return from a voyage. *Etesian* (line 46): in Greek and Latin writers, an annual, end-of-summer wind. Dryden is 'classicizing' a steady, gentle breeze from the East.

Lines 51–2: the conceit of the land's desire to move out to greet a welcome visitor was fairly common. Sir Walter Scott, in his note on a similar conceit in Dryden's *Astraea Redux*, highlights the playful fancy of the idea. 'The civility of such inanimate objects, according to the poets of this reign, was truly wonderful, considering their present insensibility.'

Lines 53–9: the Butlers, Earls and Dukes of Ormonde, were devoted royalists, and at the head of the Anglo-Irish aristocracy. They served Charles I and Charles II as Lords Lieutenant of Ireland. The second Duke, mentioned here, was the grandson of the first Duke, who is Barzillai in *Absalom and Achitophel*, lines 817–63. The 'kerns' are the native Irish peasantry. Pales (line 65) was the Roman god (or goddess, no one seems certain) of flocks and herds. Ceres was goddess of the harvest.

Lines 68–9: there seems in these lines to be an implicit comparison between the Duchess and devastated Ireland, and Helen and suffering Troy. The Trojans, in the main, decided that Helen was worth the trouble she brought.

BAROQUE STYLE. As Hoffman (see Further Reading) points out, this passage is a miniature of the voyage which is an important feature of the classical epic poem. To make small something so grand, however, involves an element of humour, and this sense of fun, of exuberance which might or might not be ironic, seems inevitably part of the baroque when it has not the total grandeur of a Milton.

'Baroque' is a term which implies a style in the service of earthly or divine greatness, involving a joyous reverence for the classical world, a torrential abundance of motifs, an energy which paradoxically transforms the statuesque into the fluid (the arts which exemplify the

Roman Baroque, a ceiling by Pietro da Cortona.

baroque best are sculpture and architecture, and the greatest baroque artist is Bernini), and a wit which makes art virtually equivalent to play and at the same time hints that there may be irony in its attitude to the greatness on which it is lavished. The baroque may be said to have its doctrinal origins in the assertion of the Roman Catholic Counter-Reformation that the senses are not the enemies of the spirit that Calvinism declared them to be.

It is interesting that W.H. Auden, a poet whose enormous facility of invention and technical command, in addition to his 'conversions' in politics, religion, and nationality, have led to his being sometimes called 'the modern Dryden', should have included this passage, as an instance of baroque poetry, in his personal anthology, *A Certain World*. Auden finds baroque the most worldly of styles (and therefore the least suitable for religious topics, as in *Paradise Lost*), but he, too, raises the issue of irony in baroque panegyric. 'At the same time, by its excessive theatricality, it reveals, perhaps unintentionally, the essential "camp" of all worldly greatness.' In my own view, Dryden is somehow able to keep the ironical potential in his theatrical and literally absurd account of the Duchess's voyage from coming into action. The reader is effectively distracted and is kept from reflecting back on the real woman and the real state of Ireland. The 'three campaigns' Dryden mentions in line 67 had left Ireland in 1697 in a state of terrible devastation. In harsh truth, the beauty of the Duchess would have been little recompense for such suffering to Ireland as a whole, however much the people of Kilkenny may have rejoiced. Yet Dryden's wit has so elevated the events into the realm of art that fancy and fact do not collide. The Duchess is quite transformed and removed from plain reality by Dryden's torrent of similes. She is, in the course of the poem, the sun and the morning star, Noah's dove and, with Dryden's usual hint of blasphemy, the Messiah, in an echo of Virgil's 'Pollio' eclogue; she drives, like Saint Patrick, all venom from Ireland; to Dryden she is the Prince in whom, as subject, he has some rights: she is the perfect blend of the four elements, and has been preserved from the corruption of sickness by a particular miracle. And so on. To look from these wonderful transformations to the 'reality' beneath seems almost ungrateful.

BETWEEN BAROQUE AND NEOCLASSIC. The form of this poem, of course, is the heroic couplet, which with Dryden was to become the great neoclassical metre of English verse. Yet in its imagery, the poem is closely related to the poetry of the Metaphysicals, where the baroque style had its greatest flourishing in English. And should we wish to remind ourselves even more of Dryden's place at the junction of seventeenth and eighteenth-century English poetry, we might compare his poem to the Duchess with that to Cousin Driden of Chesterton, also published in *Fables*, also a poem of compliment and a good one (see pp. 190–2). There, however, Dryden stays closer to the realities of the situation and produces a poem which anticipates Pope. The wit is still present, but most of the baroque exuberance has gone. Grandeur was in order in addressing a Duchess, and Dryden, in his late sixties, draws easily and with delight on a poetic style which, according to the convenient simplicities of literary history, was merely a part of his past, a style he had 'outgrown'.

Baroque: celestial commerce

When in mid-air, the golden trump shall sound,
    To raise the nations under ground;
180   When in the valley of Jehosaphat,
The judging God shall close the book of Fate;
    And there the last assizes keep,
    For those who wake, and those who sleep;
    When rattling bones together fly,
185   From the four corners of the sky,
    When sinews o'er the skeletons are spread,
Those clothed with flesh, and life inspires the dead:
The sacred poets first shall hear the sound,
And foremost from the tomb shall bound:
190   For they are covered with the lightest ground
And straight, with in-born vigour, on the wing,
Like mounting larks, to the new morning sing.
There thou, sweet saint, before the choir shalt go,
    As harbinger of heav'n, the way to show,
195   The way which thou so well hast learned below.

CONTEXT. This is the last stanza of the Anne Killigrew Ode. She died of smallpox in June 1685, having been a Maid of Honour to the Duchess of York, later Queen Mary. Dryden's elegy obviously overpraises Anne Killigrew's accomplishments in the arts of poetry and painting, but his real object is to use the occasion to exalt the sanctity and worth of the arts themselves.

FORM. The ode was by custom a form where licensed 'irregularity' was encouraged in Augustan verse, meaning in effect marked variations of line length, rhyme pattern, and metre, with a certain 'extravagance' of imagery and conceit. It is notable here, however, and throughout the ode, that the majority of lines are of ten syllables. The rhyme pattern is couplets except for two triplets (188–90, 193–5) which are in any case a normal feature of Dryden's couplet verse. Unusually, there are no Alexandrines; all the lines which are not decasyllabic are octosyllabic—a slight variation from the ten-syllable pattern. Despite the fact that he is writing an ode, Dryden sticks close to the couplet form. He makes his customary skilled use of stress variation on the basically iambic pattern. In lines 184–5, for example, the speed of the 'reassembly' of the bodies of the dead is achieved by the use of octosyllabic lines, one of which (185) has only three effective stresses. Line 186, a decasyllabic line, similarly has only three main stresses. The recurrence of the *sound–ground* rhyme (lines 178–9) in lines 188–90, *sound–bound–ground*, is unusual. The employment of repeated rhyme words occurs several times in this poem and is obviously no blemish, though later, 'orthodox' prosodists might have condemned it. The use of rhymes to bind a stanza together is well-established in the ode form; the use of repetitions may be Dryden's deliberate refinement.

TONE. One characteristic of baroque art was its element of 'celestial commerce', the near approach of natural and supernatural, inter-course between heaven and earth. Baroque artists loved the confrontation of human beings and divine personages. A St Cecilia's Day ode was an attractive subject, therefore, since, in Dryden's version of the legend, Cecilia's invention of the organ drew an angel down from heaven. Crashaw's poem on St Teresa and Bernini's sculpture are two famous treatments of such a topic. The Assumption of the Virgin and, as here, the Resurrection were other favourite events. The element of delicate irony found throughout Dryden's poem on Anne Killigrew is present here in the playfulness of his account of the raising of the dead. The Last Judgment, in the form of an English assizes, is wryly domesticated, and the flying together of the rattling bones has the element of levity coexisting with solemnity found in the baroque. The 'in-born vigour' of the poets (the phrase could be a description of Dryden himself) allows them to 'bound' from the tomb and soar like larks. Dryden makes it seem that their covering of 'lightest ground' would not, in any case, have sufficed to hold them down much longer.

'Celestial commerce' in Dryden tends to mean the drawing down of the heavenly to earth, and his Resurrection is a wonderfuly physical (and slightly comic) event. Baroque religious art in general tends, in effect at least, to use the divine to confer glory on the secular.

The benefits of retirement: 'To my honoured kinsman, John Driden, of Chesterton in the County of Huntingdon, Esquire'

One of the original poems included in *Fables* was this Horatian epistle addressed to Dryden's cousin—landowner, J.P. and M.P. Driden is celebrated in the poem as an example of a 'retired' man, one who has avoided or withdrawn from the confusion and clamour of the outside world and has established on his own estate a model kingdom whose orderliness immediately derives from the well-regulated personality of its owner. As such, the poem draws on a long tradition of country-house and retirement poetry which has as its most eminent classical forbear the Roman poet Horace. (The finest example in English is Ben Jonson's 'To Penshurst'.) Dryden's involuntary retirement in 1688 made this genre naturally attractive.

Yet 'To my honoured kinsman' is not simply a poem of retirement (in this somewhat special sense of the term). As Justice of the Peace and Member of Parliament, John Driden had to do business with the world. The poem, therefore, has a basic two-part structure in which the exemplary model of Driden's regime at home in Huntingdonshire is first described. The poet then shows how this conduct guides his cousin in his role as a politician coping with the problems facing England in 1700. (I have earlier used some lines from the latter half of the poem to illustrate what Dryden called 'my own opinion of what an Englishman in Parliament ought to be': p. 10.) The division in the poem makes it difficult to choose a single representative excerpt; the following lines, in which the poem begins to move from the 'retired' life to the political world do contain something of each element.

50 With crowds attended of your ancient race,
   You seek the champian-sports, or sylvan chase:
   With well-breathed beagles you surround the wood;
   Ev'n then, industrious of the common good:
   And often have you brought the wily fox
55 To suffer for the firstlings of the flocks;
   Chased ev'n amid the folds; and made to bleed,
   Like felons, where they did the murd'rous deed.
   This fiery game, your active youth maintained;
   Not yet, by years extinguished, though restrained:
60 You season still with sports your serious hours;
   For age but tastes of pleasures youth devours.
   The hare, in pastures or in plains is found,
   Emblem of human life, who runs the round;
   And, after all his wand'ring ways are done, ⎫
65 His circle fills, and ends where he begun, ⎬
   Just as the setting meets the rising sun. ⎭
    Thus princes ease their cares: but happier he,
   Who seeks not pleasure through necessity,
   Than such as once on slipp'ry thrones were placed;
70 And chasing, sigh to think themselves are chased.

NOTES. Lines 53–7: as a huntsman, Driden is not simply seeking sport for himself. His function as J.P. is wittily extended to the hunting field, and the fox is executed on the spot where he committed his crime, as was often done in the case of a convicted human felon. The huntsman's pleasure serves a benevolent social function.

Lines 62–7: the emblem of the hare is a reminder that man, too, is being hunted, by death, and that all human endeavour meets the same end. At this significant moment, the poet begins to introduce his wider political theme.

HUNTING AND POLITICS. Both James II and William III were enthusiastic huntsmen. (Indeed, they were 'enthusiastic' in the seventeenth-century sense of the term, fanatical.) In the references (line 67) to the setting and the rising suns, Jay Arnold Levine, the most perceptive student of Dryden's poem, sees references to these two monarchs. William has 'hunted' James from his 'slippery' throne, but knows that his own seat there is just as precarious. Even if the setting sun of James does not rise again, the inescapable huntsman, death, will eventually triumph. William was almost permanently ill, and came to believe that his regular hunting was necessary to help him cling to what health he had; thus he 'seeks pleasure through necessity' (line 68). He is an addict—of pleasure, and by extension of royal power—whereas John Driden (lines 57–61) is able to moderate his pleasures to suit his age, just as in politics he will follow a moderate course between regal autocracy and parliamentary absolutism.

HUNTING AND 'VENERY'. Driden of Chesterton, though an opponent of King William's administration, was no Jacobite. The poet acknowledges his position as a member of the loyal opposition by another series of ideas which Levine has detected. Driden was unmarried, and the poet praises the state of celibacy and satirizes the 'snare' of marriage (lines 17–35). The little kingdom of Chesterton is in a condition of calm like that of Paradise before Adam asked for a mate. King James (in this unlike King William) had been a great 'hunter' of women and attributed the loss of his throne to God's displeasure at his trespasses in that direction. The hare, which leads the king as huntsman into the poem, was an emblem of lubricity and fecundity, associated with Venus. And 'venery' was a name for the hunt, which by its suggestion of Venus came to be also a term for sexual indulgence.

In his later years, Dryden—like King James—seems to have taken with some seriousness a causal link between 'venery' and the troubles which fell upon England in 1688. (In this, Dryden and James were in agreement with William and Mary, who effected something of a cleansing of public morals in the years of their reign.) Dryden repented the lubricity of his earlier plays, and in praising the celibacy of his cousin acknowledges that to some extent at any rate the age's troubles are the age's fault.

'The Secular Masque': goodbye to all that?

According to the unreformed calendar, New Year's Day in 1700 fell on 25 March. Since the first year of the new century was, inaccurately but naturally, assumed to be beginning too, there was a celebration, and it was decided to use the occasion to help and honour Dryden. He wrote to Mrs Steward: 'Within this month there will be played for my profit an old play of Fletcher's, called *The Pilgrim*, corrected by my good friend Mr Vanbrugh, to which I have added a new masque.' This contribution to his own benefit performance is called *The Secular Masque* ('secular', Latin saeculum, an age; it is a masque for the new century) and Dryden may have taken some hints for it from Ben Jonson's *Time Vindicated*. It was performed on 29 April; Dryden died on 1 May.

The theme of time governs the masque. The main characters are Janus (god of beginnings, 'January'), Chronos (Time), and Momus (god of carping and mockery, 'fault-finding personified', according to the *Oxford Classical Dictionary*). Janus urges Chronos to hurry; the new century is in sight. Chronos enters wearily, setting down a 'great globe' which he has been carrying on his back.

CHRONOS	I could not bear
	Another year
	The load of human kind.
(Enter MOMUS laughing)	
MOMUS	Ha! ha! ha! Ha! ha! ha! well hast thou done,
	To lay down thy pack,
	And lighten thy back,
	The world was a fool, e'er since it begun,
	And since neither Janus, nor Chronos, nor I,
	Can hinder the crimes,
	Or mend the bad times,
	'Tis better to laugh than to cry.
Chorus of all three	'Tis better to laugh than to cry.

Janus then asks Chronos to display for Momus the changes which have occurred in the past age. Then enter in turn Diana, Mars, and Venus, each representing a segment of the past century. Sir Walter Scott declared that these mythological personages are linked to specific monarchs. Diana, because of her hunting, to James I, Mars to Charles I, and Venus to Charles II. Such close identifications are unnecessary. Diana represents the spirit of the first part of the century, from the end of Elizabeth's reign to the beginning of the troubles of Charles I. Mars embodies the war and turmoil which dominated the middle years until the Restoration. Venus is the spirit of benevolent procreation and amorous pleasure governing the times of Charles II and James II. These are meant to be simplifications, not rigid correspondences.

The deities sing songs describing their times, with comments by the other characters.

DIANA   I course the fleet stag, unkennel the fox,
                  I chase the wild goats o'er summits of rocks,
                  With shouting and hooting we pierce through the sky;
                  And echo turns hunter, and doubles the cry.

Chorus of all   With shouting and hooting, &c.

JANUS   Then our age was in its prime,

CHRONOS   Free from rage.

DIANA   And free from crime.

MOMUS   A very merry, dancing, drinking,
                  Laughing, quaffing, and unthinking time.

After Venus's song, Chronos comments, with a possible reference to Mary of Modena hidden under the appellation of Venus,

         The world was then so light,
         I scarcely felt the weight;
         Joy ruled the day, and love the night.
         But since the Queen of Pleasure left the ground,
         I faint, I lag,
         And feebly drag
         The pond'rous orb around.

MOMUS   All, all of a piece throughout;
(*pointing to Diana*)   Thy chase had a beast in view;
(*pointing to Mars*)   Thy wars brought nothing about;
(*pointing to Venus*)   Thy lovers were all untrue.

JANUS   'Tis well the old age is out,

CHRONOS   And time to begin a new.

Chorus of all   All, all of a piece &c.

        (Dance of Huntsmen, Nymphs, Warriors, and Lovers.)

NOTE. 'Thy chase had a Beast in view'. This strangely haunting line has always been something of an enigma. It is obviously a description of failure in hunting, and the best explanation (Alan Roper's) is that to permit hounds to hunt by sight, rather than scent, in rugged terrain, was to put them in great peril of losing their quarry.

INTERPRETATION. In one respect, *The Secular Masque* is to Dryden what *The Tempest* is to Shakespeare. It has seemed to many to be his 'last will and testament', his final judgment on his age. There is general agreement that the last lines (quoted above) show Dryden to be disillusioned with the past and in some way optimistic about the future. His death so soon after encourages these interpretations.

Yet it seems to me very unlikely that Dryden put much of himself into the masque and most unlikely indeed that, even on his deathbed, he would simply have endorsed Momus's dismissal of the entire seventeenth century. His attitude can be better appreciated if we recall that Momus is the god of carping ridicule, one who could find a flaw in anything, however perfect. His is not the spirit of true satire. Dryden had been called on to write a farewell to the seventeenth century. By using the figure of Momus, he has a character who will say the worst of it, and thus create a mood of justified dismissal, but who is not a totally reliable commentator. Since the century is gone and the future is to be faced, cheerfulness can be maintained by adopting Momus's attitude, as happens at the end. It is better to laugh, even somewhat unfairly, than to cry. The masque suggests that the early years of the century were good ones, as were the Restoration years, and that since 1688 the mood has been one of weariness and exhaustion, the fag-end of the century. These attitudes probably reflect Dryden's own. But since such careful discrimination is now out of place, Dryden uses Momus to give zest to the idea of a new beginning and a total dismissal of the past. The dominant tone of the work is one of gaiety, but the fact that time is starting on a new cycle gives a hint that Dryden expects mankind to go once more through the same cycle of good and bad times.

MUSIC. It is appropriate that Dryden's last work should have been for the theatre, and that it should have been a masque—a form almost confined in England to the seventeenth century. Since it was sung, it is interesting to note that it seems to be easier to set than some texts Dryden had written earlier. The doctrine of *rhythmus* is not over-assertive here. Perhaps Dryden had relented somewhat towards musicians. Daniel Purcell, Henry's brother, wrote music for this masque.

Versification: Dryden's prosody in practice

Unlike Pope, who employed the heroic couplet almost exclusively, Dryden used many verse forms, though his greatest work is in the couplet. It does seem best, therefore, to turn for close analysis to a passage in his most important metre.

The passage chosen consists of three verse paragraphs from the translation of *Cymon and Iphigenia*, a story from Boccaccio (*Fables*, 1700). This is one of the last of Dryden's works, and it illustrates his matured handling of the heroic couplet. The translations in couplets make up two-thirds of the writing Dryden did in this form, so concentration on the satires and poems of argument tends to leave unappreciated Dryden's employment of the couplet in narrative. This extract is a passage of narrative action. Cymon and Lysimachus, at the head of an armed band, burst into the double wedding feast of Pasimond and Ormisda, intending to carry off the brides, Iphigenia and Cassandra (lines 577–604). (In this instance, old spelling and typographical features—use of capitals and italics—are retained.)

1 Daúntless they énter, *Cýmon* åt their Héad,

2 Aňd fiňd tȟe Féast rěnéw'd, tȟe Táblě spréad:

3 Sweet Voices mix'd with ínstruměntal Sounds

4 Ascénd the vaúlted Róof, ‖ the vaúlted Róof rebóunds. (12)

5 When like the Harpies rushing through the Hall [→]

6 The suddain Troop appears, the Tables fall,

7 Their smóaking Lóad is őn the Pávement thrówn;

8 Each Ravisher prepares to seize his own:

9 The Brides inváded wi̊th a rúde Embráce [→]

10 Shréek oút for Aíd, Confúsion fills the Pláce:

11 Qúick to redéem the Préy their plíghted Lórds [→]

12 Advance, the Palace gleams with shining Swords.

13 But late is all Defence, and Succour vain;

14 The Rápe is máde, ‖ the Rávishěrs ṟemáin:

15 Two ṣturdy Ṣlaves were only ṣent before

16 To bear the purchas'd Ṟrize in Ṣafety to the ṣhore. (12)

17 The Troop retires, the Lovers close the rear,

18 With főrward Fáces, nŏt conféssing Ḟéar:

19 Backward they move, but scorn their Ṟace to mend,

20 Thěn séek tȟe Ṣtáirs, aňd wi̊th ṣlów hást děscénd.

21 Fierce *Ṟasimond* their passage to ṟrevent,

22 Thrúst fúll oň *Cýmoň's* Báck iň his děscént,

23 The Ḅláde retúrn'd unbáth'd, and t̊o the Hándle ḅént. (12)

24   Stout *Cymon* soon remounts, and cleft in two [→]

25   His Rival's Head with one descending Blow:

26   And as the next in rank *Ormisda* stood,

27   He turn'd the Point: The Sword inur'd to B̆lood,   ⎫

28   B̆ŏr'd his unguarded B̆reast, ‖ which pŏur'd a pŭrple Flood. (12) ⎬

The satires and poems of argument display the abilities of the couplet for analysis and ratiocination. There each couplet can follow the other with a steady cumulative effect, one block placed on another. The closed couplet, which is in effect a stanza, is well suited to this kind of poetry. A narrative poem in couplets, on the other hand, tends to be a challenge to the form. Forward progress by swift leaps demands something other than mere steady cumulation.

METRICAL VARIATION. The basic pattern of iambic pentameter is assumed rather than present in this passage. By my count, only eight lines are perfectly regular (2, 6, 12, 13, 17, 24, 25, 27); in the other twenty lines, some variation is being practised. One variation often employed is 'trochaic substitution', especially in the first foot. Thus, the first foot of line 1 is a trochee (˘—Daúntlĕss). This variation is often used to reinforce lines which depict vigŏrous action, as in line 11 (Qúick tŏ) and 19 (Báckwărd) and 28 (Bŏr'd his). The presence of a stress on the very first syllable gives an emphatic start, plúngĕs the reader into the line.

SUPPRESSION OF STRESS. This occurs when a syllable which would normally take a stress in the iambic pattern is too insignificant in terms of sense to bear one. (It is a basic rule of scansion that sense always takes precedence over metrical patterning. The normal pronunciation of a word cannot be changed by the poet to make it fit his metre. Thus Dryden's line, 'The sacred Receptacle of the Wood' (*The Flower and the Leaf*, line 61), enforces the stress pattern R̆ecéptáclĕ, which conflicts with the normal R̆ecéptăclĕ. Then one must find out if in Dryden's day the word was stressed as he has it in this line, and the answer seems to be negative.) If no other syllable in the line is important enough to attract the stress to itself, then the line is in effect reduced to four stresses, as here in lines 7, 9, and others. I have marked syllables with suppressed stress thus: wi̊th. The result of reducing the line to four stressed syllables seems generally to be one of rapidity (though it occurs so much in Augustan verse that it is frequently hard to give a reason for it). Another effect is reinforcement of antithesis. By having four stresses to a line, the caesura or pause can fall exactly in the middle of the line, leaving two opposed ideas in the clearly separated half-lines (line 14, The Rápe is máde, ‖ the

Ravishers remain). In a polysyllabic word such as 'Ravishers', there tends to be a predominant stress and a possible secondary stress (Ravishers). The secondary stress can be easily suppressed, which is why polysyllables are often so useful to the Augustan poet (cf. instrumental, line 3).

ALEXANDRINES. Like stress suppression, the Alexandrine (twelve syllables, or six iambic feet) is used so often by Dryden that to find a particular reason for its occurrence is often impossible. There are four of these lines in this passage (4, 16, 23, 28) and they are somewhat unusual in that each seems to have a specific purpose. The effect of echo in line 4 (three regular stresses on each side of the caesura) is achieved by repetition of words and by extending the line to six feet, which places the caesura perfectly in the middle of a long line. Lines 15 and 16 are in effect a parenthesis. The extra foot in line 16 makes the couplet 'irregular' (though regularly so) and thus acts as an aural reminder that this couplet is something of an aside. (Dryden the dramatist takes care to get his ladies off the stage and leaves his heroes free to fight.) The last two Alexandrines are the third lines of triplets. Line 23 is made to suggest the astonishment of Pasimond. He drives his sword into Cymon's back, but Cymon is wearing mail under his outer garments. The sword is 'unbath'd' in his blood, and is bent by the blow. By making the couplet into a triplet, and adding one foot to the third line, Dryden reinforces Pasimond's reaction. All should be over when the blow is struck; instead, a bent sword! (It is interesting to note that in Boccaccio, Pasimondas is armed with a wooden staff and gets no chance to use it before being killed.) Line 28 displays a common use of the Alexandrine, to act as a terminal line bringing an action to an end. The idea of the 'dying fall' extends, nevertheless, to the action. Cymon is Dryden's hero. To minimize the effectiveness of his butchery of the brothers Pasimond and Ormisda, the poet first makes Pasimond stab at Cymon's back, and then personifies Cymon's sword, which just about has to take the blame for cutting down Ormisda ('The Sword *inur'd* to blood'). The sword pierces in the first half of the line and Ormisda bleeds in the second. Cause and effect are clearly separated by a caesura and bound together by internal rhyme (Bor'd—pour'd). The alliterating pairs (Bor'd, breast; pour'd, purple) add a final touch—some would say a last straw—to one of Dryden's most baroque effects.

ALLITERATION. This is often employed by Dryden to increase emphasis still further on stressed syllables (a device which sprung rhythm made necessary in Hopkins's verse). In this passage it is notable in the last eight couplets, where I have marked the alliterating syllables beneath the line. The effect in line 18, to take a striking example, is to reinforce the determination of the ravishers, and the stress which would normally fall on 'not' is not suppressed but made comparatively less emphatic by the alliterations on the other four stressed syllables. The negative is still there, but the less emphatic stress suggests fear beneath the determination. Line 20 is a magnificent effect of united devices. Every stressed syllable alliterates, and the witty oxymoron (slów hást) forms a spondee, a foot of two stressed syllables, for which Dryden has prepared by prefacing it with a pyrrhic foot of two unstressed syllables (ańd wiᵛth). The balanced stresses of the spondee underline in sound the movement of the ravishers down the stairs.

ABSENCE OF RUN-ONS. Enjambement, a device one would expect to meet frequently in a passage of vigorous action in this form, is not used by Dryden to overrun his closed couplets. Twice, as we have seen, he expands couplets to triplets, but he never allows a run-on between couplets. All cases of enjambement (lines 5, 9, 11, 24) occur between the first and second lines of a closed couplet, and in two instances (5 and 9) the enjambement is more apparent than real, for in these cases there is a natural pause at the end of the line. The run-on at the end of line 11 is designed to isolate the emphatic verb 'Advance' at the beginning of line 12, while that at line 24 'imitates' Cymon's lethal and rapid action. Enjambement between couplets, therefore, in no way explains the undeniable vigour and rapidity of this passage. End-stopping of the vast majority of the lines is the rule. The speed of the narrative must be explained as the result of the combination of short sense units (The Rape is made...The Troop retires... Backward they move....), the use of the dramatic present tense alternating with the past tense (in one line, 24, Dryden has a present and a past together), and the use of trochaic (sometimes spondaic— Thrúst fúll, line 22) substitution in the first feet of lines. In one case (line 10), 'substitution' means the insertion of an extra stress into the line. There is no later pyrrhic foot to compensate for the initial spondee.

DRYDEN AND POPE. This passage illustrates well the ability of the heroic couplet to exist as a rhythmical theme on which the skilled practitioner could play many variations. The variations of metre within the line which Dryden uses here were passed on to a grateful Pope. Triplets and Alexandrines, however, came to seem unnecessary and inelegant to Pope, whose avoidance of them became marked. To the admirer of Pope's practice, therefore, Dryden is a poet who often found the heroic couplet restricting, and who broke up the form (and, it is implied, the 'rules') with Alexandrines and triplets, instead of accepting, as Pope did, the challenge of keeping the couplet and varying within it so skilfully as to prevent all tedium. Pope thus refined Dryden's refinements.

There was much still to do on the couplet when Pope began to write. Dryden had written it with a knowledge of the compactness of which it was capable, but not always with a realization of that compactness. In some ways he may be said to have helped the measure to revert to a freer form resembling, in rough and ready convenience, the couplets of the Elizabethans....Dryden found the heroic couplet, as he found the tetrameter, too small to turn round in, and enlarged it accordingly....It seems a law...that metre should work by expectation rather than by surprise....In his versification, Dryden often took the readiest way, trusting, as he had the right to trust, that his mounting rush of sense and sound could bear down all obstacles. His reader acquiesces since such power is a unique phenomenon, but he cannot escape, in a large measure, that nervous sense of insecurity which it is the duty of versification to tranquillize. Any variations, as Pope knew, should be made responsibly. The reader must feel secure.

(GEOFFREY TILLOTSON, *On the Poetry of Pope*)

There is no reason why Dryden and Pope should be thus run against each other, and to defend Dryden from the implied charges of burly rusticity should involve no denigration of Pope. The points Professor Tillotson makes against Dryden might, indeed, serve as recommendations to anyone beginning a reading of Augustan verse. It is not a modern assumption that versification should tranquillize and make secure. In moving from twentieth-century ideas about poetry to those held in the eighteenth by Pope, the easiest, though not the 'smoothest', way lies through the verse of Dryden.

Dryden's criticism

The following passage is an excerpt from the Preface to *Ovid's Epistles* (1680). The sentences have been numbered and separated to facilitate the discussion.

1   If the imitation of nature be the business of a poet, I know no author who can justly be compared with ours [i.e. Ovid], especially in the description of the passions.

2   And to prove this, I shall need no other judges than the generality of his readers: for all passions being inborn with us, we are almost equally judges when we are concerned in the representation of them.

3   Now I will appeal to any man who has read this poet, whether he find not the natural emotion of the same passion in himself, which the poet describes in his feigned persons?

4   His thoughts which are the pictures and results of those passions, are generally such as naturally arise from those disorderly motions of our spirits.

5   Yet, not to speak too partially on his behalf, I will confess that the copiousness of his wit was such, that he often writ too pointedly for his subject, and made his persons speak more

eloquently than the violence of their passion would admit: so that he is frequently witty out of season, leaving the imitation of nature, and the cooler dictates of his judgment, for the false applause of fancy.

6   Yet he seems to have found out this imperfection in his riper age: for why else should he complain that his *Metamorphosis* was left unfinished?

7   Nothing sure can be added to the wit of that poem, or of the rest, but many things ought to have been retrenched; which I suppose would have been the business of his age, if his misfortunes had not come too fast upon him.

8   But take him uncorrected as he is transmitted to us, and it must be acknowledged in spite of his Dutch friends, the commentators, even of Julius Scaliger himself, that Seneca's censure will stand good against him;

Nescivit quod bene cessit relinquere:

he never knew how to give over, when he had done well: but continually varying the same sense an hundred ways, and taking up in another place what he had more than enough inculcated before, he sometimes cloys his readers instead of satisfying them, and gives occasion to his translators, who dare not cover him, to blush at the nakedness of their father.

9   This then is the alloy of Ovid's writing, which is sufficiently recompensed by his other excellencies; nay this very fault is not without its beauties: for the most severe censor cannot but be pleased with the prodigality of his wit, though at the same time he could have wished that the master of it had been a better manager.

10 Everything which he does becomes him, and if sometimes he appear too gay, yet there is a secret gracefulness of youth, which accompanies his writings, though the staidness and sobriety of age be wanting.

'CHARACTER' OF OVID. The method of criticism used here is that of the 'character' of the author and his works. Dryden seems to have believed (it was a belief which sometimes led him into error) that the literary work was the product of the author's personality and of the interaction of that personality with the times in which the writer lived. This method of analysis works smoothly for Dryden because he tended to derive the character of the author mainly from his works. The argument has a near-perfect circularity. Ovid's poetical character, as it emerges from this passage, is one of juvenility. In sentence 7, Dryden finds an ingenious argument for Ovid's awareness of his own poetical immaturity. Had circumstances permitted, he would have 'retrenched' the excesses of his wit, and by so doing would have brought himself closer to Dryden's implied ideal poet, one who unites the fire of youthful creativity with the wisdom of mature self-criticism.

(In Dryden's great elegy for John Oldham, the dead poet is given the same 'Ovidian', youthful character; there, the complete poet, unmistakably, is Dryden himself.) The juvenility of Ovid emerges openly in the imagery of sentence 10, and Dryden's tone is of genuinely graceful condescension, which the reader is permitted to share with the critic.

SHARED IDENTITY OF CRITIC AND READER. The reader is drawn to side with the critic in the passage because of Dryden's assumption, at the beginning, of common ground between them. Sentences 1 and 4 are designed to elicit agreement that 'the business of a poet' is 'imitation of nature'. Ovid is shown to be a good imitator of nature because most readers find within themselves, human nature being at all times the same, the emotions Ovid describes. Ovid, like Donne, deviated from the criterion of nature only in being witty at unseasonable moments, and by not knowing when to cease, when to rein in his wit. With an implicit comparison to the drunken Noah, at the end of sentence 8, Dryden puts the critical translator in the place of Noah's sons, lesser men able to see their great father's shame but, in this case, restrained by the rules of translation from 'covering' it. The imagery of the passage, be it noted, is markedly non-Ovidian. It is restrained, almost implied—'alloy...prodigality...master' (sentence 9)—but aids the reader greatly by giving him concrete particulars to characterize the features of Ovid's style. Such a characterization nowadays would be assisted by quotation, but Dryden is concerned to give his readers a general outline of Ovid's poetical character which they can apply themselves to individual passages. In the same way, when he refers to the 'professional' critics of Ovid—'his Dutch friends' ('Dutch' being redolent of barbaric pedantry) and 'even' Scaliger—he rejects their 'learned' view that Ovid *did* know when to give over, and quotes Seneca instead and with obvious approbation. The greater name is the most 'amateur' of the critics, and has expressed the most common-sense view. (Here, as often, Dryden's Latin quotation serves to punctuate a long sentence, and is translated for the reader. Rarely does Dryden make a quotation important to an argument without translating it. The reader's 'literacy' is thus complimented without being tested.)

PROSE STYLE. The style of the passage, both as a whole and in the individual sentences, is basically accretive. An idea is stated, then modified or expanded by addition. The sentences are never long. The longest, 8, is punctuated by the quotation, and the unit of sense throughout is around thirty words. Sentence 5, for example, has seventy-one words, yet really consists of two units, one added to the other. There are a couple of rhetorical questions to maintain the pressure on the reader to involve himself in response to the author's 'speaking' voice.

The amateurishness of such criticism was Dryden's desired object. In his critical prefaces, he is making modern English literature a subject for 'polite', non-specialist discussion by persons of cultivation. Only a computer could say with exactness whether or not this passage is typical of Dryden's prose, but it does seem to me to display accurately the kind of criticism he wanted to write. And the reader who is defined by implication in this passage is the one Dryden was creating.

Dryden's plays: the critical questions

Are we to consider these plays as merely the by-product or waste-product of a man of genius, or as the brilliant effort to establish an impossible cause, or have they, perhaps, any important relation to the development of English literature?

T.S.ELIOT

Since Dryden insisted on being a full-time writer, he would inevitably have come in time to the theatre, since the writing, performing, and publishing of plays was the only kind of literary activity which had then anything of the voracity for material which periodical journalism and television have today. In Dryden's time, the theatre alone could provide a writer of great energy with something like a steady income. His first play was produced in 1663, his last in 1694. It is virtually a life's work, but it is true to say that neither Dryden himself nor the majority of his readers ever considered his plays as such. His attitude towards play-writing was always equivocal, sometimes hostile. Often he saw it as drudgery and longed to be free of the need for it. It is quite possible that Dryden himself would have asked the questions T.S. Eliot asked about that part of his own career.

Eliot found a number of good reasons for reading Dryden's plays: the need to know the whole of a writer's work, the influence (truly great) of the dramatic on the non-dramatic verse, the place of the plays in establishing Dryden's reputation, and the fact that the plays brought forth some of his best criticism. Yet all these are extrinsic reasons; none of them answers the basic question, 'How good are Dryden's plays *as plays*?'

An answer would require lengthy argument and demonstration, for which there is no room here. My own opinion, which will necessarily have to stand unsupported by evidence, is that Dryden was a better playwright than is even now generally assumed; that he is, in fact, the best Restoration playwright if all the relevant factors are given due weight. In comedy he was several times excelled. Congreve, Etherege, Wycherley, even—it might be said, *contra Mac Flecknoe*—Shadwell wrote better individual comedies than Dryden did. In tragedy only Otway might claim to have surpassed Dryden. No one wrote better tragi-comedy or heroic drama than he. Yet this all-round achievement is shaded by the uncertainty that is still felt with regard

203

to Restoration theatre as a whole. It is undeniably a coterie theatre, especially in comparison with the great theatrical age of the early seventeenth century. Comedy is seen as its best achievement, and Dryden's comedies are not his best work. The heroic play, in which he did excel, is seen as so specialized and 'unnatural' a form that it is hard to give Dryden proper credit for his achievement, which in any case is made a little suspect by the existence of *The Rehearsal*. One of Dryden's best plays, *All for Love*, appears superficially to insist on being compared to Shakespeare's *Antony and Cleopatra*, and is inevitably overshadowed, despite its quality. It is difficult, therefore, to give Dryden the exact measure of praise he deserves for his theatrical work, but it is nevertheless certain that he stands very high among his contemporaries.

In recent years many scholarly books and articles have been devoted to the plays, and while that fact may testify to nothing more than the relentless search for thesis topics, it may also suggest that a genuine sympathetic reappraisal of Dryden's plays is under way. As yet, unfortunately, academic interest has not influenced the theatre, and since no true estimate can be had of the effectiveness of a play meant for the stage but never acted, Dryden is still denied a basic piece of justice. If good productions of his major plays could be mounted, then we might find that we could give an unqualified answer to the question of their worth.

The translator: Dryden's Chaucer

Since translations make up the bulk of Dryden's non-dramatic verse, it is desirable to try to give some idea (necessarily a very limited one) of his manner as a translator. Most of the translation is from Latin, and by common consent the Juvenal is the finest work of the kind that Dryden did. Yet to make a truly informed judgment of a translation, the reader must need no translator to help him, for both languages must be known. Since knowledge of Latin is no longer widespread and since Chaucer is more appreciated now than ever before, it seems most useful here to give the reader a chance of independent evaluation by comparing a passage of Chaucer's verse with Dryden's version of it. This is not, strictly speaking, translation, yet Dryden thought of it as such and took much the same approach to Chaucer as he took to foreign poets.

Dryden's account of Chaucer in the Preface to the *Fables* should be read entire, for he there has remarks on every point likely to interest a reader, be he sympathetic to the undertaking or hostile. Dryden's belief in the progress of arts and tongues predisposed him to see Chaucer as impeded by a versification and a language not yet grown to maturity. 'He lived in the infancy of our poetry, and... nothing is brought to perfection at the first.' Dryden rejected the quite correct belief, expressed in Speght's edition of 1602, that Chaucer's verse did scan properly and that any fault was that of modern ignorance. For Dryden, Chaucer's language was 'so obsolete, that his sense is scarce to be understood', and his verses were often 'lame for want of half a foot, and sometimes a whole one, and which no pronunciation can make otherwise'. Dryden's persistence in these errors of fact and judgment explains much concerning his 'translation' of Chaucer. His theory of translation carries understanding further.

In his Preface to *Ovid's Epistles* (1680), Dryden had defined three modes of translation: 'metaphrase' or literal translation, 'paraphrase' or 'translation with latitude', and 'imitation, where the translator (if now he has not lost that name) assumes the liberty not only to vary from the words and sense, but to forsake them both as he sees occasion'. Thus an ancient poet can be made to speak as if he were a modern, and a foreigner as if he were an Englishman. This engrafted modernity and Englishness was largely a matter of language but partly a matter of style and sentiment. The imitator could take liberties with his original to bring it up to date. Dryden cheerfully admits to having excised some of Chaucer's 'redundancies' and his lowness and to have added matter of his own where he found Chaucer deficient. Given these guidelines, it is clear that Chaucer is being 'imitated' in *Fables*. The prejudice comes automatically that he is therefore being mistreated, but it is well to read before deciding.

Dryden rebuts two criticisms of his enterprise: that Chaucer is 'a dry, old-fashioned wit', not worth the trouble, or that 'there is a certain veneration due to his old language; and that it is little less than profanation and sacrilege to alter it'. The first objection will hardly arise today; the second may have become an instinctive and unconsidered reaction. We no longer *need* Dryden's version of Chaucer, but might this not mean that we can find something of independent value in it? Dryden's genuine and sincere admiration for the older poet became, through his translation, a critical advocacy which greatly helped Chaucer's rehabilitation as a great poet, and it is remarkably fitting that Dryden was buried in Westminster Abbey between the graves of Chaucer, whom he revered, and Cowley, whose denigration of Chaucer he deplored.

Chaucer: from *The Nun's Priest's Tale*

3200   Madame Pertelote, my worldes blis,
       Herkneth thise blisful briddes how they synge,
       And se the fresshe floures how they sprynge;
       Ful is myn herte of revel and solas!
       But sodeynly hym fil[1] a sorweful cas,[2]
3205   For evere the latter ende of joye is wo.
       God woot that worldly joye is soone ago;
       And if a rethor[3] koude faire endite,
       He in a cronycle saufly[4] myghte it write

As for a sovereyn notabilitee.[5]

3210 Now every wys man, lat him herkne me;
This storie is also trewe, I undertake,
As is the book of Launcelot de Lake,
That wommen holde in ful greet reverence.
Now wol I torne agayn to my sentence.[6]

3215 A col-fox,[7] ful of sly iniquitee,
That in the grove hadde woned[8] yeres three....

(Fragment VII)

[1 fil: befell; 2 cas: chance; 3 rethor: rhetorician; 4 saufly: safely; 5 a sovereyn notabilitee: an outstanding instance; 6 my sentence: my main point; 7 a col-fox: a fox with black markings; 8 woned: dwelt]

Dryden: from *The Cock and the Fox*

455 Then turning, said to Partlet, 'See, my dear,
How lavish Nature has adorned the year;
How the pale primrose, and blue violet spring,
And birds essay their throats disused to sing:
All these are ours; and I with pleasure see
460 Man strutting on two legs, and aping me!
An unfledged creature, of a lumpish frame,
Indued with fewer particles of flame:
Our dame sits cow'ring o'er a kitchen fire,
I draw fresh air, and nature's works admire:
465 And ev'n this day, in more delight abound,
Than since I was an egg, I ever found.'
    The time will come when Chanticleer shall wish
His words unsaid, and hate his boasted bliss:
The crested bird shall by experience know,
470 Jove made not him his master-piece below;
And learn the latter end of joy is woe.
The vessel of his bliss to dregs is run,
And Heav'n will have him taste his other tun.
    Ye wise draw near, and hearken to my tale,
475 Which proves that oft the proud by flatt'ry fall:
The legend is as true, I undertake
As Tristram is, and Launcelot of the Lake:
Which all our ladies in such rev'rence hold,
As if in book of martyrs it were told.
480   A fox full fraught with seeming sanctity,
That feared an oath, but like the devil would lie,
Who looked like Lent, and had the holy leer,
And durst not sin before he said his prayer:
This pious cheat that never sucked the blood,
485 Nor chawed the flesh of lambs but when he could,
Had passed three summers in a neighb'ring wood....

206

CONTEXT. The passage is taken from the moment in the story when Chaunticleer has finished refuting the contention of his wife, Pertelote, that his dream of the previous night boded no ill. The fox, who appeared in the dream and who later is to seize Chaunticleer, is now introduced to the story.

METHODS. In *The Nun's Priest's Tale*, Chaucer combines with the success of genius two literary devices, beast fable and mock heroic. Each of these is well-adapted to humour and satire, since each presents human actions in an unfamiliar light and exploits the difference between what actually happens and the style in which it is described. Thus it is ludicrous that a cock and a hen should have a full-dress, medieval debate, replete with learned authorities, on the portentousness of dreams. It is even more ludicrous when the beast characters behave like figures in a heroic poem.

Dryden's version of Chaucer relies almost entirely for its individuality on amplification. Only rarely, despite his claims, does Dryden omit anything of Chaucer's. His usual method is to add further to what Chaucer has said, and in so doing, of course, he often makes Chaucer's delicate irony coarser, and eliminates those delightful moments when Chaucer says just enough and no more. Thus when Chaunticleer ends his account of the death, foretold by a dream, of St Kenelm, Chaucer has him say: 'By God! I hadde levere than my sherte [I'd give my shirt] / That ye hadde rad his legende, as have I.' The lapse from the dignity of hagiography to the homely phrase is just right. Dryden ends the speech by adding further to the grave citation of authority, and the effect is less good. 'The tale is told by venerable Bede [not true, incidentally], / Which at your better leisure you may read.'

IMPROVEMENT? Dryden cannot hope to improve on Chaucer, but he can retain Chaucer's mastery while transforming the poem into a 'contemporary' one. His choice of poem to 'translate' and his additions to it show what it was that Dryden loved in Chaucer. In *Mac Flecknoe* and *The Hind and the Panther*, Dryden had developed his own forms of mock heroic and beast fable respectively. He loved the poetry of learning and loved to make gentle fun of it. He makes considerable additions—and corrections!—to Chaucer's already long astrological passages, for example. And he loved the fine comic perspective on human life which Chaucer creates and which in Dryden's hands could so easily, and so well, become the blunter, or more cutting, weapon of downright satire. When he said of Chaucer that he was no great inventor, 'the genius of our countrymen in general being rather to improve an invention, than to invent themselves', Dryden may properly have included himself in that generalization. He cannot really improve on Chaucer, but what he adds has often something of genius in it.

THE PASSAGES. In Chaunticleer's speech to Pertelote above, Chaucer quite unfussily, and in four lines, restores his gloomy protagonist to happiness. Dryden, however, is eager to heighten the sense of mock hubris which precedes Chaunticleer's seizure by the fox. First he particularizes Chaunticleer's remarks on the birds and the spring, converting Chaucer's simplicity into something like pedantry with his very eighteenth-century descriptions of nature—personification (line 456), wit (line 458) and all. He then increases Chaunticleer's pride by adding the lines in which the cock draws the invidious comparison between himself and puny mankind, though he ends with a superb bathetic line, 'Than since I was an egg I ever found'.

Both authors emphasize the inevitability of fate, though Dryden's version is more pointedly classical, as in the switch from God to Jove. Chaucer is followed in his wry assertion of the truth of his tale and in the sly reference to women's credulity in their fondness for stories of Lancelot. This last point, however, becomes the occasion for one of Dryden's typical amplifications. He says that 'our ladies' hold Lancelot's story in a reverence as great 'As if in book of martyrs it were told'. This line would inevitably have been seen as a reference to John Foxe's *Book of Martyrs*, a work of early Anglican hagiography which was quasi-biblical in its authority among Dissenters. The reason for this reference becomes apparent at once: 'A fox full fraught with seeming sanctity'. What follows is a satirical bestiary account of the fox as religious hypocrite and particularly as the stock caricature among Tories and High Churchmen of the canting, greedy, and unscrupulous Dissenter. (Line 481 makes him, by virtue of his refusal to take an oath, a Quaker, a member of the Society of Friends, founded by yet another Fox, George (d. 1691), a name well known to Dryden's readers.) The suggestive economy of Chaucer's simple 'col-fox' is gone, replaced by a very seventeenth-century fox in saint's clothing.

FRUIT AND CHAFF. A marked and interesting difference in tone and attitude between the two poets can be felt when the moral is drawn at the end of the tale. Here is Chaucer's ending.

> Lo, swich it is for to be recchelees
> And necligent, and trust on flaterye.
> But ye that holden this tale a folye,
> As of a fox, or of a cok and hen,
> 3440   Taketh the moralite, goode men.
> For seint Paul seith that al that writen is,
> To our doctrine it is ywrite, ywis;
> Taketh the fruyt, and lat the chaf be stille.
> Now, goode God, if that it be thy wille,
> 3445   As seith my lord, so mak us alle goode men,
> And brynge us to his heighe blisse! Amen.

NOTE. Line 3445: the identity of this 'lord' is unknown.

Dryden gives his conclusion its own subheading.

The Moral

810   In this plain fable you th'effect may see
          Of negligence, and fond credulity:
          And learn besides of flatt'rers to beware,
          Then most pernicious when they speak too fair.
          The Cock and Fox, the Fool and Knave imply;
815   The truth is moral, though the tale a lie.
          Who spoke in parables, I dare not say;
          But sure, he knew it was a pleasing way,
          Sound sense, by plain example, to convey.
          And in a heathen author we may find,
820   That pleasure with instruction should be joined:
          So take the corn, and leave the chaff behind.

NOTE. Line 819: the 'heathen author' is most probably Horace in his *Ars Poetica*.

    Chaucer's moral comes with perfect appropriateness. *The Nun's Priest's Tale* is notably well designed to provide a portrait of the Nun's Priest himself. He is given a homiletic approach and a love of learning, combined with wit, humour, and piety. His apology for the use of a beast fable to convey his truth (lines 3438–43) reveals no underlying insecurity in his own mind. The actual moral (lines 3436–7) is simply presented.

    Dryden does not have the advantage of a characterized narrator, and his rather forceful insistence that the story does have a moral and is not mere frivolity perhaps shows some uneasiness on this score. (The reception of *The Hind and the Panther* may have crossed his mind.) In repeating the Nun's Priest's assurance that such a tale could serve good ends, Dryden adds significantly to the 'weight' and number of his authorities. Chaucer's Saint Paul is exchanged for Christ (line 816) and the classical authority of the 'heathen author' is superadded. (Dryden's refusal to name Christ may be real or affected modesty, or it may be a response to the hostile, moralistic criticism he suffered near the end of his career.) Moreover, the moral itself is expanded from two lines in Chaucer to four (lines 810–14) and has already been anticipated in the body of the story (474–5 above) in lines which Dryden added. These changes were perhaps suggested by a slight sense of insecurity on the translator's part; their effect is to make Dryden's narrator seem more severe, more sternly moralistic, than Chaucer's perfectly balanced Nun's Priest.

Part Five
Reference Section

Short Biographies

BUCKINGHAM, GEORGE VILLIERS, SECOND DUKE OF, 1628–87 [Zimri]. The biblical Zimri to whom Dryden alludes scandalized the Israelites by pagan worship and by an affair with a Midianite woman (Numbers 25). Buckingham was notorious for a love affair with the Countess of Shrewsbury, whose husband he killed in a duel. He was fabulously wealthy, and enormously in debt. In the early Restoration, Buckingham was an important minister of Charles II, but later joined the opposition. He helped Shaftesbury use the Popish Plot against the Court, but dropped out of political life as Shaftesbury increasingly asserted his leadership. One aspect of his 'variousness' is *The Rehearsal*, in which he is said to have had much assistance, including that of Samuel Butler, author of the character 'A Duke of Bucks'.

BUSBY, RICHARD, 1606–95. Dryden's headmaster was himself a King's Scholar at Westminster School and from there passed on to Christ Church, Oxford. He became Master of Westminster in 1638 and held the position until his death. During the Civil War Busby retained his post despite his well-known royalism and allegiance to the Church of England. At the Restoration his loyalty was acknowledged by further ecclesiastical preferments and, a signal mark of honour, he carried the ampulla at the coronation of Charles II. Two of Dryden's sons followed their father as King's Scholars at Westminster, and in 1693 Dryden dedicated his translation of the fifth satire of Persius to Busby. Many stories were told of him, a typical example being his alleged refusal to remove his hat when Charles II visited the school, lest the boys should think there was any man in the world greater than Dr Busby. Most of his own literary works were school editions of the classics, carefully expurgated, and 'published solely for the pious purpose of enabling his own pupils to imbibe the beauties without being polluted by the impurities of the ancients' (*D.N.B.*). His influence over Dryden in such matters does not seem to have been great.

CHARLES II, 1630–85; succeeded his father in 1649, but was unable to reign until the Restoration of 1660. The Civil War and the years of exile were obviously great formative influences on Charles, but his character developed on very different lines from those of his father and brother. He was generally sensual, self-indulgent, and lazy, but could on occasions be firm, businesslike, and even principled. The

Duke of Buckingham, "Zimri".

cases of the Treaty of Dover and the Exclusion crisis illustrate Charles's political conduct in representative, because opposing, ways. In 1670 he made a treaty with Louis XIV, publicly agreeing to an alliance with France against Holland. In secret clauses, moreover, Charles agreed to convert to Catholicism, to receive subsidies from Louis, and to use French troops in the religious conversion of England. Charles took Louis's money, as he was to do again, and was converted to Rome on his deathbed, fifteen years later. But he wisely never attempted to convert England to Rome. In the Exclusion crisis, however, when the easiest course at times would have been to abandon James, Charles showed great tenacity, waited out his opponents, and then moved decisively against them. At his death the throne seemed secure and Charles had earned a reputation for political shrewdness and courage. On the whole J.H. Plumb gives the best overall summary of the reign:

> Whatever charm Charles II may have possessed, he certainly lacked, in strong contrast to Louis XIV, single-minded dedication to the business of government. It was the unbuttoned ease, the air of summer relaxation that he brought to the monarchy, rather than his sexual licence, that undermined the awe and respect of his courtiers, servants, and supporters and provided so much grist to his enemies and to those who wished to belittle the monarchy.
>
> (*The Growth of Political Stability*, 1967)

In literary patronage, Charles's behaviour was damagingly inconsistent and sporadic. He had a great ally in Dryden, but failed to make the best use of him. 'There never existed in England that close contact between the Court and the arts that is such a marked feature of French life at this time' (Plumb). Dryden was Poet Laureate, but he was irregularly paid and infrequently employed. He tells us that he received several hints from Charles for various works, but the best anecdote of this type comes from Pope and is unverified. It is probably just a nice story, indicating a type of closeness between King and poet that perhaps *should* have existed.

> One day, as the king was walking in the Mall, and talking with Dryden, he said, 'If I was a poet—and I think I am poor enough to be one—I would write a poem on such a subject in the following manner:' and then gave him the plan for it.—Dryden took the hint, carried the poem [*The Medal*] as soon as it was finished to the king, and had a present of a hundred broad pieces for it.
>
> (SPENCE, *Ancedotes*)

CONGREVE, WILLIAM, 1670–1729. Congreve was educated at Kilkenny School and Trinity College, Dublin, and was a contemporary and friend of Swift at both places. He tried the law, but he never became a qualified lawyer. It was probably Congreve's classical scholarship that recommended him to Dryden, and the older man invited the younger to be one of the 'Eminent Hands' to translate Juvenal. As the *Juvenal and Persius* was about to be published in 1692, Congreve showed the manuscript of his play *The Old Bachelor* to Dryden and Thomas Southerne. Southerne later wrote that Dryden said 'he never saw such a first play in his life, but the author not being acquainted with the stage or the town, it would be pity to have it miscarry for want of a little assistance'. So Dryden, Southerne, and the politician and Kit-Cat Arthur Maynwaring set about 'assisting' Congreve, and the play was a great success. Congreve was thenceforward a leading play-wright, though his greatest work, *The Way of the World*, which Dryden did not live to see, was poorly received, in part perhaps due to the attack on Congreve by Jeremy Collier. Congreve wrote no more plays and gradually moved out of literary life.

In his poem 'To My Dear Friend Mr Congreve, On his Comedy called *The Double Dealer*', Dryden designates Congreve as his literary heir, and that estimate was fairly generally shared. ('Late, very late, may the great Dryden die / But when deceased, may Congreve rise as high': Charles Hopkins, *Epistolary Poems*, 1694.) Dryden's genuine admiration for Congreve was as generously repaid. Dryden asked Congreve to 'Be kind to my remains', and when Congreve edited a six-volume *Dramatic Works* of Dryden in 1717 he wrote a character of the older poet in the epistle dedicatory to the Duke of Newcastle.

> He was of a nature exceedingly humane and compassionate, easily forgiving injuries, and capable of a prompt and sincere reconcilia-tion with them who had offended him. . . .
>
> His friendship, where he professed it, went much beyond his professions, and I have been told of strong and generous instances of it, by the persons themselves who received them, though his hereditary income was little more than a bare competency.
>
> As his reading had been very extensive, so he was very happy in a memory tenacious of every thing that he had read. He was not more possessed of knowledge than he was communicative of it. But then his communication of it was by no means pedantic, or imposed upon the conversation. . . . He was extreme [*sic*] ready and gentle in his correction of the errors of any writer who thought fit to consult him, and full as ready and patient to admit of the reprehension of others in respect of his own oversight or mistakes. He was of very easy, I may say of very pleasing access, but something slow, and as it were diffident in his advances to others. He had something in his nature that abhorred intrusion into any society whatsoever. Indeed it is to be regretted that he was rather blame-able in the other extreme, for by that means he was personally less known, and consequently his character might become liable both to misapprehensions and to misrepresentations.

To the best of my knowledge and observation, he was, of all the
men that ever I knew, one of the most modest and the most easily
to be discountenanced in his approaches, either to his superiors or
to his equals...no man hath written in our language so much, and
so various matter, and in so various manners, so well.

DRYDEN, LADY ELIZABETH, 1638–1714. Dryden's wife was the youngest
child of the Earl of Berkshire. Little is known of her; she is a shadowy
figure in a life that has many shadowy places. Her father provided
her in 1662 with a dowry of £3,000 in the form of a grant which was
to come to him in instalments from the King. In subsequent years,
Lady Elizabeth and her husband had to petition the Treasury for
this money; they were, finally, successful. Twenty years after her
marriage, Lady Elizabeth was libelled by Dryden's enemies in a
number of lampoons. Since in 1663 she had been of marriageable age
for what was, in those days, a long time, it was suggested that she was
sexually lax and that when Dryden married her she was already a
'teeming matron'. Others suggested that Dryden's was a shotgun
wedding, with the bride's brothers as the enforcers. These are *only*
rumours, as is the tradition that it was an unhappy marriage. The
best support for the gossip is a letter of Lady Elizabeth's to the Earl
of Chesterfield in 1658 which suggests that she was an independent
young woman, *possibly* on intimate terms with the Earl. Whatever
the truth may be about her relationship with her husband, Lady
Elizabeth clearly shared with him a great affection for their three
sons, all of whom died before her.

JAMES II, 1633–1701; as Duke of York, came to the throne in 1685;
went abroad in 1688. James II had, to his ultimate misfortune, a very
different temperament from that of his brother. He was convinced
that his father had been too yielding in his dealings with the Parliamentarians, and to supplement his own natural determination, or
rigidity, he had qualities of industry and thoroughness which made
him powerful in seeking his own way. Unlike Charles, he lacked
humour and the ability to ride out a storm. He had soldiered in the
service of both France and Spain during his exile from England, and
he served his own country well as Lord High Admiral.

    James became a Catholic in the 1660s, and thenceforth displayed
the zeal of the convert. His religion made his removal from the succession the main aim of the Whigs in the early 1680s, but Exclusion
failed and James mounted the throne in 1685 in an atmosphere of
great good will. His policy of removing the civil disabilities of his
co-religionists was pushed far enough to antagonize his best supporters, the Church of England and the Tory gentry, and he was effectively removed from the throne by his nephew and son-in-law, William
of Orange.

    James's espousal of toleration for both Catholics and Dissenters has been seen by some twentieth-century historians as a genuine conversion which put him far ahead of his time in his attitudes. The traditional view is that James had no real sympathy for Protestant Dissenters and used their support as a cynical expedient to forward an eventual attempt to convert the whole nation to Catholicism, an argument that has been reasserted in response to the modern and more favourable view of James. What seems certain is that, if James was sincere in offering toleration, his actions made his professions incredible and his removal was the only course left to his opponents, who by then represented the will of the nation.

KNELLER, SIR GODFREY, 1646–1723. Kneller was born Gottfried Kniller in Lubeck, Germany. He was a student of mathematics at Leyden University in Holland, but opted for painting. Rembrandt was one of his teachers. Kneller made his journey to Italy between 1672 and 1675, and in 1676 came to England, where he was patronized by the Duke of Monmouth and the King. In 1688, he became joint Principal Painter to William and Mary, and sole Principal Painter in 1691, a post he retained till his death. He was knighted in 1692 and was made a baronet in 1715. He built himself a splendid house in Middlesex, which is now Kneller Hall, the Royal School of Military Music.

Kneller's career exemplifies the dominance of English painting by foreign-born artists which extends from Holbein to the time of Hogarth, and includes such names as Rubens, Van Dyck, and Lely. It was by portraits alone that a painter could prosper and achieve the wealth and social status (Deputy Lord-Lieutenant and J.P.) that Kneller obtained. Much of his work, particularly in his last years, was mediocre, but, like any artist, he deserves to be judged on his best, and that certainly includes the famous Kit-Cat series and his last portrait of Dryden, which is now at Trinity College, Cambridge.

MAECENAS, GAIUS CILNIUS, born *c.* 70 B.C. Maecenas might be described as 'the patron saint of literary patrons'. As a friend of the Emperor Augustus and an eminent figure in Roman life, he was in a position to offer powerful support and guidance to several poets of the period, such as Virgil, Horace, and Propertius. His form of patronage is described thus by the *Encyclopedia Britannica* (eleventh edition, 1911):

> His patronage was exercised, not from vanity or a mere dilettante love of letters, but with a view to the higher interest of the state. He recognized in the genius of the poets of that time, not only the truest ornament of the court, but a power of reconciling men's minds to the new order of things, and of investing the actual state of affairs with an ideal glory and majesty. The change in seriousness of purpose between the *Eclogues* and the *Georgics* of Virgil was in a great measure the result of the direction given by the statesman to

the poet's genius. A similar change between the earlier odes of Horace, in which he declares his epicurean indifference to affairs of state, and the great national odes of the third book is to be ascribed to the same guidance. . . . But if the motive of his patronage had been merely politic it never could have inspired the affection which it did in its recipients. . . . Much of the wisdom of Maecenas probably lives in the *Satires* and *Epistles* of Horace.

Modern classicists may regard this as a very simplified account of the reality, but, as a description of an ideal of patronage, it finds fulfilment in the English eighteenth century. Lord Bolingbroke provided Pope with much intellectual guidance of just this sort—he suggested, for example, that Pope should 'imitate' Horace—but Pope did not see such advice, which he took, as 'patronage' at all, since that term implied in his day financial dependence and flattery. Dryden never seriously sought intellectual patronage from any individual and was content with the nexus of cash and flattery which he manipulated with such skill. He might, indeed, have found that form of the relationship preferable to the intellectual servility which might, uncharitably, be detected in Pope's attitude to Bolingbroke.

MONMOUTH, JAMES SCOTT, DUKE OF, 1649–1685, [Absalom]. Monmouth was born in Holland, the eldest son of Charles II by his mistress, Lucy Walter. After the Restoration, the King was able to indulge his love for his favourite child, making him a duke, giving him precedence over all but royal dukes, and showering honours upon him.

Monmouth was good-looking and athletic, but poorly educated and not intelligent. He was a wild libertine, once ordering the slitting of the nose of an M.P. who had insulted the King and once causing the death of a beadle in a brawl. He was a competent soldier and as captain-general of the forces earned some victories and much praise. His popularity with the public, reinforced by his Protestantism, made him the antagonist of James, Duke of York.

Lucy Walter (d. 1658) had embarrassed the King by claiming to be his lawful wife. With the Exclusion crisis, the project of adopting the 'Protestant Duke' of Monmouth as Charles's heir caused the King to declare that he had never married Monmouth's mother. Nevertheless, Monmouth 'campaigned' for the throne, claiming that a mysterious black box contained his mother's marriage lines. Often banished, he never finally lost favour with the King, but he came increasingly under Shaftesbury's influence. His own political abilities were small. In 1680–82 he toured the countryside, building up his popularity. After the failure of Exclusion, Monmouth was involved (to what degree is uncertain) in the Rye House Plot to murder Charles II and York. In 1683 he fled to Holland. In 1685, after his father's death, he landed at Lyme Regis and claimed the throne. He was crowned at Taunton, but James II's army destroyed his forces at Sedgemoor. Monmouth was arrested, condemned, and most incompetently beheaded on Tower Hill.

OATES, TITUS, 1648–1705, [Corah]. Oates, remarkably unlearned despite much opportunity (Westminster, Merchant Taylors', Cambridge), nevertheless had what liars are proverbially said to need, a good memory. He managed to get ordained despite his lack of a degree, but was soon in trouble for scandalous behaviour. He signed on as a naval chaplain but was dismissed for homosexuality in 1676. In 1677 he was received into the Catholic Church, though he later claimed that this was a feigned conversion merely to get inside information. He was sent to the Jesuit college at Valladolid in Spain, but proved so ignorant of Latin that he was sent back to England. He then got himself accepted at St Omer, the English Catholic school in northern France. There he had a very difficult time and was expelled in 1678.

On returning again to England, Oates decided, with the help of a half-crazy clergyman, Israel Tonge, to take advantage of his experiences as a 'Catholic' to publicize a great Jesuit plot to overthrow the English monarchy. The success of the Popish Plot made Oates for a time very important, but after the failure of Exclusion the 'saviour of the nation' began to find life difficult. The Duke of York was awarded damages of £100,000 against him for *scandalum magnatum*, and, in default of payment, Oates was gaoled. He was then tried for perjury, 'a trial every bit as unfair as that of any of his victims' (J.P. Kenyon), and, perjury not being a capital offence, was sentenced to a series of floggings obviously meant to kill him. But Oates survived and after the Revolution of 1688 was released from prison and eventually received a pension. He married a rich widow, became a Baptist preacher, and, typically, lost his position after a scandal.

Oates's physical appearance impressed all who saw him. His neck was short, his chin immense, and he had a harsh and sing-song voice. In one sense, however, he did benefit his country. His floggings in James II's reign were remembered in the Bill of Rights of 1689 and helped make 'cruel and unusual punishments' unconstitutional in Britain and the United States.

PURCELL, HENRY, 1659–95. Purcell's father was a gentleman (choirman) of the Chapel Royal at Westminster in 1661 and the young Henry was soon a chorister there. At the age of eighteen he was made composer in ordinary to the King, in 1679 organist of Westminster Abbey, and in 1682 one of the organists of the Chapel Royal. Purcell composed music for Court festivities, both secular and religious, and was soon in wide demand. He wrote, without conflict, for both church and theatre, and his amazingly large output and the range of his talents entitle him to the honorific 'various', so often applied to Dryden.

SHAFTESBURY, ANTHONY ASHLEY COOPER, FIRST EARL OF, 1621–83, [Achitophel]. Cooper became an M.P. in 1640 and in the early years of the Civil War fought for Charles I. He changed sides in 1644 and eventually became a supporter of Cromwell, with whom, however, he broke in 1656. He helped bring about the Restoration and was created a baron in 1661. Though sometimes opposed to the policies of Charles II, he served him in government until 1673, when he was dismissed. Thenceforth he led the opposition, mainly by trying to prevent James, Duke of York, from succeeding to the throne. To this end he made unscrupulous use of the Popish Plot. The failure of Exclusion enabled Charles to arrest Shaftesbury on a charge of high treason. Though released by the grand jury, his power was broken, and to forestall further prosecution he went into exile in Holland, where he died.

The motives of Shaftesbury's actions in politics are still matters of contention. He left very few personal papers which might have explained his reasons, and in the absence of such rebuttal Dryden's portraits of him have attained a quite extraordinary ascendancy. Poetic genius has been reinforced by historical accident; every historian who writes of Shaftesbury has to contend with the image of the 'false Achitophel'. Since that portrait is so well known, and is presented elsewhere in this book, it will be only fair to state here some of the arguments which have been set out in Shaftesbury's defence, particularly those of his modern biographer, K.H.D. Haley.

Shaftesbury was neither a republican nor, worse, a democrat. He had supported the Restoration because he disliked military autocracy and feared mob anarchy. John Evelyn, who knew him, reports that he said he would support the principle of monarchy 'to his last breath, as having seen and felt the misery of being under a mechanic [plebeian] tyranny'. But for Shaftesbury, monarchy was the rule of a king guided by a parliament of men of property who, in the final extremity of a conflict between the king and themselves, should have ultimate supremacy. For Shaftesbury there was no divine right of kingship, and no form of government was sacred. The king held his office by the withdrawable consent of his great landowning and trading subjects, 'the people'.

Shaftesbury supported religious toleration of all Protestants, but he also supported the idea of an established Church with a right to tithes. He upheld the Test Act of 1673, which restricted public office to Anglican communicants. There seems to be no truth in the allegation that he was a religious hypocrite for political ends. (Charles II's nickname for him, 'Little Sincerity', still sticks, nonetheless.) His opposition to Catholicism stemmed from the political doctrines associated with that faith. For him, Catholicism meant tyranny and he strove to keep James from the throne because he believed James would be a tyrant.

Ranke, the great German historian of England, said that Shaftesbury 'seized the ideas which had the greatest future', and pointed to his long association with John Locke as a mark of lasting greatness. Modern students of Locke's political writings see his friendship with Shaftesbury as a two-sided, creative partnership, out of which grew the constitutional theories which eventually triumphed in Britain and North America. The final abandonment of the divine right of kings and the acceptance of Parliament as the sovereign power of the nation may owe as much to Shaftesbury as to Locke. His place in the evolution of Locke's ideas is only now coming to be estimated with some accuracy.

The good side, however, should not distract attention from the worst act of Shaftesbury's career, his use of the Popish Plot. No one will ever know whether he believed in the Plot, but sincere or not, he manipulated it ruthlessly in the cause of Exclusion and sent many innocent men to their deaths.

Locke's friendship with Shaftesbury was cemented when he supervised a successful surgical operation in 1668 for the removal of a cyst from Shaftesbury's liver. For the rest of his life, Shaftesbury wore in his body the drainage tube Locke had caused to be inserted into the wound. It is entirely typical of late seventeenth-century political propaganda that in the writings of his enemies, Shaftesbury's tube should have become a giant 'tap' and that his complaint should have been described as venereal in origin. At the end of Dryden's opera, *Albion and Albanius* (1687), a tableau appears. Fame stands on a globe which in turn stands on a pedestal.

> On the front of the pedestal is drawn a man with a long, lean, pale face, with fiend's wings, and snakes twisted round his body. He is encompassed by several fanatical, rebellious heads, who suck poison from him, which runs out of a tap in his side.

SWIFT, JONATHAN, 1667–1745. Swift was a kinsman of Dryden (a second cousin once removed) and in a very typical way took pride in the relationship while publicly proclaiming his distaste for Dryden and Dryden's work. The legendary explanation for this animosity is a story of Dryden reading some of Swift's verses and saying, 'Cousin Swift, you will never be a poet'. There is no basis for the story; it is a myth, invented to explain the otherwise inexplicable. Dryden, the translator of Virgil and a supporter of the 'Moderns', appears in Swift's *Battle of the Books* wearing Virgil's armour, which is far too large for him. The elaborate system of prefaces and dedications in *A Tale of a Tub* is a sarcastic parody of the prefaces and dedications which 'encumbered' many seventeenth-century books, Dryden's *Virgil* again conspicuous among them. From the tone and nature of Swift's remarks it is reasonable to infer that his purely literary disagreements with Dryden were founded on something more personal than Swift's protective love of good writing. The best guess at an explanation involves the *Virgil*, since in the preparation of that work Swift saw the careers of several of his friends and equals, such as his schoolfellow Congreve, and Addison, advanced by their alliance with his own kinsman, yet that kinsman extended no favour to Swift, who was at the time in some anguish over his choice of career and his search for patronage. Of all the attacks that Dryden's reputation sustained, none is quite so mean and supercilious as one preserved in a letter of Swift's in 1735. In correcting some verses sent to him, Swift pounced on a triplet *à la* Dryden.

> Dryden, though my near relation, is one I have often blamed as well as pitied. He was poor, and in great haste to finish his plays, because by them he chiefly supported his family, and this made him so very uncorrect; he likewise brought in the Alexandrine verse at the end of the triplets. I was so angry at these corruptions, that above twenty-four years ago I banished them all by one triplet, with the Alexandrine, upon a very ridiculous subject. [Swift refers to the last lines of his poem 'A Description of a City Shower', which parodies several lines from Dryden's *Virgil*.] I absolutely did prevail with Mr Pope, and Gay, and Dr Young, and one or two more, to reject them. Mr Pope never used them till he translated Homer, which was too long a work to be so very exact in; and I think in one or two of his last poems he hath, out of laziness, done the same thing, though very seldom.

Pope, too, might have found this hard to take.

TONSON, JACOB, 1655–1736. Tonson was a man of considerable education who knew Latin and French and could produce passable verses of his own. He ('Tonson the Elder') was for the latter half of his career in partnership with his nephew, also called Jacob Tonson ('the Younger') who, to confuse matters still more, died in 1735, one year before his uncle.

Tonson was a most successful business man, worth at least £40,000 at his death. His association with Dryden was 'the bedrock of his career' (Kathleen Lynch), and many famous contemporaries were published by him: Congreve, Prior, Addison, and Steele, for example. He produced editions of such older writers as Shakespeare (notably Rowe's pioneering edition of 1709), Spenser, and Milton—the sumptuous and successful 'Fourth Edition' of *Paradise Lost* in 1687. Tonson was a 'polite' publisher, keeping as clear as he could of the frequent scurrilities and scandals of Grub Street. His success made him instrumental in the 'refining' of early eighteenth-century letters in England.

Tonson was a lifelong Whig, and helped found and run the most famous of literary clubs, the Kit-Cat, which became an influential political body in the reigns of William III and Queen Anne. Politics, however, did not come between him and Dryden, though their relationship was at times embittered. Dryden on one occasion threatened to lampoon Tonson in verse, and sent him a triplet as a sample.

> With leering looks, bull-faced, and freckled fair,
> With two left legs, and Judas-coloured hair,
> With frowzy pores, that taint the ambient air.

When he retired from business in 1720 and set up as a country gentleman, Tonson got to know Alexander Pope well and thus became one of the few men to have been well acquainted with both Dryden and Pope. He left no real memoirs, which is a great pity. He was a bachelor —married, it was said, to his trade.

Acts and Movements

DECLARATIONS OF INDULGENCE. These were declarations (by Charles II in 1662 and 1672, and by James II in 1687 and 1688) relaxing the penal laws against those, both Protestants and Catholics, who refused to be members of the Church of England. Charles and James both claimed these powers as part of the royal prerogative.

DISSENTERS. The Restoration term for those Protestants who refused to be members of the Church of England.

EXCLUSION. The project of excluding James, Duke of York, from the succession to the throne because of his Roman Catholicism.

JACOBITES. Those who stayed loyal to James II after the Revolution of 1688 and who transferred their allegiance to his son, James Edward Stuart, the Old Pretender, after his father's death in 1701. 'Jacobus' is the Latin for 'James'.

NON-JURORS. Clergymen who refused to take the oath of allegiance to William and Mary, and who were thus deprived of their livings.

ROYAL PREROGATIVE. The large, acknowledged, but troublesomely ill-defined powers that the King could exercise without consulting his Parliament.

Further Reading

> The character of Mr Dryden, both as a writer and as a man, has been drawn by men of great learning, integrity, and candour, but in such different lights, that it is impossible to make any of them a guide in forming a summary of it for our readers.
>
> *The British Plutarch,* 1795

The following suggestions are divided into two lists. The first consists of works which can be recommended as providing information to take the reader on the first stages beyond this *Preface*. The second gives, chapter by chapter, those works to which I am indebted for what is said here and which are individually more specialized than may be desirable for most readers.

I

Editions of Dryden's Works

The standard edition of all Dryden's *Works*, when completed, will be that published by the University of California Press. (The volumes now available have been of great assistance to me.) In the meantime, James Kinsley's edition of the *Poems* (4 vols, Clarendon Press, 1958) is the most convenient complete edition of the verse. It is available as a paperback (translations and notes omitted) in the Oxford Standard Authors series and I have given line numbers for Dryden's poems from this edition. Kinsley and George Parfitt have edited a volume of Dryden's criticism (*John Dryden: selected criticism,* Oxford Paperback English Texts, 1970). Convenient and well informed editions of some of Dryden's best plays are available in two volumes edited by L.A. Beaurline and Fredson Bowers, *Four Comedies* and *Four Tragedies* (University of Chicago Press, 1970).

Letters

The *Letters* were edited in 1942 by Charles E. Ward (Duke University Press). On first inspection, the small number and frequently terse nature of Dryden's letters cause disappointment. Yet the letters are invaluable and on close examination provide more insight than might be anticipated. Ward has included letters addressed to Dryden —a very useful accompaniment.

Biography

The standard biography is also by C.E. Ward (University of North Carolina Press and O.U.P., 1961). This is often more valuable for its footnotes than for its text and is sometimes infuriatingly hard to use. (It is often difficult to work out the exact dates of events, for example.) Yet Ward is careful to separate fact from conjecture, and the deliberately dry flavour of his biography is preferable to the fanciful tone of those biographies (such as that of Kenneth Young, Sylvan Press, 1954) which provide spurious 'colour' by taking rumour as fact.

Bibliography

Hugh Macdonald's *Dryden Bibliography* (Clarendon Press, 1939) is one of the best reference books on Dryden. Its usefulness is by no means restricted to matters purely bibliographical.

Ideas

Phillip Harth's *Contexts of Dryden's Thought* (University of Chicago Press, 1968) is essential and supersedes Louis I. Bredvold's *The Intellectual Milieu of John Dryden* (University of Michigan Press, 1934), though Bredvold's chapter on Toryism is still helpful.

History

The standard histories of the period are David Ogg's *England in the Reign of Charles II* (O.U.P., 2nd edn, 1956; paperback, 1967) and *England in the Reigns of James II and William III* (O.U.P., 1955; paperback, 1969). Both are lucid, full of vivid detail, and concerned with far more than simply political history. John Kenyon's *The Popish Plot* (Heinemann, 1972) gives an account of an episode of great importance in the period and in Dryden's literary career.

Criticism

Three volumes seem notably more successful and useful than many others on Dryden: Earl Miner, *Dryden's Poetry* (Indiana University Press, paperback, 1971), Arthur W. Hoffman, *Dryden's Imagery* (University of Florida Press, 1962), which is concerned with far more than its title might indicate, and the collection edited by Bruce King, *Dryden's Mind and Art* (Oliver and Boyd, 1969). This last, being by several hands, is inevitably uneven, but brings together some of the best essays on Dryden..

II
Works consulted, in addition to those listed above.

Chapter 1. Early Career

John Aubrey, *Brief Lives*, ed. O.L. Dick (Secker and Warburg, 1949). G.F. Russell Barker, *A Memoir of Richard Busby* (London, 1895). S. Budick, *Dryden and the Abyss of Light* (Yale, University Press, 1970). W.T. Costello, *The Scholastic Curriculum at Early Seventeenth Century Cambridge* (Harvard, University Press, 1958). M.H. Curtis, *Oxford and Cambridge in Transition* (Clarendon Press, 1959). Paul Fussell, *The Rhetorical World of Augustan Humanism* (Clarendon Press, 1965). K. Hopkins, *The Poets Laureate* (Bodley Head, 1954). John Locke, *Some Thoughts Concerning Education*, 1693. C.A. Patrides, *The Cambridge Platonists* (Stratford-upon-Avon Library, 1969). *The Diary of Samuel Pepys*, (1660) ed. R. Latham and W. Matthews (G. Bell, 1970), vol. I. M. Purver, *The Royal Society: concept and creation* (M.I.T. Press and Routledge, 1967). G.M. Trevelyan, 'Undergraduate life under the Protectorate', *Cambridge Review*, 22 May, 1943. B. Willey, *The Seventeenth Century Background* (Chatto and Windus, 1934).

Chapter 2. Making a living

John Barnard, 'Dryden, Tonson, and the subscriptions for the 1697 *Virgil*', *Papers of the Bibliographical Societe of America*, LVII (1963). K. Lynch, *Jacob Tonson, Kit-Cat Publisher* (University of Tennessee Press, 1971).

Chapter 5. Religion

Robert South, *Sermons* (2 vols, Bohn, 1850).

Chapter 6. Politics

Fredson Bowers, 'Dryden as Laureate: the cancel leaf in *King Arthur*', *Times Literary Supplement*, 10 April, 1953. W.J. Cameron, 'John Dryden's Jacobitism', in *Restoration Literature: critical approaches*, ed. H. Love (Methuen, 1972). L. Proudfoot, *Dryden's 'Aeneid' and its Seventeenth-Century Predecessors* (Manchester University Press, 1960).

Chapter 7. Establishing an Idiom

O.F. Emerson, 'John Dryden and a British Academy', *Proceedings of the British Academy*, (1921). Paul Fussell, *Theory of Prosody in Eighteenth-Century England* (Archon, 1966). R.D. Jameson, 'Notes on Dryden's lost prosodia', *Modern Philology*, xx (1923).

Associations with MacFlecknoe

1 Bedlam
2 Barbican
3 Bunhill Fields
4 Watling Street
5 Pissing Alley

Tyburn

12

5

Lincolns Inn Feilds

9

8

15

7

10 *Covent Garden*

11

6

R   I   V

E.

H

14

T

13

200   0   400   800   1,200 Yard

Map of

NSTER AND THE BURROUGH OF SOUTHWARK

EY ARE NOW STANDING Anno Dom. *1707.*

6 Dorset Gardens Theatre
7 Dryden's home in Gerrard Street
8 Dryden's home in Longacre
9 Duke's Theatre
10 Rose Alley

11 Theatre Royal
12 Tonson's Shop
13 Westminster School
14 Whitehall Palace
15 Will's Coffee House

Chapter 9. The Kindred Arts

E.J. Dent, *Foundations of English Opera* (Cambridge University Press, 1928). J. Hagstrum, *The Sister Arts* (University of Chicago Press, 1958). J. Hollander, *The Untuning of the Sky* (Princeton University Press, 1961). I. Jack, *Augustan Satire* (Oxford paperback, 1966). D.T. Mace, 'Musical humanism, the doctrine of rhythmus, and the St Cecilia Day Odes of Dryden', *Journal of the Warburg and Courtauld Institutes* XXVII (1964). R.E. Moore, *Henry Purcell and the Restoration Theatre* (Harvard University Press, 1961). R.M. Myers, *Handel, Dryden, and Milton* (Bowes and Bowes, 1956). J.D. Stewart, *Sir Godfrey Kneller* (G. Bell, National Portrait Gallery, 1971).

Critical Survey

W.H. Auden, *A Certain World: a commonplace book* (Faber, 1971). T.S. Eliot, *John Dryden...three essays* (New York, 1932). J.A. Levine, 'John Dryden's Epistle to John Driden', in *Dryden's Mind and Art*, ed. B. King (see above). A. Roper, 'Dryden's *Secular Masque*', *Modern Language Quarterly* XXIII (1962). J. Sutherland, 'Prologues, Epilogues, and the audience in the Restoration theatre', in *Of Books and Humankind*, ed. J. Butt (Routledge and Kegan Paul, 1964). A.N. Wiley, *Rare Prologues and Epilogues, 1642–1700* (Allen and Unwin, 1940).

Reference Section

William Congreve: Letters and Documents, ed. J.C. Hodges (Macmillan, 1964). K.D.H. Haley, *The First Earl of Shaftesbury* (Clarendon Press, 1968). J.H. Plumb, *The Growth of Political Stability: England 1675–1725* (Macmillian, 1967). *Correspondence of Jonathan Swift*, ed. F.E. Ball (Bell, 1913), Vol. V.

General Index

Index to Dryden's Works

235